(e)Pedagogy – Visual Knowledge Building

Stefan Sonvilla-Weiss

(e)Pedagogy – Visual Knowledge Building

Rethinking Art and New Media in Education

PETER LANG
Bern · Berlin · Bruxelles · Frankfurt am Main · New York · Oxford · Wien

Bibliographic information published by Die Deutsche Bibliothek
Die Deutsche Bibliothek lists this publication in the Deutsche Nationalbibliografie; detailed bibliographic data is available on the Internet at ‹http://dnb.ddb.de›.

Printed by support of the European Commission and the Federal Ministry for Education, Science and Culture in Vienna.

Cover Design: Stefan Sonvilla-Weiss, "Eye can fly"

ISBN 3-03910-609-0
US-ISBN 08204-7001-5

Hochfeldstrasse 32, Postfach 746, CH-3000 Bern 9, Switzerland
info@peterlang.com, www.peterlang.com, www.peterlang.net

Contents

Introduction

Networks of any kind of human interaction are as old as human existence. Present-day life, at least in the western world, implies continuous flexible processes of social, professional and private affiliations, commonly paraphrased with postmodernist life-concepts and strategies. Extreme individualization – intended or unintended – coexists with heterogeneous desires and aspirations. Novel paradigms reveal how social interaction and community building could be organized and adapted to personal life-stages and programmes that are the forthcoming and challenging questions at present and in the near future.

During the last decade "community building" and "networking" have become among the most popular keywords alongside the tremendous evolvement of ICT since the advent of the WWW.

"How does it work that any two people in the world can be connected via 'six degrees of separation'?" The "Small World" Project from Columbia University (http://smallworld.columbia.edu/) suggests that we might live closer together than one could imagine.

Network theory followed "chaos", and recent research results astound us as to how complex networks of any kind of organizational structure (from sexual contacts to freshwater food) unfold similar patterns such as the structure of the world wide web. A most surprising result emerged, for example, when hundreds of thousands of web pages were scanned utilizing the number of links each of the pages contained. Instead of a bell-shaped curve with a few pages and less links on the left side and a few home pages with more links on the right, scientific research found that there is a certain discrepancy between a few pages with more than thousand links and the majority of web pages scarcely linking to two or three other pages.

From today's perspective the research results seem to be rather plausible if we compare the overhang of private home pages containing very few links with the major hubs like Google, Amazon and eBay. Contrasting former mathematical network theories and assumptions, the latest cognition in network theory stresses the concept of "preferred combinations", which could be exemplified by social networks as well: people who normally have a large circle of friends tend to make contacts much easier than loners. The rich become richer.

Transferring the idea of creating a hub, such as the one I intend to unfold by publishing this book, is to illuminate and to demonstrate scientific and programmatic excerpts from an international community of researchers, practitioners, teachers and scholars working in interrelated fields such as Aesthetic Education (Ästhetische Erziehung), ePedagogy Design – Visual Knowledge Building, Visual Education (Bildnerische Erziehung), Art Education and Media Pedagogy and Interdisciplinary Artistic Education (Intermediale Bildung).

The unifying umbrella under which the various viewpoints and thematic issues may well be subsumed and deployed is the new international MA study programme "ePedagogy Design – Visual Knowledge Building" headed by the University of Art and Design Helsinki, Finland, in cooperation with University Hamburg, Germany, and University INHOLLAND Rotterdam, Netherlands.

My intention in bringing together leading edge visionaries from various European countries, schools and disciplines underpins the necessity of reflexive and critical discourse towards paradigmatic changes in the pedagogical rearrangements, in regard to interdisciplinary visually- and socially-oriented knowledge building processes in informal and formal educational settings.

Thus I extend my gratitude to the authors who helped me to compose such an intriguing network of excellence in that field.

Stefan Sonvilla-Weiss
Helsinki, July 2004

Transfairness

(About the fair transfer of the very elementary understanding of the basic structures in increasing the intellect-related and emotion-related density of visual messages)

Gerhard Hickisch (translated by William R. Purviance)

Not far from now children and teens will celebrate retro parties and will take the flat picture worlds of their ancestors to heart. TV sets of the past will offer the same retro kick as the flat image information systems conveyed by their grandparents' various media systems. The current retro charm of a vinyl record will find its future equivalent in the retro charm of the flat information structures such as DVDs, which, on special occasions, they can look through with the same interest some of us devote to our attraction to old photographs.

On flat screens, maybe one by two meters in size, children and teens will turn to stereoscopically perceivable graphic and picture structures and will interactively control their features with ease. Navigation through the sea of information will be a central issue for the suppliers as well as for the consumers of information. Three-dimensional stacks of information levels, representing a variety of portals leading to different information (documentation, news, entertainment, infotainment etc.), can be moved and altered to any spatial position at will. With simple commands each of these levels may take up its own format-filling screen and split it into three-dimensionally perceivable images.

The availability of three-dimensionally displayed image information for everyday use will represent the biggest media jump in the 21st century, no matter what kind of engineering technique it is based on. The media wall in the living rooms of industrial nations will be a standard (just as TV sets are today). It will be used as a computer monitor as well as a medium for realtime picture communication to stereo-optically transmit conference calls during working processes or for the entertainment distributors to make use of it.

The recording and the consumption of stereo-optically perceivable image information will be on the same level as for instance the use of stereosound nowadays. The recipients of the future will be able to form a sculptural picture in the true sense of the word by themselves. Normal movies and pictures will only provide a single space information concerning the distance to the projection, and will be perceived as strange as, for example, a silent movie in the movie theater nowadays. Just as you can decide to make a movie or take a photo without color today, you will have a choice in the future to integrate stereo-optical information into a movie or photo at will. Nevertheless, perception methods will shift. The stereo-optical perception routines packed into information perception will become the omnipresent standard to transfer visual information.

The institute for Computer Graphics and Vision of the Technical University of Graz has, in collaboration with the University Clinic of Graz, developed a half-translucent, virtual and three-dimensional representation of specific liver tumors. Priming surgeons with the aid of this technology, the layered computer tomographies of a certain patient are digitally and virtually discernible. A stereo-optically presented 3d image showing the position of the liver tumor is possible and the respective user of this virtuality can, with a real data pen, turn it and twist it in any position to be able to have an exact image of the basic conditions expected in the upcoming tumor surgery. What is the position of the tumor in respect to vulnerable systems surrounding it? What is the best way to reach it and which complications could be encountered during this surgery, by looking at the exact size and position of this tumor?

For many decades the use of stereo representation in medical science and sciences in general represented a real possibility of increasing the density of visual information. Through the use of stereo-optics and with the aid of stereo movies 50 students simultaneously are able to practice surgeries, as if they were taking part in the surgery themselves. Photos of metal structures, taken with a scanning electron microscope (SEM), basically become information only by means of achieved and conditioned stereo perception. Molecular structures are presented unmistakably and well-defined by stereo images. Whenever it is a matter of scientific representations mediating precise information in relation to space, then this already existing trend towards stereo-optical presentation will evolve to its fullest extent. Virtual space worlds will play a major role in the education of doctors in the future. For training purposes the virtual representation of liver tumours is already made available today.

What do these predictable technology jumps mean for art teachers (art pedagogues, creative teachers, specialists in the organization of teaching processes in the visual culture) in the future? What do they themselves have to prepare for? How do they have to prepare the children and teens entrusted to them? How should the university training centers react to these foreseeable prerequisites of those new visual cultures? Which qualifications should the students be given on their way into the future? Which transfer of competence is an indispensable basis to cope with the challenges of adequate didactics of the future visual culture? And how can this future be connected with the ample resources of recent years and even the past?

Technological developments always demand a fundamental knowledge of technology. The obvious conclusion is that the mediation of this fundamental technological knowledge itself guarantees the emancipation of the children and teens towards the new technologies. This conclusion can have unfortunate consequences for art education, if the teachers of the subject search for their own comprehension in the transfer of technological knowledge. The transfer of operating program knowledge, when using electronic tools, should neither exceed the time scope nor the content scope the teacher is allowed to receive in his professional didacticism. On the other hand, every form of reality refusal, revealed by negating the use of the new technologies, will, in the end, also inevitably place the education of art aside, when thinking about how directly and voluntarily children and teens will engage and get involved in these new media.

But what can a teacher in the field of art really offer to deal with the expansion of the efficiency of media in a didactically valuable way?

I have been teaching design for twenty years at the University for Art and Industrial Design in Linz to prepare students for being teachers in art education. For ten years I have been trying to integrate electronic media into the range of the creation and reflectance media in the field of art education. I have gained a good overview of the creative possibilities of vector and pixel graphics and have also dealt with the design of flash animations and websites (see www.hickisch.at). I teach electronic imagery as well as manual design, and for these reasons I want my contribution in this publication to be as practical as possible, because I see myself, primarily, as a practitioner in teaching design and art education.

For a start the most important thing, my credo:

The program lessons for the use of electronic tools are very time-consuming. If art pedagogues set off to include these lessons in their teaching catalogue, they voluntarily contribute to make themselves mere assistents of teaching information technology. The center of dedication must be resident in the practice and reflectance of design. The program lessons must be limited as far as possible to core impulses, which provide just enough knowledge so that the emancipation of students is technically guaranteed in the creation and reflectance area. The basic structures of increasing the intellect-related and emotion-related density of visual information must be pursued. The focus of attention must be put on the explanation and the possibility to experience proven visualization strategies enveloping some thousands of years of use. These strategies should be illustrated and intensified.

1.1 Increasing the intellect-related density of visual information

The surgeon who, with the aid of a virtual space image, wants to investigate the position and the condition of a liver tumor rightly expects an objective correctness of the visual information presented to him. The tumor is displayed spatially in its position to the liver. Its own color distinguishes it clearly from the color of the virtual liver. The differentiation of the colors has to exclusively fulfill objective functions. The surgeon neither should be inspired by the coloration to experience an intended emotion, nor should the spatiality serve the stereo virtuality of attracting his sensuous perception for its own sake. The stereo space information is considered to be far better than the monoscopically experienced image information (all flat projections of pictures on flat image information systems) in relation to information density. The surgeon actually sees the space itself and not just an illusion on a flat image area. His information about the tumor is denser and less misleading, his investigation of the contextual subject leads to an unequivocal result. The technology of the robotic sight (i.e. TU Graz: Institute for Computer Graphics and Vision) raises the presurgical state of the surgeon's consciousness. He gets an optimized supply to his own intellectual demand for clarifying the situation expected in the forthcoming surgery.

The virtual holographic image of the liver tumor constitutes a peak value of those specific visualization strategies which should provide for the distinct transfer of information by the means of image structures. The technological development of digital virtuality and holography allows the final presentation of the form- and color-structures. The recipients' navigating through the virtual space makes the displayed objects accessible from all sides and excludes ambiguities and misunderstandings.

Long before the development of these technologies, the masters of visualization strategies in many different centuries compensated for the loss of information, which the presentation of figures on flat screen systems inevitably implicates because of loss of stereo optical perception, with promising design methods. (Leonardo da Vinci's text about a practice for young painters describes this problem basically as follows: *If two towers are overlapped by a wall in such a way that only their upper halves are visible, and if these two towers look equally wide and equally high, but we know that the left one is much farther away from us than the right one, how can we portray that in a picture? – Emery Kelen, "Leonardo da Vinci"*. It is not necessary to point out that, when looking at the position of the towers spacially or when viewing the virtual space representation through stereo-optical sight, the case would clearly be resolved. Leonardo da Vinci also wrote about stereosight in a way that impressively proves his understanding of this.

The comparison of the following six pictures *(1a, b, c: a by Mag.art. Leo Kislinger at a Photoshop seminar, made in the seventh semester / 2: Cardinal Albergati, Jan van Eyck / 3: details of an Egyptian mural painting / 4: nude, Peter Paul Rubens / 5: manipulation of 4 / 6: nude, Pablo Picasso)* may appear, at first sight, as a random selection of very different images. Nevertheless, the six examples are related by a visualization strategy where each of the six images, more or less separated by time and style, is associated to the others by a fundamental form-presenting relationship and could be identified as a compensation method because of the loss of information due to the image representation on flat image carriers. If two eyes provide more information about the perceived objects than only one (i.e. the objective of a camera), why should this undeniable fact not expand the boundaries of flat image displays to three dimension (at least the illusion of space) as a construction method for image structures? The mixture of different views of substructures in complex image formation is one of the oldest compensation methods of image design with a high information density. The presentation of complex forms in multiple perspectives transmits the illusion of reality via the use of a devised and developed multi-flat pictogram.

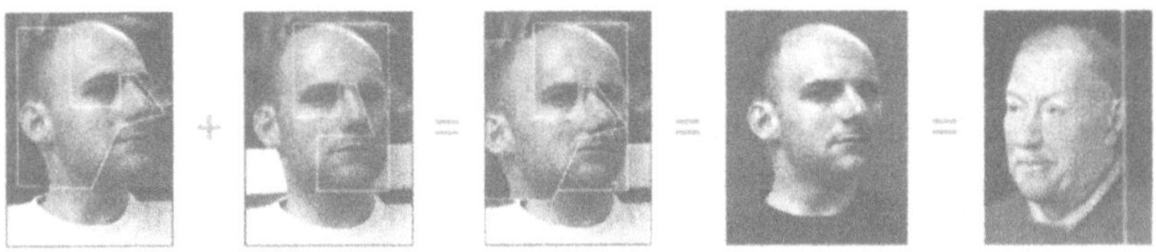

1a 1b 1c 2

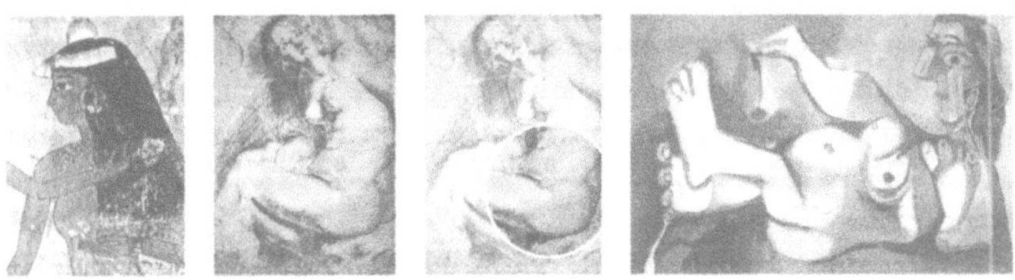

3 4 5 6

Leo Kislinger has made a Photoshop manipulation of his brother, to illustrate, with the example of the portrait, the strategy of mixing typical aspects of important subinformation (from 1a and 1b). The result (1c) does not look manipulated at first sight; nevertheless it shows the sum of blending different perspectives. In the side view the nose is the better defined sign, the mouth is better defined from the front. Both eyes are not intersected, the distance from eye to ear is stretched to offer room for the cephalic sign on the image carrier, in order to allow adequate volume. The electronic postexecution of a known reliable visualization strategy of Gothic and Renaissance portrait paintings serves the sensuous illustration of a very much concealed compositional construction principle of the so-called old art. Youngsters, who would grant the portrait of Jan van Eyck (2) the quality of photorealistic equivalence, should recognize by looking at Leo Kislinger's picture series that van Eyck was not a master of copying reality, but was, by all means, an exceptionally deliberate master inventing image structures suited for image carriers, whose sophisticated composition should be appreciated. Van Eyck merged his graphic subforms (eyes, nose, mouth) according to the criteria of the densest information to an apparently realistic looking overview, and so inconspicuously that most recipients interpret his image structure as an imitation of the seen reality.

The conditions of image carrier systems had to be mapped precisely and be taken into consideration according to the conversion of the seen reality into a fictitious picture form to develop this impression of pretended reality on the image area.

When Pablo Picasso constructs his female act (6), where the rear as well as the front can be conceived, he thereby allows us a glance into the workings of his composition. His visualization strategy is clearly exposed to the recipients. And still, it is densely related to the creation strategy of "comprehensive" information, just as Jan van Eyck (and Antonello da Messina, Andrea Mantegna, Raphael, Albrecht Dürer, Hans Memling, Hans Holbein – to name a few) made use of. The difference lies in surrendering the illusion of reality, which Pablo Picasso has not used in this picture. Peter Paul Rubens' work (4) shows high-quality information on the human pelvis, because Rubens merged the back view with a side view of the pelvis (compare with manipulation 5). He illustrated the body in a most comprehensive way. In basically the same way, and centuries later, Picasso has chosen to offer a surround view of the female act, and still, clearly more concealed, concerning the exposure of a conceivable image, a conceivable imitation of a seen reality. Van Eyck and Peter Paul Rubens decided to blur their composition tracks; by apparent loyalty to reality, Picasso has moved his design methods confidently to the foreground in picture 6, and Leo Kislinger has with didactic intentions illustrated the photo strategy of perspective mixing.

Basically all examples have the same intention: increasing the density of the intellectually detectable information and the compensatory balance for the loss of the stereo sight by means of the simultaneous display and blending of different perspectives. This combination (composition) of different views can evidently and in self-reference be expressed or extremely hidden, as for example in picture 1c, which may not be recognized immediately as a montage without the neighboring pictures 1a and 1b. Picture 3 shows the strategy of visual information density with the combination of views more clearly than picture 1c. The Egyptian mural paintings are strictly developed in relationship and dedication to the flat image area and still offer an excerpt of multiperspective sight in their whole area, an effect which, in an attractive way, connects the image flatness with the increase of information with the aid of multisight (more than one eye) of the elective image theory of combinations. Pablo Picasso has, with his picture of the naked woman (6), cited the basic Egyptian principles of the viewpoint of blending.

Condensing the information value of a graphic representation by claiming visualization strategies, as for example the multiperspective image theory of combinations, which can possibly be used to visualize landscapes (for the opening and closing of aspects and the blending of different views in one image composition), has played a significant role and has for all times served mainly one function: to compensate the ceasing values of information (because of the loss of stereo optic sight).

The fact that the technologies of the future will make this compensation unnecessary, because they will guarantee stereo-optical space information, does not mean that the quantity of visualization strategies, going beyond the blend of viewpoints, could not increase the power of potentials to elevate the uniqueness of visual information.

The fundamental structures of human visual perception will also have to be made available in future. The findings of the creative contact with those fundamental structures should still be introduced and be accessible in practice and in theory. The density of visual information may be technologically perfected to some extent; however, even in fifty years the knowledge will imply the assistance of design methods. The communication of this experience, where this digital cognition will surely support its users interactively and virtually in gaining more knowledge, will play a major role. The articulation of these knowledge areas with regard to content and form will certainly constitute the most significant field of work in the science of art education in the future. Electronic media will optimize the illustration of those conclusions, which will go back far into the past of the development of visualization strategies. The merger and the utilization of the knowledge for the application of innovative technologies will span a golden bridge, whose sustainability will account for the development of new visual cultures. The success of this bridging will lie in the hands of the future specialists in visual cultures, who, whatever they will be called, will have enjoyed an education, about whose structure the trainers of visualization experts should already think today.

Merely transferring skills in the technical application of electronic media will guarantee too little competence for a valuable creative efficiency. A much too one-sided movement of the educational science of art in the direction of functional qualification of the students as users of electronic tools will turn out counterproductive. It would be clearly more purposeful to enlighten the disciples on the optimization conditions for the transfer of intellect-related visual information by design form and color structuring processes. By which design methods and by which means of effective guidance can the perception of the recipients be brought to a definite result of assimilating information? How is the recipient led, with the variety of signs, symbols and pictures, exactly in the way, intended by the meaning of information transfer? Who steers the ship of information reception through the cliffs of misunderstandings and ambiguities in the sea of signs towards the safe beach of a clearly provided message? What do the nautical aids look like? Who is in charge of the navigation? Does the recipient really have the rudder in hand or does he follow a perfect course which experienced specialists for visualization have suggested and planned very consciously?

1.1/1 Perception guidance as a core strategy to increase the intellect-related density of information

Children and teens should be given full access – in theory and reality – to all design methods. The functionality of those methods can be covered objectively, and the steering system of the information assimilation for the recipients is therefore justified. Intellectual insight into the fundamental tools of the perception leaders, who guarantee all design techniques of the intellect-related density of information, must be disseminated. This presentation of the control methods of perception processes can form the basis of a liberal education of children and teens which enables them to realize the basic structures of visual information manipulation they encounter daily. Every admission of information implies the result of an abundance of manipulation methods, no matter how seriously (or unsound) it is presented.

In any case, the manipulation of the recipients presents the most elementary meaning of the design of visual messages. The title page of the "Frankfurter Allgemeinen Zeitung" (a quality newspaper) is meant to manipulate the recipients just as effectively as the title page of the "Bildzeitung" (a tabloid). The choice of messages is structured here and there. Text blocks form unities of information; headlines become optical focuses. In both formats visual guidance systems become the inevitable navigational requirement for the readers. The manipulative strength of designed articulation of text information is beyond any doubt, but for the art pedagogues it is analytically very difficult to explain, because they work in a field beyond the competence levels of the text designer.

During didactic work with children and teens it must be brought forward that manipulation processes are necessary tools for the design of information transfer and have to be explained. The manipulation of the recipients reflects the honorable purpose of visualization professionals. Very rarely are the consumers conscious of suitable visualization methods for those manipulation tools, whose powerful application regulates their admission of information.

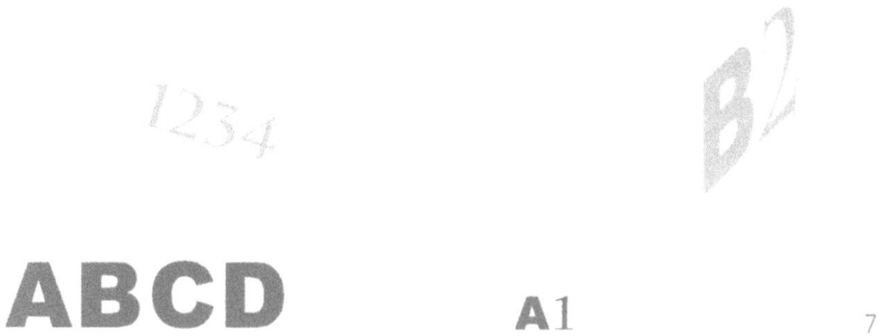

The symbols ABCD and 1234 are perceived as separate unities of information. Two different fonts in two different point sizes and different gray tones and adjustments build blocks of information which are distinguished clearly from each other by the different parameters of the formal articulation of the involved symbols. The A1 and B2 symbol pairs consist of symbols of different symbol families, and although one of the two symbols is respectively related with that of the second symbol pair, the control methods of information transfer ensure that no recipient raises the character relationship to the adjustment factor for his perception (this would result in both symbol pairs AB and 12). The Gestalt laws used make up for too large an effect (similar or identical figure signs – in this case similar size and tone overregulate the formal analogy; parallelism and closeness), so that the recipients could not experience a different perception than the one desired.

The described optical perception laws of figures (Wolfgang Metzger, "Laws of sight", Frankfurt am Main, 1975) offer an excellent platform for objectivity in art education.

1.1/2 The regulation of the unequivocal perceptibility of figures on flat image carrier systems as a condition for a functioning perception guidance

The strategy of the controlled perception of picture figures through regulation of content- and form-based context decisions, which are stretched between these figures as controlling forces and bonding strength, can only expand to its fullest capability if those figures are perceived clearly, as what they are to be: as clarified figures, whose emblematic statement is transported unmistakably. The flattening of picture figures during their projection on flat image carriers can result in misunderstandings with the interpretation of their message.

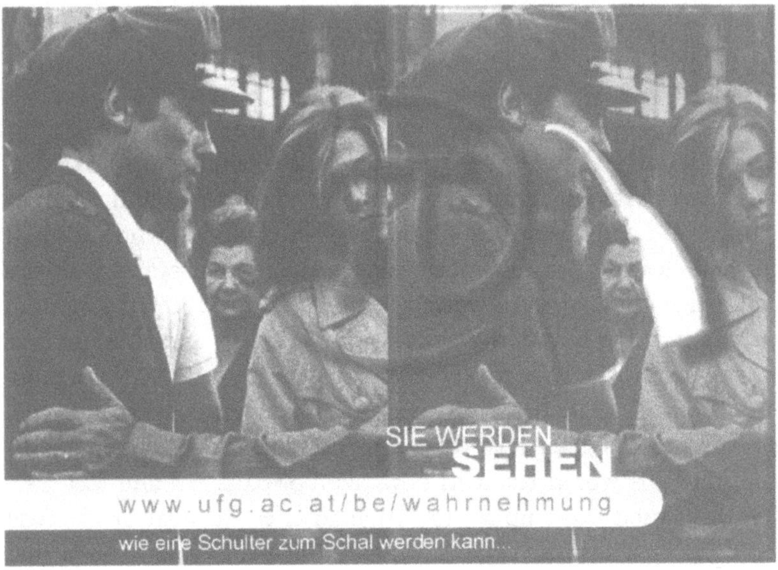

8

For this interrelation the objective description of Gestalt forming is useful in the terminology of Gestalt psychology, not only for explaining systematic controls for the transfer of information by figure arrangements, but is also suited extremely well for the proof of unintentional information, which, e.g. in photography, very often arises from the loss of stereosight. The photograph of the young Alain Delon in conversation with a director (8) offers a very persuasive unintentional figure, resulting in a most effective and powerful form in the image area: a white scarf which originates from Alain Delon's white shirt collar and the shoulder of a man behind him. The Gestalt laws of "nearness", "good continuation" and "similar or same figure qualities" force this kind of figure perception. During "Science Week 2002" a web site was presented by an art education team of the University of Art and Industrial Design Linz with "perception" as its topic, which deals with the general framework of the visual perception of flat level picture information split into three categories (stereo sight / Gestalt laws / context: www.ufg.ac.at/be/wahrnehmung).

Especially photography, which is granted the most persuasive reproduction of reality by children and teens, leads to many ways of deception by often irritating the distinct transfer of information. Unintentional figure losses and unintentional figure formations form the barely described and also barely perceived day-by-day business of photographic images.

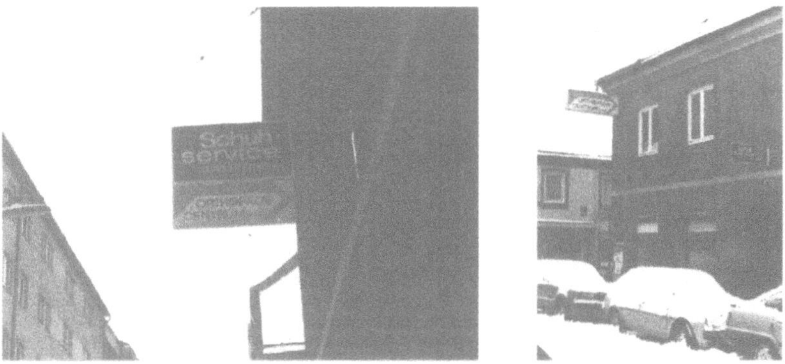

9

The left picture suggests the admission of information that two signs are mounted at the same height, while the right picture gives you the clarified information that the dark sign is smaller and mounted considerably more to the front than the bright one (9). The laws of good continuation and unity cause this figure formation of the left picture. The collapse of the real space zones into the projection on the flat image carrier of the photo causes the misunderstanding.

In future such misinformation will be avoided with the use of holographic media. It is yet of great importance to know the origin of potential misinformation in figure transfer on flat picture systems, because only this knowledge can enlighten the strategies used by the image designers of the last centuries who applied them to navigate the ship of their visual message against the wild currents of information cloaking by unintentional figure formations or figure losses or rather irritating space position misconceptions, to the shore of an explicit picture form (which has not always succeeded).

To promote children's and teens' comprehension of the complexity of such objectives should constitute an indisputable educational target, because the hedonistic acknowledgment of ingenious design methods of the fine artists of all times (as well as the visualization artists at PIX-AR Studios and Industrial Light and Magic) opens new doors and ways of encountering art for our children. To understand the graphic solutions of the past and the present can qualitatively deepen reception behavior.

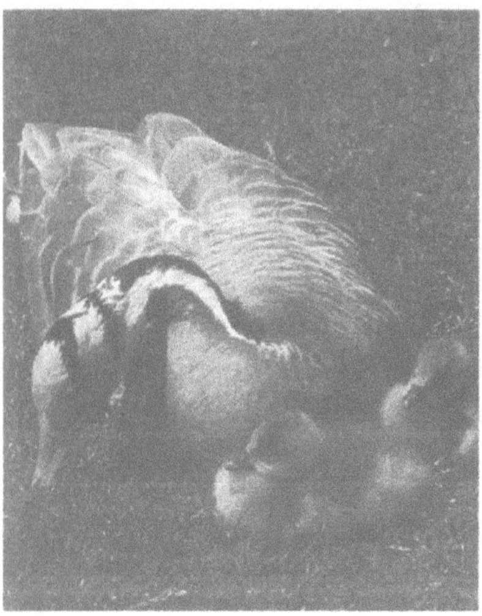

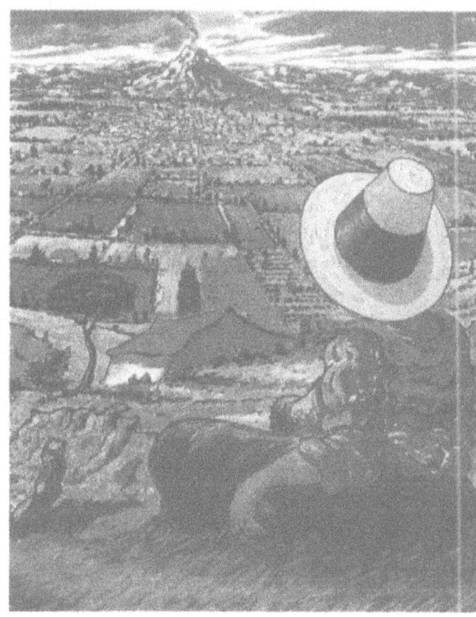

10/11

Regulating the optical importance between the picture figures and their respective surroundings makes up the most important manipulation form of conspicuity control and the space positioning of figures on flat image systems. Because of the same regulation of optical importance the dominant black-and-white divided goose head (10) comes into a highly lifted space position, likewise the painted hat (11). The explicit closeness of the two figures and their conciseness against their surroundings detach the figures out of their image coherency and cause an unintentional rupture of the figures, whose elements can no longer be spatially connected. Looked at from the viewpoint of intellectually coherent information transfer the spatial illusion on image areas constitutes an absolute multimedia problem (in the sense of spanning all types of media). Photography, hand drawing and painting are media normally used without stereoscopic information, and can only then provide clear space information if the result of regulated styling and brightness-darkness control (color control) is presented by means of the given figure values. In all these media imitative illustration heads towards a mass of misunderstandings, which need not be the topic of analysis from the level of the subjective sense of beauty by visualization experts, but can be a matter of objective emancipating education by scrutinizing the objective information value.

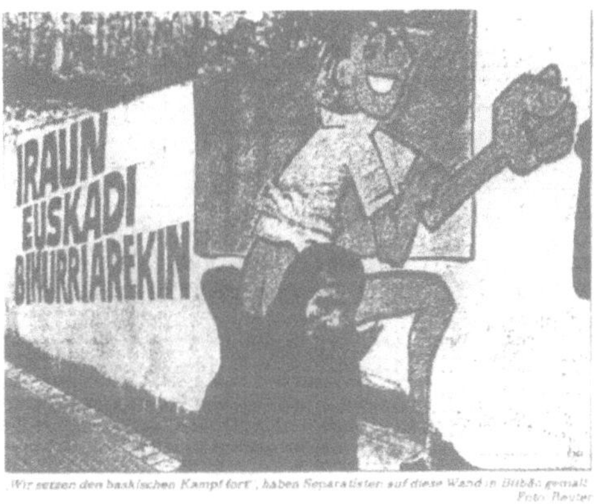

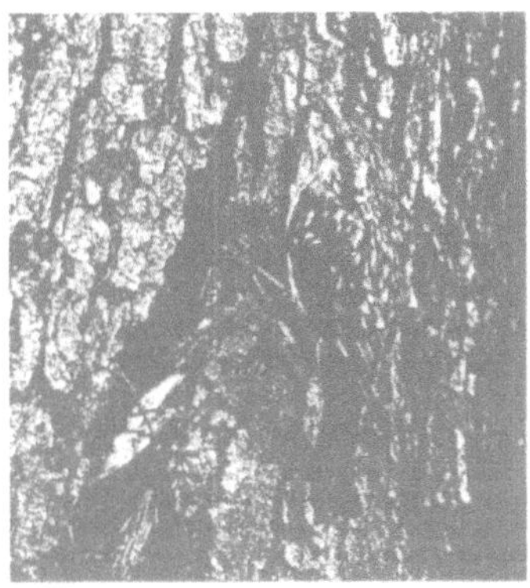

12/13

The photo document (Reuter, #12) shows an impressive fusion of different picture varieties resulting in an unintentional cumulative form. The old woman in the picture foreground seems to carry a painted picture figure in a basket on her back. "Unity", "similar or identical figure attributes" and "good continuation" cause this image form. The exclusion of stereo-optics and the presentation through a linear depth of focus (which does not exist that way in the real visual process) join space zones which were never connected, and create unintentional compositions from this form melting (or figure loss, as seen in the picture of the small bird, #13). And it is here that the emancipating education of visual culture should begin: in explaining the power of the most important figure-creating organization tendencies of human visual perception. Those who do not realize the power and the strength of those Gestalt laws will not escape them anyway. The more conscious the exposure to those Gestalt-building forces, the more a designer can change from the victim's role (which is rarely recognized) into that of the culprit. Design should not be the result of element interactions which the designer neither knows nor copes with, but rather a document of his comprehension of the structure-building framework of image articulation.

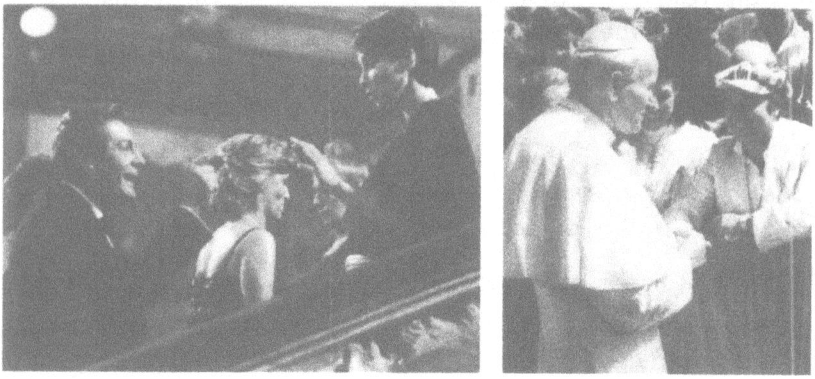

14 / 15

Frozen pictures are strange enough. But if they offer information which conveys contents never intended, we are in need of action. Should the consumption of visual culture be allowed to imply the trained and sensitized perception of its recipients or is it enough to be corrected by the intellect (because what cannot be must not be), which rectifies every visual offer, until the message anchors in the right port? With intellect focused information density every correction should be unnecessary, but still, the exact medium with the highest acceptance for accurate information transfer, the medium of photography, exhibits an almost unbelievable need for intellectual finishing touches by the recipients.

Marcello Mastroianni and the woman facing him seem to be touching a lady's hairdo in the background ("good continuation", "unity" and "symmetry", 14). The Pope seems to have an extremely long nose (15), formed into a figure unwillingly by the figure characteristic of a woman's nose in the background. Such false figure formations are on no account limited just to the medium of photography but constitute a basic problem of the realistic and exact transfer of image information on flat image carriers.

The stereo optical representation of spatial circumstances raises the value of image information quite considerably. Interestingly enough, the bonding strength of the Gestalt laws in different relation systems of human visual perception results in different conclusions when interpreting the visual information choices (the pulsating triangle on the internet starting page leads to the "you will see" button download, where the "perception pdf" offers more text on this subject). In the following pictures the rise of information density can be seen for yourselves and experienced stereoscopically by utilizing a small hand mirror in the following way: look directly at the left picture with the left eye and drag the mirror image of the right mirrored stereoscopic picture with a light panning of the hand mirror precisely onto the picture non-mirrored and directly seen left. The correct position of the mirror can be seen in picture 17 (also stereo-optically).

The seemingly strict vertically ordered point rows (16) left show the scheme for the effect of the Gestalt law of "nearness". Because of the denser nearness in the vertical order the points are perceived as vertically lined up. In the stereo-optical presentation the same law is responsible for the nearness of the horizontally lined up point order perception (after all, diametrically different information). The different relation systems of perception (mono-optic and stereo-optic) lead to extremely different pieces of information about the position of the points shown.

With the transfer and explanation of the effect of image-building organization trends in human visual perception, children and teens can be given access to the elementary potentials of the image formation craft. Teens should recognize that the construction of planned figures on flat image areas always requires the result of the regulatory and structuring definition of form and color value relations of figures in respect to their surroundings. The term "composition" should be explained in the analysis of intellect-related transfer by visual information as a "cooperation" of several visualization strategies. These strategies as a

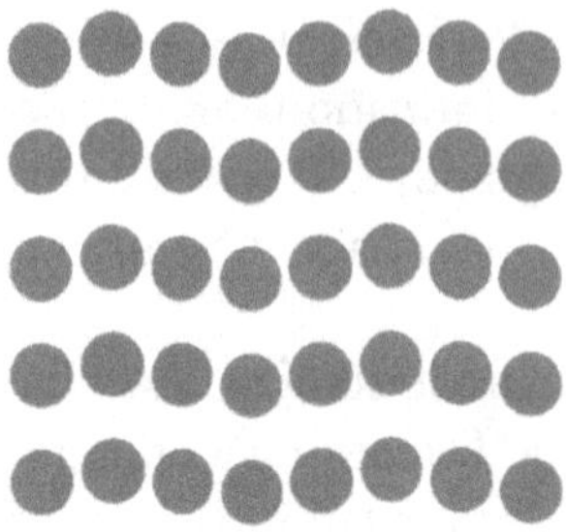

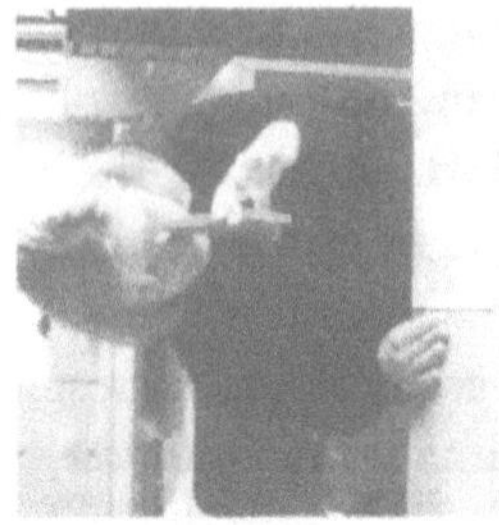

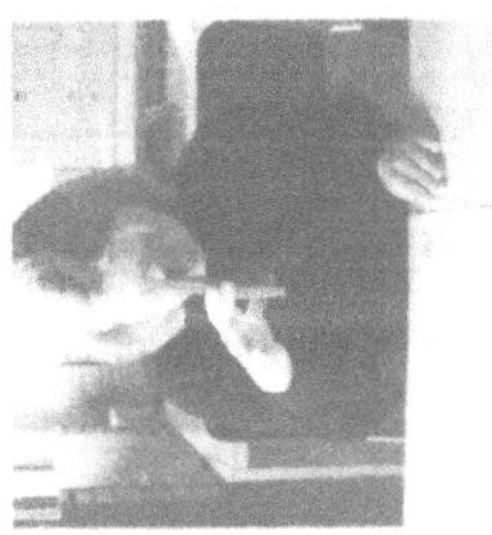

16/17

stratification of form, color- and brightness-conciseness by means of the hierarchy of emphasis and significance as well as by means of space stepping definition, or the strategy of the formal summary of the elements of information, which should be seen in a correlation of contents, will have to be made clear as tools of that guided perception intended by the image creators.

1.1/3 Perception guidance by controlling the context with regard to content and form

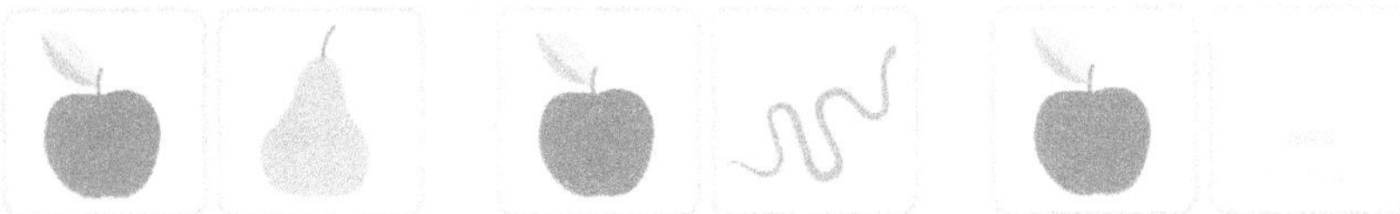

18/19/20

To successfully direct the perception of the recipients, it is not enough just to know how to articulate a clearly legible figure on a flat image plane. The control methods for content- and form-related context direction are highly effective instruments for steering the perception system of the recipients. To successfully adopt content-related context direction means to accurately obey the contextual interdependency of the signs and to evaluate for yourself the transfer or density of a certain message (see also: "the one-armed kontextbandit", from: "you will see", context, www.ufg.ac.at/be/wahrnehmung).

The three sign pairs (18, 19, 20), possessing formal resemblances (this strengthens the effect of the content-related context change), three times display one and the same apple sign, which is differently colored by the varying neighboring second signs (law of "nearness") in the interpretation of its contents. Of course, these different interpretations made by different contextual accompaniments require adequate knowledge of context (the temptation by the snake, Apple computer, e.g.). But this clarification illustrates a significant achievement in directing by the navigators of content-related contexts. Provided that these image figures are to be interpretable in regards to content the combining of sign and image values asks for an appropriate appraisal of its mutual influence, concerning the content message of such sign combinations. As soon as it is clear which sign choice leads to what kind of content result, the formal context regulation will decide how distinctly and effectively the desired transfer of a content message will work.

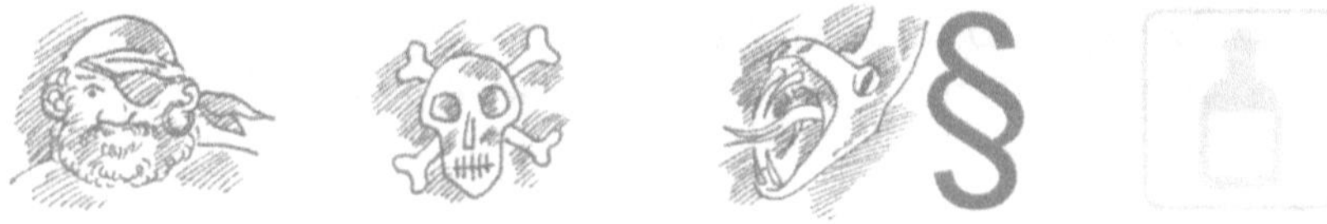

21/22/23/24/25

The three hand drawings (21, 22, 23) are perceived as belonging together in regards to contents and form. Although the section mark (§, 24) is very close to the snake image (law of "nearness"), there is barely a connection with regard to contents between them. The formal articulation difference of the section mark separates it much too clearly from the image of the snake, whose formal resemblance dominates together with the two neighboring hand drawings. This example illustrates that formal relationships can look family-forming and that through this kind of form relation the visual order of the sign admission by the recipients can be determined decisively, when using such form relations. In spite of the distance from the three apple-sign pairs, the design of the small bottle sign (25) brings the form parameters of the three pairs to mind. Even over a large distance it belongs, so-to-speak, to its family, though in contents it has not much in common with the messages of its relatives. No one would put the sign of the bottle in relation to one of the hand drawings, and yet it is intended that way, as the following illustration should prove.

26
The poison bottle as a content- and form-combination of different sign families

The form-related context of design formation in image figures decides how to read the composition these figures build up with each other and to each other. Which figure has to do with which other figure? How is this relation explained in contents? Or just why do the contents demand this formal coordination of these figures? Such important compositional questions are based on the analysis of the interdependance of content- and form-related context direction. In addition, formal management of context includes classic strategies of visualization such as the stratification of how noticeable colours and forms are in relation to their surroundings (the regulation of the relationship of figure and background) for the purpose of directing the pithiness and regulating the position of all the creating elements involved and all the approved strategies of directing the planned sight by steps of composition such as relationship of measurement to format, proportion, rhythm, arrangement of direction, etc.

Only if those conditions of the design construction and the controlling of design relations of several shapes to each other are clear (concerning the parameters of the design clarity of image figures on flat image carriers and concerning their content- and form-related context definition), the transfer work can – in a first step – concentrate on the content density of intellect-related information transfer.

1.1/4 ConZENtration as a core strategy to increase the intellect-related density of visual information

If you have learned the prerequisites an image area needs to create clear design relations you can deal with the conZENtration of its picture information as a strategy to condense its message. The distinct articulation of sign fields on flat image carriers must be accepted as a prerequisite for innovative image drawing creations. Otherwise, many efforts in concentrating image contents by means of ideas for content density are offered and sold below their value as more or less readable constellations of form.

The word concentration (27) written in this way or as conZENtration demonstrates a useful attempt to transfer content density and the great importance of concentration as a self-awareness strategy of Zen Buddhism (Walter Jerey, visualization study, 1995).

27

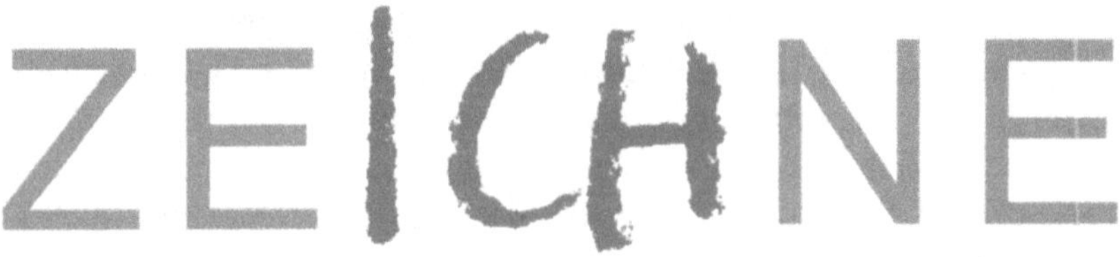

28

In her visualization practice of 2000 Barbara Scheuchenstuhl summarized the information “Ich zeichne (I draw)” in the word ZEICHNE (28) and in this way illustrated essential motivations of character setting by the means of character articulation of the letters in the word ZEICHNE (the German word “ICH” means “I” in English).

ConZENtration and reduction are likely most important parameters of a content-motivated information density. Sifting out gold, separating chaff and wheat, melting the useful optical representatives of contents into an innovative setting of signs: all this is to be accomplished if one strives for a content density surprising the recipients by sign articulation or new sign creation on one hand, and on the other hand the recipients are neither too challenged nor left in any uncertainty. Restricting to a few signs which represent their message centrally and precisely advances the recipients more quickly towards the goal, to the perception of the information transferred.

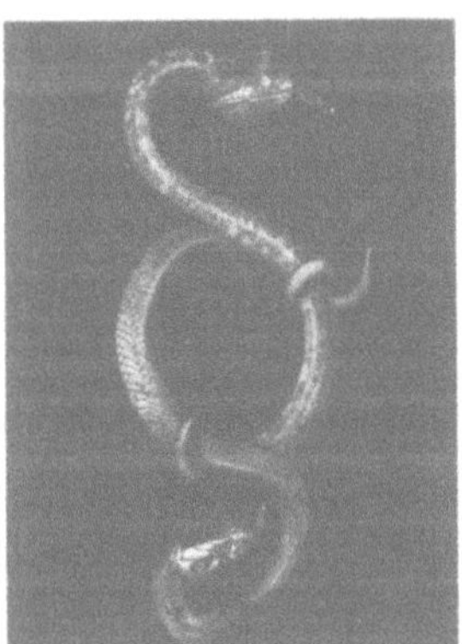

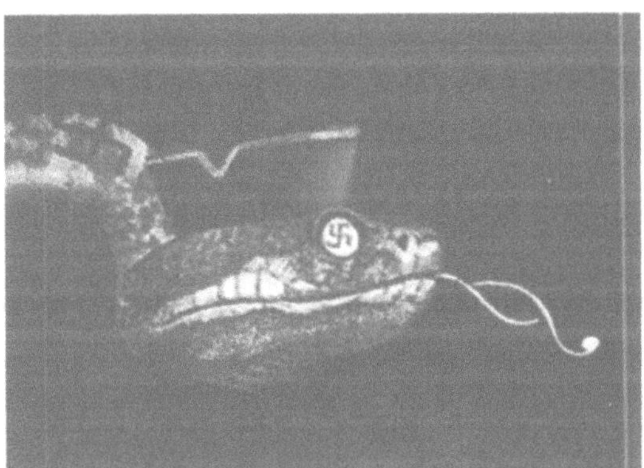

29

"They writhe and they turn and they call themselves German judges": with this critical visualization John Heartfield has picked out the role of German justice at the time of National Socialism as a central theme (29). He has condensed his intellect-related information by the invention of a section mark sign built through two snakes wound each other. The judge's hat and the section marks as snake tongues complement the picture symbol, which surprises the recipients in its originality, and which together with its title unmistakably transfers its message. Concentrating on an effective image invention gives the critical content transfer a sharpness which could probably not be offered by an overloaded assembly of image figures. "Less is more." This key sentence of design teaching applies to this example in an extremely persuasive way. Thus a kind of intellect-related density of the visual information can consist of protecting the concentration of the message by reducing the symbol/sign repertoire.

Many examples cover the usefulness of this restriction strategy. However, this should not block another important and true possibility of concentration: density by clustering many things. "More can really be more."

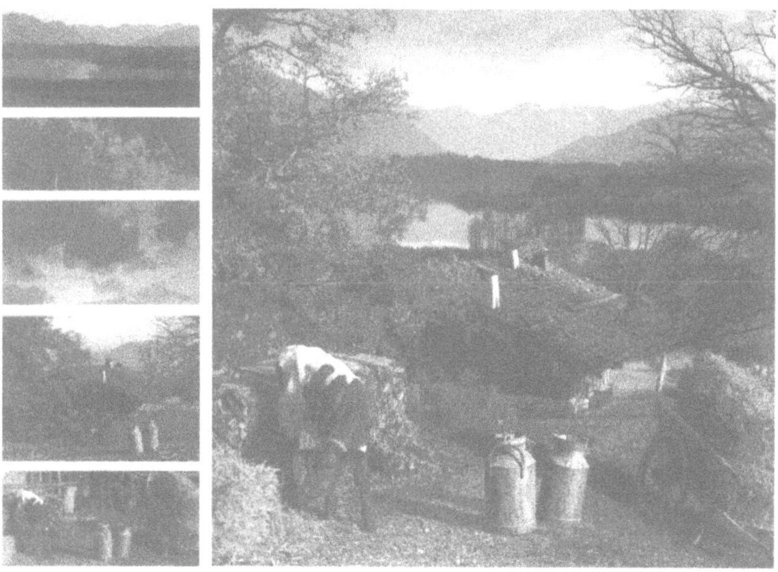

30

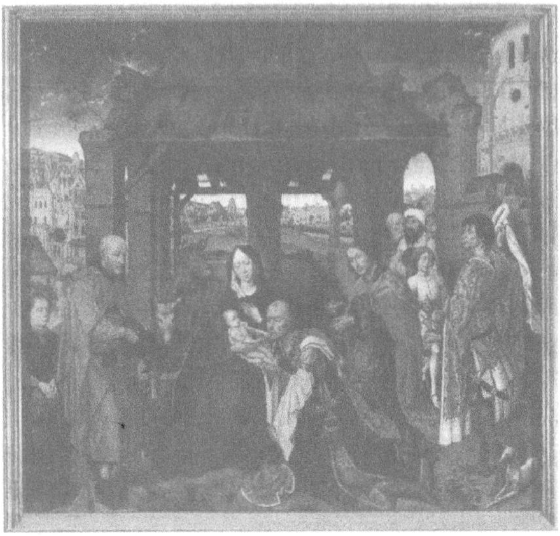

31

The idyllic advertising photo manipulation (30) is the result of fusing useful representatives of regional and country idyll. A representation was attained from several photos of different perfect figures, which provides a fictitious picture as a concentrated load of sustainable subsigns. The technical and formal execution of this picture manipulation at a high standard guarantees its density of persuasion. The painted representation of the Three Magi (31) also functions as an arrangement of the most indispensable elements. In both cases you cannot speak of reduction, but concentration is still present as a visualization strategy. While John Heartfield uses concentration as a means of restriction on a supersign as with the example of the snake sign section mark and therefore protects the density of information by reduction, the last two visualizations have both been made possible by the application of the concentration as a package of many pieces of information, which, with their dense accumulation, mutually effect each other for the desired effect.

The intellect-related density of visual information can be objectified very well and is extremely well suited for teaching processes. The formation of unambiguous figures on flat image areas, the basic conditions of content-related and form-related context direction achievements which take care of more or less complicated image structures, and the methods of concentrating sign repertoires used to guarantee content density of visual messages, all these configuration measures can be excellently covered and illustrated in numerous valid examples.

1.2 Applying electronic media in the teaching processes on increasing the intellect-related density of visual information

As with all other media applications, employing electronic media will be justified didactically in two ways: electronic media as creative media in the teaching processes of the educational theory of art on one side and electronic media as an ideal reflection and visualization media on the other.

With the resource "flying classroom" (a unity of 12 multimedia highend laptops and suitable auxiliary devices such as beamer, scanner and printer) a team of the art education class in Linz (Hickisch, Proprentner, Schreibelmayr) has developed 13 model lessons for the sensible application in the didactic subject of electronic media (devised by 13 participants of a praxis lesson), and tested them during school. The results of this testing were documented and displayed on the internet. All media necessary for the exercises (in each case one lesson lasting two hours) can be downloaded from the Internet: www.fliegendes-klassenzimmer.ufg.ac.at.

All interested persons can request a data CD for 13 lessons from the home page. The CDs contain three booklets covering the three subject areas (Hickisch: Electronic Media for Beginners / Proprentner: Internet Design / Schreibelmayr: Art Work Analysis by Applying Electronic Media) as PDF files.

1.2/1 Electronic media as reflection and illustration media in the teaching processes concerning increasing intellect-related densities of visual information

Electronic media are extremely suited to making comprehension and insight, in an almost playful and most simple way, even in interactive form, easier. For transferring knowledge and qualifications simple didactic Flash movies can be of good use: for example "the little movie about the great Gestalt laws" (from the Gestalt laws category "you will see", www.ufg.ac.at/be/wahrnehmung), or the "one-armed context bandit" (also from "you will see", section "Context"). The following examples present the repertoire of didactic Flash animations from the flying classroom: "a little movie about script" (Hickisch/Barna/challenge) and the movie about the most important possibilities of acquiring conciseness "How to create a dominant figure" (Schreibelmayr/Bammer/challenge). An extremely simple interactivity is the basis of all these media. Of course, the Internet sites themselves are also didactic media, because they offer an overview for potentially interested parties. The multimedia-based conditioning of these and other contents requires much time as well as adequate budgets.

In the future imparting knowledge will operate with interactive and multimedia-based teaching methods and studying aids. Virtual knowledge spaces will open up possibilities didactic specialists should already be thinking about.

1.2/2 Electronic media as creation media in teaching processes on increasing intellect-related densities of visual information

Whenever children and teens use electronic media as creation media practically, there is a risk that the transfer of using this functional program knowledge requires a lot of time. That is why prepared cut out figurations (electronically cut out) are used in the context section of both class schedules of the flying classroom, so that the kids can quickly begin working. The primary goal of these teaching units is to transfer the understanding of context direction and not the transfer of program knowledge of how to cut out electronic forms in Photoshop.

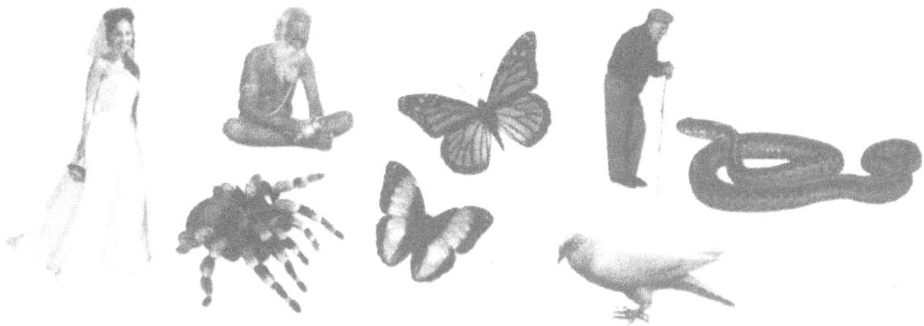

32

In her class schedule "Image montage: a sight performance" (Hickisch/Riebe) Anna Riebe makes seven human figures and seven animal figures, all cut out nicely and cleanly, available for the context direction of "sceneries" (32). In the image editing program Photoshop a scenery image can be chosen from a group of 20 photos, completely different in contents, as background. A human figure and an animal figure are placed on the stage. The contextual interaction of the chosen contents is to be observed and described accurately. Furthermore, an attempt should be made to leave just one figure and exchange the rest (scenery and a second figure e.g.) in such a way that the remaining figure in regards to content is perceived differently from the the first attempt of image order. The goal of this teaching unit is to provide the process of picture montage as a sight performance with a directing achievement by selecting the acting signs.

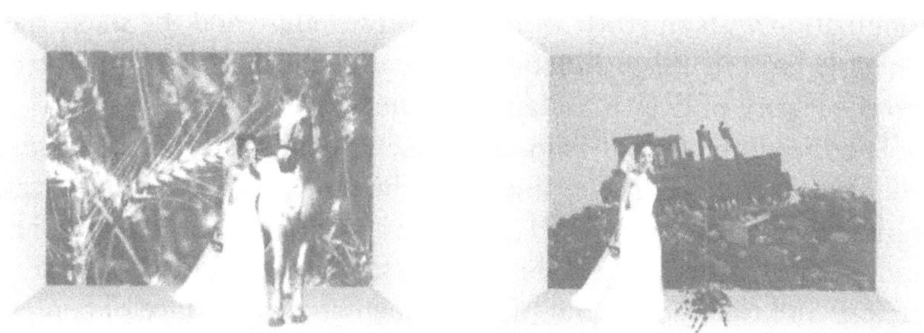

33

In this student's work (33) the stage figure "bride" is presented in two different surroundings which contribute to color the message of the whole stage appearance. The environment with positive image signs (the grain ears of the scenery and the figure of the white horse) makes the recipients understand the scenery in a different way from the same bride's figure in front of a waste dump and a gigantic spider. In this context practice the students can mirror and adjust the size of the available figures and therefore gain elementary experience with the design of formal context (if the bride is facing away and standing far away from the horse, it will provide different information about the scene than if the bride is standing close to the horse, etc.).

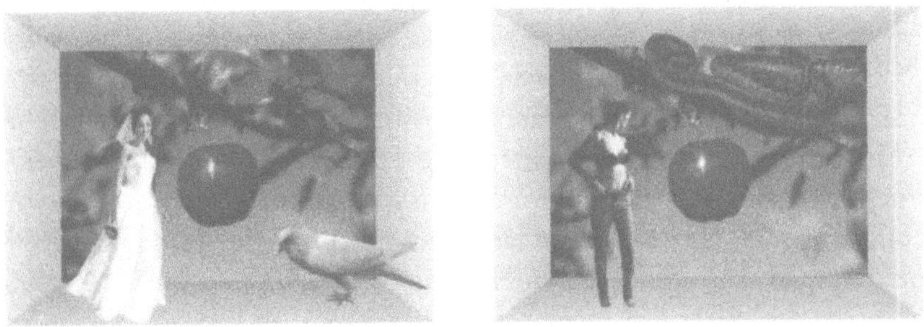

34

The bride, the white pigeon and the shining apple together express acceptance of life. The positively assigned staggered pieces provide a "piece" of pleasant life in their combination (composition). In this combination the apple is not necessarily read as a symbol of temptation. In the combination with an erotic woman's representation and the snake sign the apple loses its fill-in function for vitality and health and is forced into the legend of Eve's temptation by the snake (34).

The meaning of the lesson "montage: a sight performance" is not about transferring computer fluency to the students, but about increasing knowledge and experience in dealing with context controls. The quintessence of the lesson is about the basic clarification of design connections and the filtering out of the elementary importance of contextual direction. Hereby the comparison of scenery and static montage fulfils an appreciable and didactically fertile function.

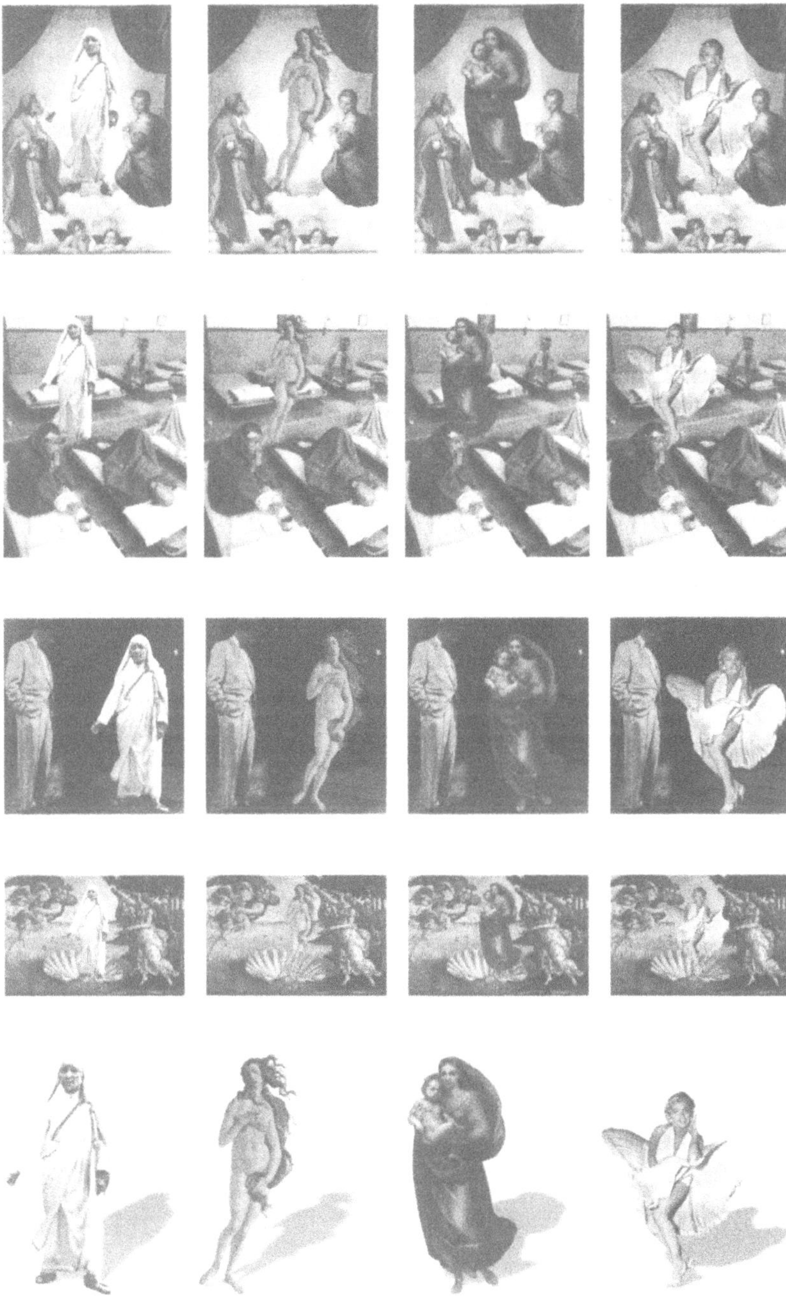

The class project "Exchange with icons of femininity" by Regina Time (Schreibelmayr/Time) similarly operates with ready-to-use cut out picture figures which can be taken out of their contexts and put in respective contexts with other figures. Four icons of femininity (Mother Theresa, Marilyn Monroe, Botticelli's Venus, Raffael's Madonna, 35) are shown in their own original contexts but also in the contexts of other icons. In this way the students can observe the contextual interaction between the same and the varying surroundings by playfully exchanging the figures. The four icons of femininity represent four pictures of women; pictures, which by all means turn out to be very different. The students should recognize that the pictures (images) of these four women are enriched with contents and meanings the figures bear when extracting them from their original surroundings and integrating them into foreign surroundings. How quickly a picture of a woman can become a decal of the woman can be shown with Botticelli's Venus on a yoghurt cup (36). The icon strength of Venus is to be transferred to the (yoghurt) product. The capitalistic consumer society promises the power of Venus to all who enjoy the milk product. The students should comprehend the manipulative contact with picture figures and the commercialization of pieces of art for non-art business interests by the self-applied transfer of the cut out women's figures in any contexts.

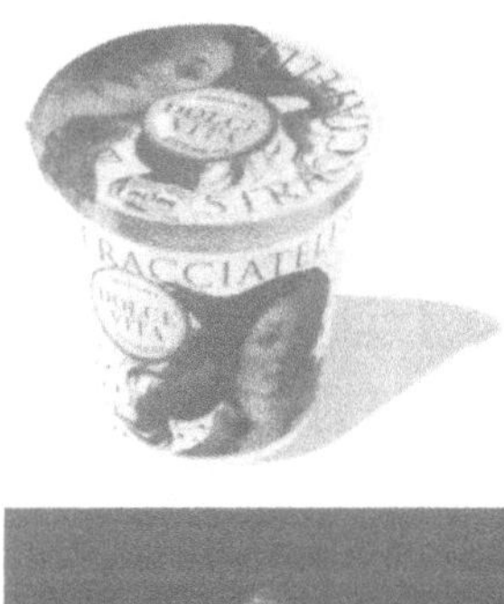

36/37/38

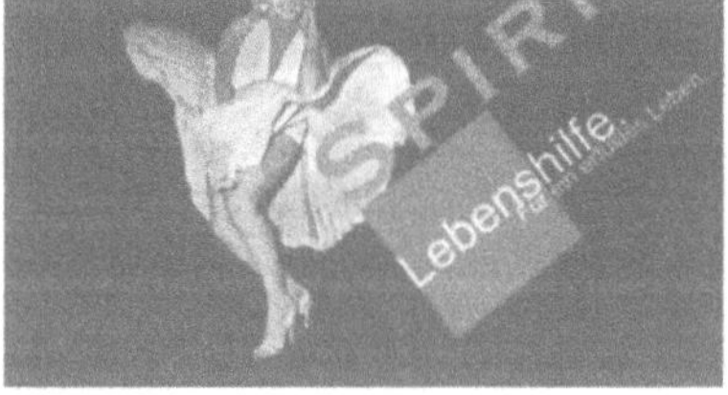

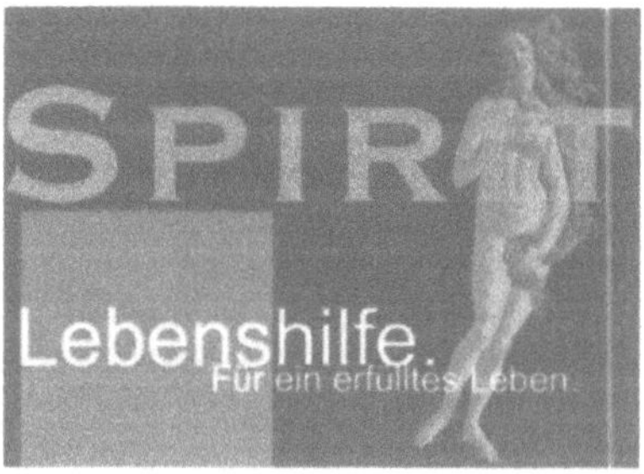

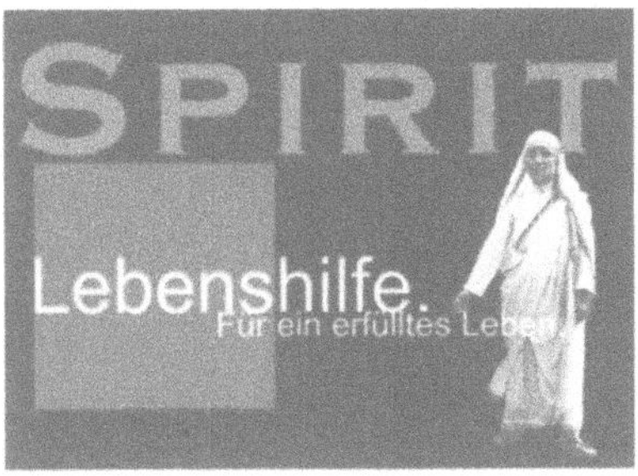

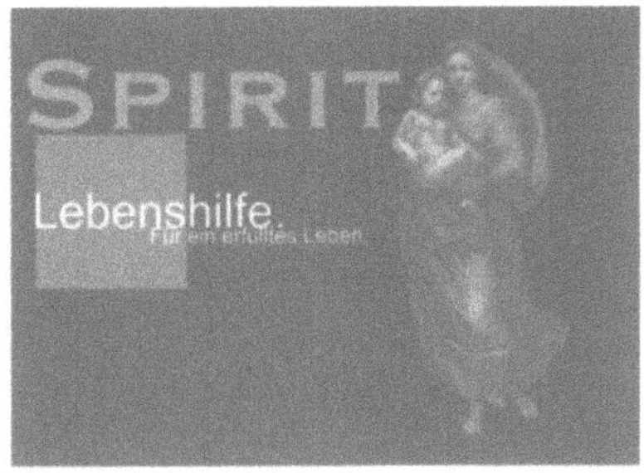

39/40

In the second part of the two hour lesson the students employ pre-made text and sign values which are to be complemented with one of the icons of femininity (37–40). In this way advertising posters are created for a mineral water, a hair shampoo, a theater performance and for a community of spiritual interest. With easy program commands the students can decide on the arrangement of the available design elements, but above all should be able to describe how the message of the posters is changed when the chosen icon is exchanged for another. The students should realize that the choice of contents alone shows a relevant design achievement.

Veronika Bammer's lesson plan "How to create a dominant figure?" is devoted to the transfer of the most elementary strategies of conciseness. By editing an electronic working sheet (vector graphic art file) the students should get to know the most important possibilities of controlling the conciseness of design elements (control of position, size, brightness, colour, direction and form of these elements, 41–46).

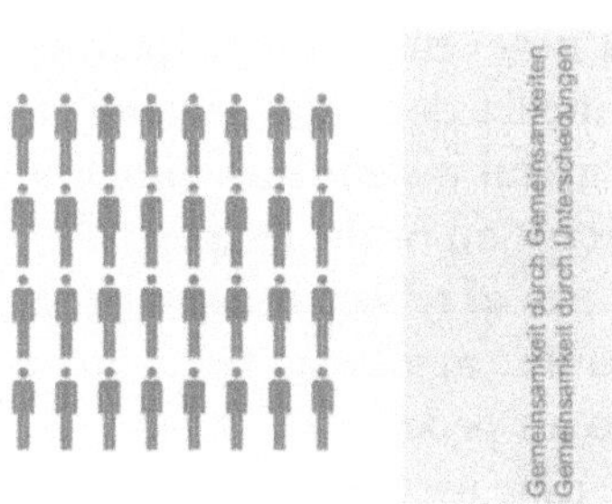

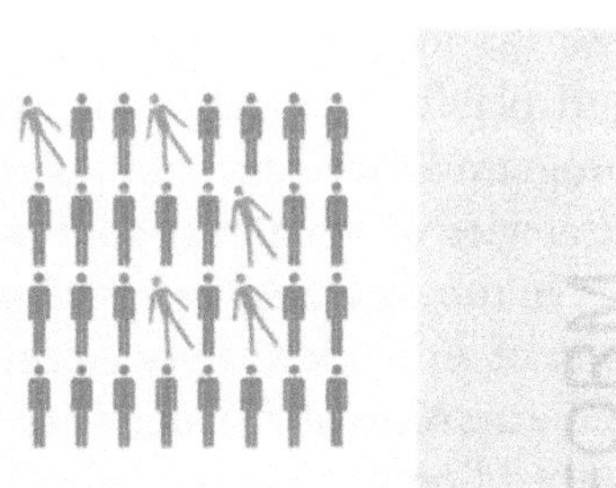

41/42

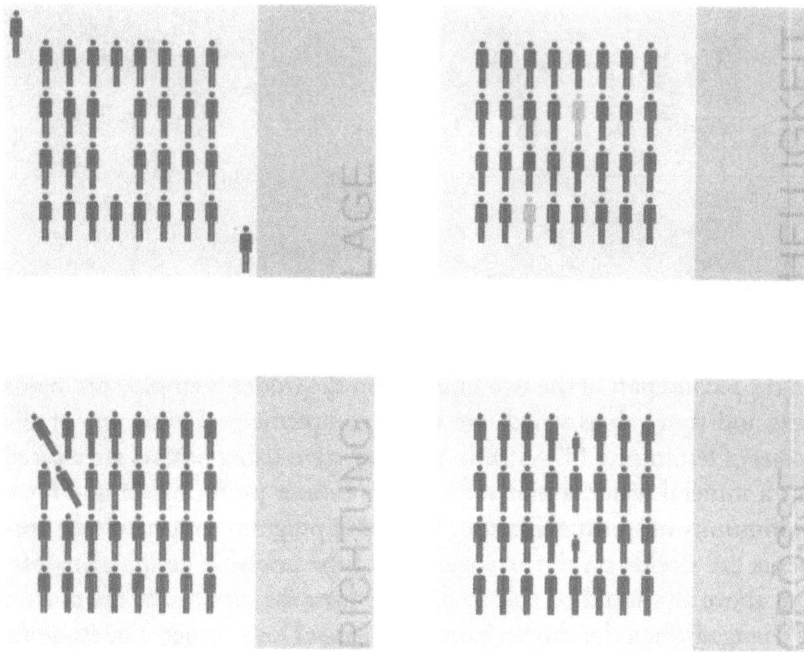

43/44/45/46

Afterwards the students can easily manipulate the brightness of the central figure from Goya's "Shooting the Guerrilla" ["The Third of May, 1808"] (47) in Photoshop. In the same way they may transform the low visual importance of another person into high conciseness. Changing the conciseness ratio changes the perception of the graphic communication (48). The relation between main and minor character reverses and the recipient's sight is caught by a new center. This experimental and playful application of electronic media does not demand much program knowledge and guarantees a useful insight into visualization strategies which aim at guiding the perception of the recipients.

In the creative area as well as in the area of reflectance and presentation of art work-analytic findings, electronic media can reveal an essential extension of didactic possibilities to art pedagogues. As long as the imbedding of electronic media and the time used for it can be justified with professional didacticism, it represents a valuable supplement to designing specialized teaching methods. Teaching methods intended to

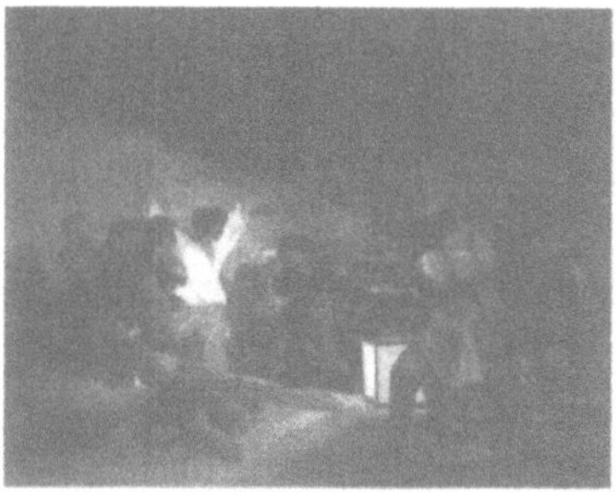

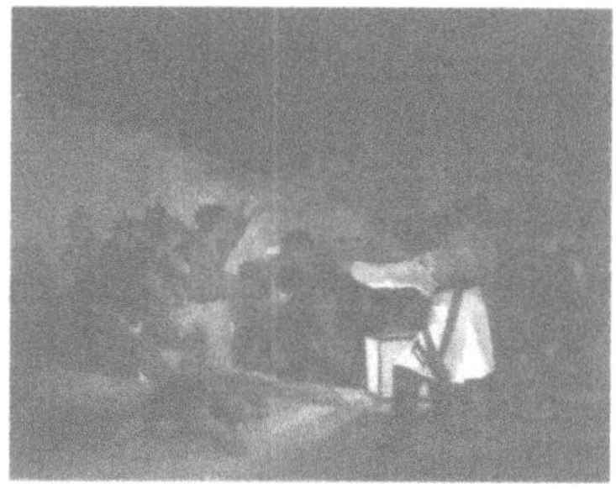

47/48

integrate electronic media didactically can only be realized at the expense of time consuming preparations. To make the design-related parts of art education directly accessible to children and teens without any time delay, all media must be presented in a user-friendly and didactically optimized way. This enormous preparation effort will be rewarded with quickness and a vast variety in the students' works, something that cannot be guaranteed with any other medium nowadays and with such a persuasion density (think of picture editing). The students should gain insight into the methods and strategies of the professional users of electronic media, which should enable them to be emancipated enough to face the top achievements of the picture navigators.

When using such an emancipation process, it should also be pointed out that the historical connection of visualization competence to the most significant representatives of fine art will no longer be the norm. The competence centers for visualizations will rather shift from the art universities to technological and medical institutes where scientific visualization tasks are worked upon, as well as to gathering places such as the PIXAR studios or ILM (Industrial Light and Magic, George Lucas's visualization company responsible for the Special Effects of the Star Wars saga). Such high performance training centers possess sufficient budgets to effectively accompany the development of new program resources with the recruitment of visualization specialists, who are most experienced designers. Only in this way will top visualization performances be achieved, such as "Finding Nemo".

While in the Gothic and Renaissance periods peak values of visualization were to be found in fine arts, nowadays the relevant developers of visualization hardly ever reside within fine arts. The leading role of scientific visualization centers in the continuation of virtual realities as density tools for visual information can no longer be denied. Whereas in the 15th century artists gave the scientists tools for the visual coping of their information transfer, nowadays this seems to be reversed. And visualization centers such as PIXAR studios or ILM represent core areas of the movie industry that have actually made the market-oriented production of picture worlds their day-to-day business.

And without any intention of wanting to understand the technological know-how of these visualization centers, there is definitely a fundamental difference between the academically oriented research levels and the entertainment oriented picture studios of the flourishing movie industry: If the density of intellectually aligned visualization is the main subject and almost sole purpose in the area of the academically motivated articulation of explicit visual information, the visualization professionals of PIXAR studios work on the density of the intellect-related transfer of information as well as on the density of emotion-related information transfer. Several marine biologists and ocean current researchers were involved in the development of convincingly animated underwater picture worlds ("Finding Nemo") and by their professional skills ensured the credibility and the content-related persuasiveness of digital picture creations. The fact that the recipients' emotions are addressed and tempted to develop specific feelings in certain movie scenes, possibly by controlling the color, brightness and darkness ratios of the movie, is due to the proficiency in visualizing the emotion-related steering system of the viewers' perception by successfully emphasized design processes.

2.1 Increasing the emotion-related density of visual information

Creating image information implies that guidance of perception is wanted at any time and in any case. The successful or, in the ideal case, the optimized visual information transfer calls for such a guidance of perception by applying designing methods. Content-related and form-related context management determines the recipient's perception of the sign order. The articulation of clear image signs which unmistakably transport their statement of contents in the image area is without any doubt part of the intellect-related information density. The deliberate control of the guided recipient's view also represents the result of an intellect-related sign order achievement.

The choice of signs responsible for the transfer of a certain message in their respective content context is already part of a smooth transition area between the intellect-related and the emotion-related work of information density. The choice of a laughing child for transferring an advertising message should address the recipients' emotions, just as the conventional melancholic rain scene is always used when the emotions of the movie's main actors need an external reflection of their inner existential orientation.

The actual emotion-related density achievement may have already been started by mentioning the sign whose assignment should affect the viewers' emotions, but the choice alone is not enough. The mode and method of the formal (bright and dark, colored, acoustically accompanied, multimedia-based etc.) articulation will decide the issue. How sympathetically the laughing child in the commercial really influences the viewers' emotional world, how disturbing the dramatic rain scene really is, is decided by the parameters of the formal translation of the chosen sign repertoires.

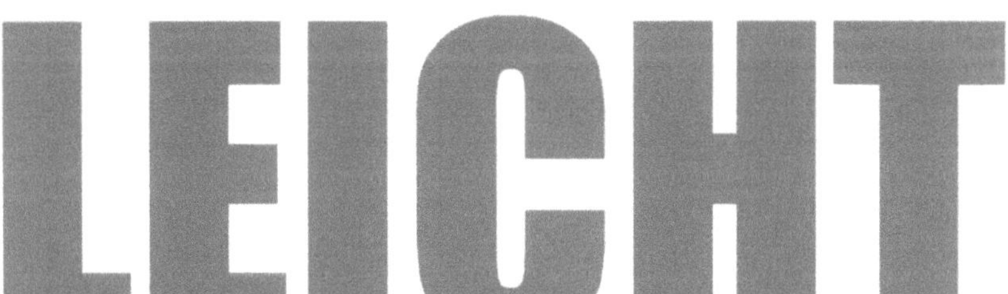

49

The guidance achievements in designing intellect-related information densities of written information originate from the regulation of the letter arrangements. The distances between the signs should guarantee an undisturbed reading fluency, the spacing cadence serves as a sign adoption relief as well as an adjustment for the interlinear space. The best texts show the qualities of a successful font in which the formal relationship of the family members represents an extroverted union of signs. However, if these formal analogies admit the individual uniqueness of each sign, these are, in perception-theory, the best conditions for an efficient font.

If only the optimization of perceptibility of a text as a design intention was the main aim, throughout Europe two to five fonts would be absolutely sufficient. If the sole purpose of text designers was the optimization of legibility, with the support of intellect-related density methods they would cover all requirements of the character design functions.

Many students show a rather moderate interest in the didactically oriented information transfer of design education. Often their point of view is that motivation for questions about arranging forms and signs might remain aloof without hurting the inhabitants of the ivory towers. Especially those students who most resolutely deny the meaning of analysing design processes and their general conditions would never put up with a reduction of the font choices in their computers to just five. But really, why not? If the optimization of character legibility can be guaranteed, why should the refusers of the ivory towers not live with such a restriction?

Maybe there are demands (as well as or just from their point of view) for letter forms which guarantee other qualities than just the optimization of their legibility?

The word LEICHT (the German word for lightly, 49) can be easily read. The letter signs responsible for its legibility are clearly distinguishable from each other and still formally related so much to each other that the association of the sign group is without doubt. They not only provide the intellect-related sign identity of the letter interpretation but also have an effect, a quality of impression: the signs look bulky and heavy. This effect implies an emotion-related perception of the signs. During each perception process such an emotion-related perception will sometimes be more and sometimes less effective. The only question is to what extent the conveyed contents of a visually perceived message should be transferred over the meta-level of the quality of impression of the applied form and color repertoire.

The heavy effect of the word "lightly" (in German: leicht) counter-contrasts the quality of impression of the letter signs with the meaning of the information they transfer. The signs could look very light just as well and therefore underline the contents of the message formally. The formal strengthening of transferred contents represents an ancient challenge for the articulation specialists of visual messages and for millennia resulted in strategies to increase the emotion-related density of visually perceived information.

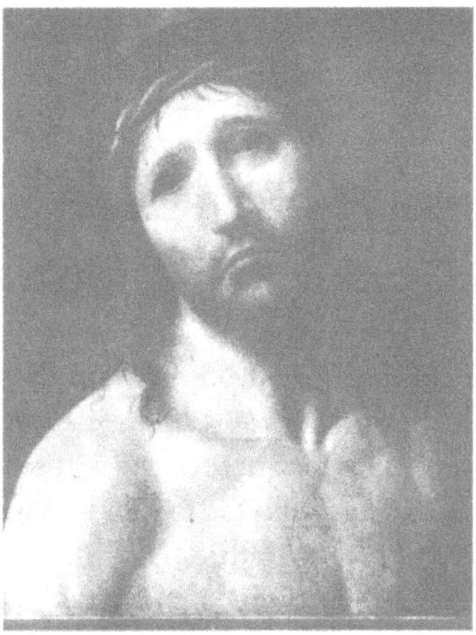

50

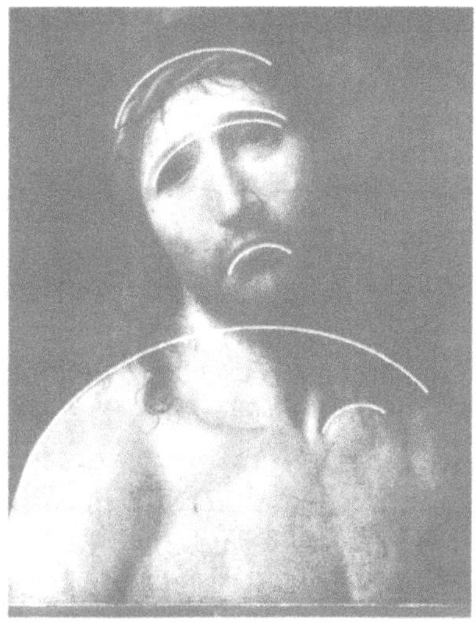

51

The portrait of the tormented Christ of Antonello da Messina's figure shows a suffering person with a crown of thorns (50). The symbol of the mouth is created by using a sickle, clearly pointing downwards, which refers – unmistakably by contents – to the emotional situation of the tortured person. To underline the effect of this sickle, Antonello da Messina repeatedly used the sickle form pointing down in his composition and without attracting too much attention by using this design method (as shown in 51). The curve of the eyebrows and the forehead as well as the form of the collarbone and the direction of the shoulder contour are clearly developed out of the concept form of the mouth and effectively intensify his suffering gesture.

Antonella da Messina composed with disguise and hereby granted the recipients a chance to absorb the contents of the representation very directly and undisturbedly. His methods of design are so unobtrusively embedded in his visualization that many viewers give the picture credit for its near reality resemblance, even if it is a clearly detectable invention. The invention of this sign builds upon the strategy of strengthening a picture statement by repeating the form values decisive for contents as well as formal relations of the elements of composition.

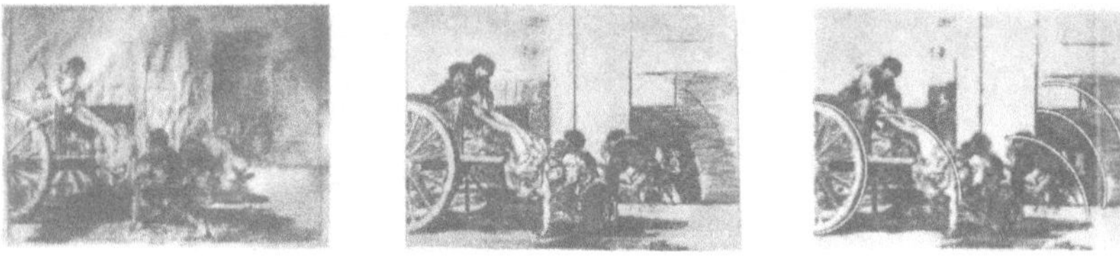

52/53/54

This strategy is excellently seen in the comparison of both phases of a Francesco Goya etching. The taking down of a corpse is intensified in the second version of the work (53) by repeating the curve of the corpse's figure in the architectural opening in the background (as shown in 54). In the first version (52) Goya drew a door which is traditionally limited horizontally and vertically. The comparison of both versions documents Goya's compositional approach and illustrates the use of a visualization strategy of the emotion-related information density by the formal repetition of important design elements.

Students should recognize that the control of form and color parameters of a visual composition can be used not only for the purpose of relating configuration elements to each other, but also serves to construct a directed emotionalizing total effect which when combined with the contents can emphasize and dramatize its message.

2.1/1 Electronic media as reflectance and illustration media in teaching processes concerning the increase of emotion-related information densities

The regulation of dimension-, form-, brightness/darkness- and color-ratios in image designs can be demonstrated extremely well by using electronic media. With didactic intentions examples from the historical and the current image cultures can be manipulated to visualize design decisions through the method of comparison. This way didactic media can be developed whose use by the teachers can optimize and simplify the transfer work. Form, color-, dimension- and brightness/darkness ratios can be altered to demonstrate the purposefulness of applying these modifications. Such alterations can guarantee the student's interactions with didactically processed image materials in an almost playful way. The result of these interactions should benefit the students with an insight into visualization strategies, a benefit that cannot be assured by any other medium at such speed and illustration quality. The selective efficiency of control factors to evoke moods and expression values by directing efforts of form and color utilization in visual communications can be proven by means of electronic media in an entertaining and vivid way. (see: "A little movie about script" – impression quality/ Hickisch/Barna; "Feeling Blue" – Schreibelmayr/Wiesinger; "Corporate Identity" – Proprentner/Nenning)

Didactic teaching material developed by electronic media will give the students didactic impulses in a persuasive and an objective way. The production of these teaching materials could be the responsibility of universities. A substantial part of the fundamental research in art pedagogy could be devoted to the distribution of electronic media as carrier systems for didactic illustration processes.

2.1/2 Electronic media as creative media in the teaching processes of increasing emotion-related information densities

Hands-on experience with the form- and color-structures control by direction achievements of the proportion, form, brightness/darkness quality, color and rhythmics makes comprehending the direction achievements of others easier. Electronic media facilitate this hands-on experience of children and teens and offer didactic possibilities guaranteeing insights into design processes, which in many ways account for the recipients' emotional reaction to the offered image structures and their design backgrounds. Students can experience themselves that the control of the perception-related admission of information is not only limited to the regulation of the intellect-related reception of information but also essentially serves the emotion-related reaction of the recipients.

"text samples" by Ulrike Barna (Hickisch) allows basic insight into the control forms of the emotion-related design decisions with the articulation of text information. The increase of expression can damage the readability of the text and the other way round, as shown in the two articulations of "wild" (see 55 and 56).The measures of obtaining optimal readability of written information (rational concentration of information) represent a creative power which does not always point the same way as the power of emotional concentration of information. Harmonizing these often diametrically opposed powers means a challenge to any professional processs of creating optimal visual information.

55 (WYD or WILD?)

WILD 56

Daniela Nenning's "Corporate Identity" points to the determining importance of color for the emotion-related admission of Internet pages and offers youngsters a wide range of color control methods to playfully test the design of websites. Manfred Wiesinger's "Feeling blue" allows students the mimesis of their self-portraits, effectively assisted by applying color.

All three class lessons call for the use of electronic media without asking students for any special operative knowledge. A few commands enable a didactically valuable trial of design methods quickly and simply. And only when its indispensability is verified does the specialized didactic application of electronic media legitimize the high expenditure of media-based preparations. The enormous consumption of time such efforts require allows the plausible conclusion that the production of well-structured media packets could be the responsibility of the universities.

3.1 Transfairness

The relay race of human consciousness through space and time always implies the successful transfer of information to be perceived visually. Society has never depended on this information transfer to the same extent as nowadays. The great importance of a sensitization and emancipation of children and teens for and by the content and formal bases of this information transfer and the media-based technologies which allow the same has never been as easy to be verified and argumentatively justified as today.

Paradoxically many decision-makers in educational institutions react to this analysis with a reduction of art pedagogy lessons. The esteem of the subject and its objectives decreases by the same magnitude by which its objectified importance increases.

Transfairness is a word-creation that describes the essential objectives of emancipating lessons by the faculty of art pedagogy by concentration of information. Fairness in the transfer of information could in many ways be intended as a basis of a humane culture of information and be made a subject of discussion. The transfer of visually perceivable information calls for enlightened recipients who know and understand the basic structures of the conditioning of sign/symbol fields for the purpose of transferring content messages. Transfairness calls for emancipated recipients who recognize the necessity of manipulation processes in favour of guaranteeing information transfer, but who also have to know its most important tools in theory and practice. Transfairness calls for a fair articulated information transfer as a result of the professional working achievement of fair visualization strategists. The recipients' acknowledgment of elementary fundamental rights should co-define the professional ethos of the visualization captains, so that they do exercise their leadership (which they must have as: conditio sine qua non) not demagogically, but with a sense of responsibility and respectability.

The control over a fair information transfer lies especially in the hands of art pedagogues, who should set as an important emancipating objective the qualification of children and youths as potential control authorities in the transfairness of future information transfer. A society which renounces training awareness of manipulation tools to articulate visual messages allows a less positive interpretation of the term transfairness, which means trans fairness, i.e. beyond fair behavior. This form of transfairness is less desirable and it would already be an advantage if the positive potential of this concept creation were developed so much that the identification of the fair transfer objective by information would be dominantly connected to the term transfairness. Future art pedagogy could protect transfairness simply by providing and explaining the criteria and tools of fair information transfer.

Last but not least the term transfairness could characterize the fair transfer work of the art pedagogues as well. Fair transfer work by visual culture specialists assumes that this work is divided as strictly as possible into objectified knowledge transfer and opportunities for reflectance, which, in an even more complex manner, should form the subjective and individual encounter of children and teens with the media and works of visual culture.

Nearly all pieces of information which can be presented didactically processed on the subject of the intellect-related transfer by visual information are objectified assets of knowledge, objective knowledge which can be communicated and tested. It would be absolutely fair to make students aware of this fact and to show them the general validity of this actual knowledge by suitable media and methods.

Multimedia-based areas of knowledge will be able to cover this upcoming illustration need. Multimedia-based (soon also holographic) visualization of the basic structures of the intellect-related density of visual information will represent a functioning instrument of a fair emancipation of children and teens on the topic of transfairness with the articulation of visual messages.

An essential component of fair transfer, a transfairness of didactics, will be the fair separation of objectified transfer of knowledge and working with subjective experience. Students are to recognize and experience that their subjectivity is seen as an untouchable property of their individual art experience, without the need for their art pedagogues to withdraw the treatment of the emotion-related transfer of visual information exclusively into the undefinability of unclear moods.

The effect of colors and forms as well as the effect of tones and sounds will be a major topic in the subject of medical research, whose results will also be utilised therapeutically. Humans are emotional beings, who as oscillation systems show a natural dependence on the oscillation relations surrounding them. The upcoming optimization of this oscillation by a humane design of residential and work-rooms shows a significant, economically relevant prophylaxis against conceivable disease patterns.

But even if essential parameters of the effect from form and color structures on the emotionality of the recipients are known, they should also be able to experience free space and freedom for their emotional reactions to cultural events. They need not feel in a predefined and planned way. On the other hand, they should also recognize that it is often the intention of the creators of emotion-related information density to cause a planned and steered emotional reaction in the minds of the viewers. For this planned emotionality of the recipients the creators have ways and means at their disposal which can be explained, at least in their outlines, and can also be illustrated.

The experience of emotions by artists was over and over again an occasion for their "wanting art" to evoke emotions in the recipients by design achievements. Even if some design methods can be described objectively, luckily the transfer process of emotions by means of art cannot be comprehended rationally and described completely. It would be more than fair if a fair transfer work of fair art pedagogues pointed out these areas of incomprehensibility and the objectified regulation of eluding imponderability of artistic expression forms. It would be more than fair, if a fair transfer work of fair art pedagogues could do without proposing interpretation of works of art to children and teens where subjective interpretations seem to be objective facts.

The fair transfer, the transfairness of the most important parameters of the intellect-related and emotion-related density of visual information, whose articulation could impress by transfairness, could elevate art pedagogy of the future to an indispensable mediator between intellect and emotion. And offering children and teens a sustainable bridge spanning the abyss between intellect and emotionality would be more than fair.

4.1 Unprovable remarks on "Criticism of the New Media" by Uwe Jochum

The differentiation of the intellect-related and the emotion-related density of visual information cannot be defined so exactly that the fluent transition and the mediation values which develop between the poles of the intellect-related and the emotion-related design methods will never be able to demand their rights. These design methods have often interwoven and merged.

However, this changes nothing of the fact that this differentiation could represent a sustainable model of all visual culture phenomena integrating the didactic approach, which would concentrate not only upon the area of free art but also take into consideration all remaining applications of visual conditioning of information.

This sentence completes the contribution to transfairness; and to be fair I must point out the fact that the following text acts as a small attachment meant only for readers who can really enjoy wild hypotheses.

I think of Uwe Jochum's "Criticism of the New Media" to be an important, relieving book. I think his representation of the conditions that constitute human life is unquestionable. There is only one point in which I might contradict Jochum's statements. As each of my critical remarks that I can throw onto the scales has no objective weight, without a gram of proof, what remains is to offer my personal experience of decades in a mental construction, a picture without any relation to reality for all those who have not experienced the reality which lies behind this picture.

The more efficient electronic media become, the more the attempt to guarantee virtual life gains in depth of focus. Interfaces are developed which in parallel with reality offer definable and shapeable virtual reality, according to their own laws. The use of these virtual realities ranges from computer games to artistic interactions with artificial worlds and sceneries.

Gifted users of the electronic media, disguised as created representatives, so-called Avatars, go to adequate communication platforms to meet other Avatars, other participants of the electronic masked ball. The better the general technical conditions are developed, the easier one can experience those contacts in real time and with a high frequency of participation. In future you will also be able to perceive such meetings in three-dimensions. Holographic pictures will show the meeting of holographic dolls interacting in real time.

At the same the attractiveness of such communication forms represents its largest deficiency as well: the knowledge of all parties involved of the conditions and rules of the game. Each player knows about his role of playing a figure. Each of the thread-pulling puppeteers knows that, represented by his doll, he will meet other dolls whose puppeteers he cannot know. At any time nevertheless each of them knows of the other puppeteers and of the doll's activities. The play with the game and other players is transparent at any moment. Each player knows that each Avatar is handled by a puppeteer behind it. Each puppeteer of an Avatar knows that no player will one day think of his Avatar to be an autonomous being, because he knows the true nature of animating an Avatar-figure from his own experience.

What if, however, it became technically feasible to develop an Avatar game, in which the participants are integrated into their Avatars so forcefully and convincingly that they would believe, while playing, they are this Avatar? Would this game be liked? Who would like to play this game and for what reason?

What would happen if there could be such sophisticated technologies that interfaces could be created in a complexity we cannot imagine today? If there could be interfaces which would grant the Avatars entry to complex activity- and development-playgrounds?

What would happen if such an interaction-scenery could be created for developing consciousness? What if creating such interfaces for spiritual evolution was a form of art of beings which we cannot imagine because at the moment our consciousness can neither project nor portray such forms of being?

What if each "player" and "user" of this interface "world" played with a huge number of Avatars, whose experiences are not purely of a playful nature and not only for the sake of entertaining the player? What if the purpose of such experiences were to change the puppeteers of the Avatars themselves? What if there were an interaction between the Avatars and forms of consciousness playing with them? An interaction which would strongly transform and evolve the players? If this transformation resulted in such an increase of the players' consciousness that one day they would be employed to create and care for those consciousness-supporting interfaces? Voluntarily and with great devotion, knowing the sacred seriousness of this game?

What if electronic media with unimaginable capacities were necessary to guarantee such interfaces technically?

What if we were Avatars of something that we might rightfully call ourselves and we did not know any better?

What if we were Avatars of ourselves, and had forgotten?

What if there were Avatars that would become aware of being puppeteers of Avatars? If they remembered other Avatars of themselves and if they could gain insight into the real meaning of the interface in which they may be one Avatar of many right now?

What if an Avatar of himself that can work on the enhancement of his consciousness with the aid of the most complex electronic media, wrote a book indicating the boundaries of the electronic media available, above all, in the area of production and utilization of virtual realities labeled “Criticism of the New Media”?

What if playing with Avatars called for players and custodians who would all be of divine origin? If religion was really the reconnection of all forms of consciousness to their divine origin?

What if the acceptance of magnificent technologies and varied characteristics of the many different forms of consciousness ought not to negate religious faiths in many different worlds except that the perception of the Creation would be more complex?

What if an Avatar became aware of himself and could not restrain from presenting such an exposed opinion in an article about electronic media?

Literaturverzeichnis

“Gesetze des Sehens” (Laws of sight), Wolfgang Metzger, Frankfurt am Main, 1975
“Leonardo da Vinci”, Emery Kelen, DuMont Buchverlag Köln, 1979.
“Kritik der Neuen Medien” (Criticism of the New Media), Uwe Jochum, Wilhelm Fink Verlag, 2003.
“Fliegendes Klassenzimmer / Heft 1” (Flying Classroom / issue 1), Gerhard Hickisch, Bildnerische Erziehung Linz, Universität für künstlerische und industrielle Gestaltung Linz, August 2003.
“Fliegendes Klassenzimmer / Heft 2” (Flying Classroom / issue 2), Katrin Proprentner, Bildnerische Erziehung Linz, Universität für künstlerische und industrielle Gestaltung Linz, August 2003.
“Fliegendes Klassenzimmer / Heft 3” (Flying Classroom / issue 3), Wolfgang Schreibelmayr, Bildnerische Erziehung Linz, Universität für künstlerische und industrielle Gestaltung Linz, August 2003.
www.fliegendes-klassenzimmer.ufg.ac.at, April 2003.
www.ufg.ac.at/be/wahrnehmung, April 2002.

Illustrations

1a, 1b, 1c: photomanipulation by Mag. Leo Kislinger / term paper / visualization strategies / seventh semester, 1997
2: Kardinal Albergati, Jan van Eyck, page 93 / “Van Eyck” / Otto Pächt / Prestel 1989

3: Egyptian painting, 18th dynasty, during the regency of Thutmosis IV (1401–1391 B.C.) / "Die ägyptische Kunst" / Michalowski Kazimirz / Herder Verlag
4: female nude, Peter Paul Rubens (school) / Studie zu einer "Susanna im Bade", München, graphische Sammlung / "Aktzeichnungen großer Meister" / Verlag Kurt Desch 1974 / page 253
5: photoshopmanipulation of 4 by Gerhard Hickisch
6: female nude, Pablo Picasso / "Pablo Picasso" / Carsten Peter Warncke / volume 1, 1890–1936 / Benedikt Taschen Verlag 1993
7: text and numbers / illustration by Gerhard Hickisch, 2004
8: Alain Delon / "Alain Delon" / Rein A. Zondergeld / page 53 / Wilhelm Heyne Verlag München / 1984
9: two signboards / photos by Gerhard Hickisch, 1987
10: head of a goose / playing card with animal picture
11: hobby painting printed in "Daily All" / 1994
12: old woman with basket / foto in Oberösterreichische Nachrichten / 1992
13: camouflage bird / foto by Gerhard Hickisch
14: Marcello Mastroianni / still picture from the movie "The Two Lifes of Mattia Pascal" / 1985
15: the pope / photo in a newspaper
16: point arrays / illustration by Gerhard Hickisch
17: stereophotos by Gerhard Hickisch
18, 19, 20: contextillustrations by Gerhard Hickisch
21, 22, 23: drawings by Gerhard Hickisch
24: Arial
25: illustration by Gerhard Hickisch
26: illustration by Gerhard Hickisch
27: konZENtration / Walter Jerey / term paper / 1994
28: zeICHne / Barbara Scheuchenstuhl / term paper / 2000
29: "Sie winden sich und drehen sich und nennen sich deutsche Richter", John Heartfield / page 170 / "John Heartfield" / Wieland Herzfelde / VEB Verlag der Kunst 1971
30: advertisement for Alpha Laval / "Viennapoint: Paintbox 2" / Andreas Fitzner – Albert Winkler / page 242–243 / paintbox artist: Karl Hoffman, photographer: Jürgen Müller / Prestel Verlag 2000
31: Columbo altar / Rogier van der Weyden / "Flämische Meister" / Dirk De Vos / page 83 /Dumont 2002
32: context figures / photos by Anna Riebe 2003
33: student projects by 16 year old pupils / 2002
34: student projects by 16 year old pupils / 2002
35: context variations / Regina Time / 2003

36: photo by Wolfgang Schreibelmayr / 2004
37: student projects by a 17 year old pupil / 2003
38: student project by a 17 year old pupil / 2003
39: student project by a 17 year old pupil / 2003
40: student project by a 17 year old pupil / 2003
41: vector graphic by Veronika Bammer / 2003
42: student project by a 14 year old pupil / 2003
43: student project by a 14 year old pupil / 2003
44: student project by a 14 year old pupil / 2003
45: student project by a 14 year old pupil / 2003
46: student project by a 14 year old pupil / 2003
47: The shooting of the guerillas / Francisco Jose de Goya / "Der Prado Madrid" / Jose Antonio de Urbina / Verlag C.H. Beck München
48: manipulation of "The shooting of the guerillas" by a 14 year old pupil
49: illustration by Gerhard Hickisch
50: The tortured Christ / Antonello da Messina / "Antonello da Messina" / Jan Lauts / Verlag Anton Schroll & Co in Wien / 1986
51: visualisation of the composition of the tortured Christ (Antonello da Messina) by Gerhard Hickisch
52: sketch of "Cartload for the graveyard" / Francisco Jose de Goya
53: etching of "Cartload for the graveyard" / Francisco Jose de Goya
54: visualisation of the composition of the etching "Cartload for the graveyard" (Francisco Jose de Goya) by Gerhard Hickisch
55: illustration by Gerhard Hickisch
56: illustration by Gerhard Hickisch

"Aesthetic Operations" – a perspective in art and media education

PIERANGELO MASET

At the core of art education is an experimental situation, one in which materials, perceptions and concepts can be acquired, and connections to the world and the self can be experienced. That would be the case, at least, if *art* were art education's central subject. It is art that can intensify our methods of thinking and acting, and only art has the capability to reflect on and demonstrate our actions from a different – aesthetical – point of view.

Since the pedagogically-orientated seventies, and not only in Germany, developments in "art" teaching have gone hand in hand with a noticeable failure to respond to the new challenges of contemporary art. One gets the impression that only a few involved in teaching art have even noticed the damage caused by the use of art for pedagogical purposes. In this article I hope to make clear that the pedagogical problems of art education can only be solved by means of art and not vice versa. This is because the artistic mentality comprises all the methods and discourses that are necessary for art education.

If there is a question that concerns art education today, it is whether or how art education can evolve an artistic mentality. The concept *Aesthetic Operations* attempts to facilitate contemporary art education by demonstrating the "mentality" of artistic, aesthetic or educational work. Mentalities connect production with perception, and producer with recipient. To connect and communicate are goals of art, as well as goals of art education, though clearly art has evolved faster and more radically than art education. This is one of the main problems we have to face when we discuss contemporary art education.

1. The Transformation of the Autonomy of Art

The following thoughts were developed with much support from my friend and colleague Michael Lingner from the *Hochschule für Bildende Künste* in Hamburg, who has been working for some years on the problem of the autonomy of art.

The way art has been produced and received is still dominated today by the idea that "art-ness" is the result of an object's specific qualities. These qualities are seen as the product of craft, and the resulting object is defined as the "work". This leads to the expectation that the work by its mere existence guarantees the presence of art. The quality of a work of modern art is judged according to the degree to which it results from decisions made by the artist that fulfil the criterion of being of the highest *improbability*. These qualities are attributed to the artist's free and individual *choice* of ideas, materials and forms. Such a choice demands an extraordinary amount of *self-determination* from the artist, which in turn is needed to underline the authenticity and uniqueness of the work. Originality is seen as the unrepeatable expression of the *autonomous* artist's personality and of the autonomy of art.

If art is defined as the specific material presence of an object produced by artistic craft, it is clear that the appropriate way to receive it is by *observation* or *meditation*. As long as this restriction is valid, aesthetic autonomy is exclusively restricted to the art object and the artist. In the art of the 1960s an attempt was made to make art more independent of the aesthetic *qualities* of the art object transferring it onto the *experience* of the recipients. Once the "objects" are conceived for the active participation of the receiver, they lose their status as "works" and become *tools*. With their (in principle) inexhaustible variety of action, receivers now also function as generators of improbability making the role of the artist and their work relative. Michael Lingner argues that the new focus of aesthetic practice is no longer the autonomy of art or of the artist, but *autonomy through art*. When the public contributes and acts, the point is no longer to fulfil a certain objective set by the artist. Aesthetic action becomes primarily a process-orientated and communicative activity that is aimed at the complexity of situational and personal givens.

According to Niklas Luhmann, communication takes place as a "processing of selections". As a result each communicating person is forced to make continuous factual decisions and take actions that refer to possible addressees. Thus for example in planning an exhibition it has become more important to offer the best conditions for the social *interaction* between the participants.

This differs from earlier practices by making an explicit link to day-to-day scenes such as eating and playing or sports and astrology, which art had once considered taboo. As a result the public no longer needs to feel insecure or inhibited when faced with the pretension of having to understand "art". In his book *Invention du Quotidien – L'Arts de faire,* Michel de Certeau pointed out early on that the practices of everyday life could be transformed into aesthetic strategies. These strategies are close to the strategies of an art-orientated art education, and if we want to evolve an aesthetic mentality, we need forms of mediation that have an artistic character. The transformation of art's autonomy makes the development of an art-orientated, art mediation possible.

2. Art via Art

Recently it has become evident that new forms and methods developed by art have transformed the concept of art. One significant characteristic of the art of the nineties was the revival of "institutional analysis" and "institutional critique" which used scientific methods and forms of research and presentation. Also evident was a strong interest in exploring socio-cultural contexts and cultural manifestations that were outside the art system. Art enhanced forms and methods of communication and drew attention to mediation as a necessary dimension.

Modern art is very much art about art, which is only possible through the mediation of *art via art*. When in 1913 Malevich showed his Black Square, it was a symbolic end point of art. But he also did something for the continuation of art – he invented a new concept. In the early nineties the artist Allan McCollum quoted Malevich's operation. He multiplied the Black Square as "Plaster Surrogates" and filled whole galleries with copies of it. One might say that he used Malevich's work for his own operation. Consequently, Malevich's work is mediated by McCollum's. Through this mediation the continuation of art was made possible. And this was not the end: in 1991 Andrea Fraser radicalized McCollum's work in a video where an actress performed the comments of various gallery visitors in front of McCollum's Plaster Surrogates.

Contemporary art has discovered mediation as one of its essential dimensions and it is very important that any art mediation or teaching is aware of this fact, since the basic operation of art is communication. Even the most self-referential works of art have to communicate. At the very least they have to communicate that they are self-referential. We have reached the point where the traditional subject/object constellation of art education practices has become obsolete. Contemporary works of art operate differently. I am interested in facilitating access to works of contemporary art and I am convinced that many of the "works" themselves suggest ways of doing this.

3. Against a "Culture of the Crude"

The current focus in our schools on effectiveness and the multiplication of educational goods has a dangerous side effect: the culture of the crude. Consumerism and a lack of sensitivity are not a direct consequence of the current curriculum, but the result of an economy-orientated mentality. The hidden agenda of our current school system is the consuming customer. Intolerance, lack of social behaviour and vandalism are not only the excesses of a disoriented youth but also the result of the domination of the culture of the crude for which measurable and consumable objects are more important than social behaviour and aesthetic perception.

The successful concepts of the seventies (in Germany: "Ästhetische Erziehung" and "Visuelle Kommunikation") unfortunately reduced art education to an increasingly measurable and predictable entity. In this context Dietmar Kamper has noted, "This mediation of art and literature as 'subject' secretly transforms everything into a poison, a slow poison that immunizes pupils from becoming interested with enthusiasm and engagement in literature and art."[1]

1 Kamper, Dietmar: *Zwischen der Logik des Selben und der Wahrnehmung des Anderen* (Interview with Martina Koch and Pierangelo Maset), in: *KUNST + UNTERRICHT*; Heft 176, October 1993, p. 44.

Passionate work on the concept of art is the intrinsic purpose of mediation in a theoretical and practical sense because the concept of art determines whether an aesthetic content can be perceived at all and also whether one can evolve a mentality that corresponds to art. The concept of art even determines the manner in which oil paint is put on a canvas. The German author and art educator Gert Selle argued in a recent article that art education has always had the problem of operating in traditional institutions with fixed structures that do not have very much in common with the improbability of art. Though it can do its best and try to develop the aesthetic autonomy of the pupils, in the end there is always a compromise with the institutional demands.[2]

Art education is situated in a field of contradiction between the freedom of aesthetic work and the task of work in an institution, which is the result of certain expectations concerning the institution 'school'. No wonder that in recent years art education as a technical operation has become the norm. This has led to a narrowing of artistic content, even when 'successful' and 'viable'. The real impulse of art – the free play of form and imagination – suffers under the regime of technical operations. Here art education is a long way from art. It uses the glamorous label 'art' for pedagogical purposes that are far more central than artistic content, and shows little feeling for an aesthetic mentality.

4. The Concept "Aesthetic Operations"

The notion *operation* here is used differently but not in opposition to its use in system theory. In system theory since Niklas Luhmann *operation* means the reproduction of an element of an auto-poietic system by other elements of the same system. There is no system without a specific kind of operation and on the other hand, there is no operation without a system to which it belongs. According to the theory of auto-poiesis every existing element must be linked to the operations of the system and any possible object only exists because a system constitutes it as a

2 Selle, Gert: *Das Eine oder das Andere. Über eine minimalistische Didaktik der ästhetischen Irritation*, in: *BDK-Mitteilungen*, Heft 3/2003, pp. 4/5.

unity. On the level of auto-poiesis the main problem of the system is reproduction, and reproduction requires existing operations to be linked with new operations within the same system. Operations are the guarantee needed for each system to reproduce itself.[3]

The notion of "operation" that I would like to propose stems from the Italian art critic and curator Achille Bonito Oliva. In his flamboyant book "Eingebildete Dialoge (Imaginary Dialogues)"[4] he introduces for example the *Operation Duchamp*, the *Operation Warhol*, the *Operation Maradona* and the *Operation Holy Ignatius of Loyola*. With the juxtaposition of these names Oliva's intention is clear: one "makes use of" an operation, i.e. of a well-known artist like Andy Warhol to facilitate an aesthetic process. Warhol's most important operation was perhaps the "serial". Via Warhol one can use the serial as an aesthetic impulse, but in one's own processing of this operation the result can or should be different from Warhol's. You can even "do Warhol" in order to go in a completely different direction. It is evident that there is an *Operation Warhol* or an *Operation Maradona*. It is the operative scheme of a specific artistic or aesthetic work. There is always a nucleus of such a work and a mental disposition that leads to specific methods and operations. If one locates this nucleus, one is able to determine the operation of an artist, or the operation that was necessary to produce a work of art or an artefact. *Operation* should have a number of connotations (for example: *act, efficacy, influence, force, agency, procedure, process, transaction, campaign*) since the concept "aesthetic operations" deals with the openness of art and art processes, which should not be diminished by any prescriptive definitions. The few definitions to be found in dictionaries can all be applied.

Aesthetic operations can also be used to interpret works of art. Locating the operational scheme of a work of art is a manner of unfolding its meanings. Take for example Balthus Klossowski – the French painter who died in 2000. He was one of the most important painters of the twentieth century. His operation was the application of some formal principles of the Renaissance under the artistic conditions of moder-

3 Cf. Baraldi, Claudio/Corsi, Giancarlo/Esposito, Elena (ed.): *GLU. Glossar zu Niklas Luhmanns Theorie sozialer Systeme*, Frankfurt/Main 1997, pp. 123ff.

4 Oliva, Achille Bonito: *Eingebildete Dialoge*, Berlin 1992, pp. 29ff.

nity. Through this shift he evolved a singular position in painting that is still a challenge for art historians today.

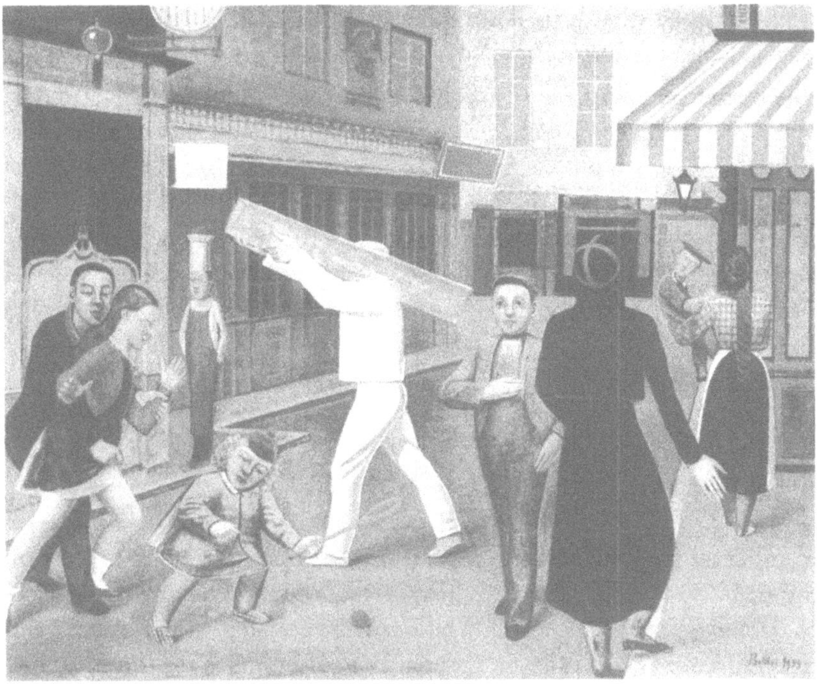

Balthus: *The street*, 1936

An aesthetic operation is not just a method but a cluster of methods, procedures and techniques. Each artist uses at least one characteristic aesthetic operation that can be traced back through art history. Watching and reflecting on art's operative schemes (modus operandi) is very productive because you are watching and reflecting from the perspective of art making. With aesthetic operations you are always asking: What mentality is behind that work of art? I hope it is clear now why aesthetic operations go far beyond lessons and training. They are not just a technique for teaching pupils, but a way of evolving an artistic mentality. When we teach art, we should be aware that art is not just a 'subject' and that it is necessary to show the potential for artistic mentality. This has to do with the openness of human existence, an openness in which the difference of *the other* might emerge. To teach pupils, it is necessary to plan, but also to be aware that the experimental aspect of art education, because it deals with processes of the highest improbability, implies that not everything can be planned. *Aesthetic operations* resist a technical approach to teaching and affirm the risk of openness. The mediation of art is a very complex process; you can only – and this is my main argument – mediate art if the mediation itself has an artistic character.

These operations are directed at methods, procedures and techniques applied in art and everyday aesthetic practice. They go beyond existing methods, procedures and techniques, because they are not consistent. They leave out or attach at least one important element of an existing operation.

5. Operation and Participation

In order to mediate aesthetic operations, mediation should be part of the operation itself. Consequently mediation should have an artistic character. This means searching for an improbable form. It can be a material form as well as an immaterial form of acting or communication, for example. In a seminar with the title "SMS = Stop Making Sense", students were faced with the task to do something with a 20×20 cm canvas. I introduced the project with a presentation demonstrating the different uses of the canvas in art history: the figure/ground constellation (Leonardo da Vinci), the presentation of the canvas's back (René Magritte), the all over (Jackson Pollock), the three-dimensional attack on the canvas (Robert Rauschenberg), the cutting into the canvas (Lucio Fontana), and so on. The empty as well as the full canvas can be a pictorial metaphor for an artistic mentality. The use of the canvas is a central problem in the history of art and a way of deciphering artistic mentality. The *Operation Canvas* did not concentrate on a particular artistic position. It took the canvas as the general space of inscription for a creative work with material.

An operation always has a distinct setting with some rules: 1. The construction of large three-dimensional objects on the canvas was not allowed. 2. The respective student who received the canvas each week was obliged to create something "new" on it.

Each week the canvas was exhibited on a pedestal. We discussed the result, photographed it, and put it on the Internet. The main difficulty for the students was getting a "new" idea once many ideas had already been used. Barbara Schaefer got the canvas when it was completely covered with concrete. In the village where she lives she used the concrete slab as a pedestal for performances with her neighbours. Many improbable things happened, i.e. different constellations of people around the pedestal and presentations with significant objects on the pedestal. There was even some ironic use of the pedestal: someone showed their pet chicken. For the participants it was a kind of a game that they took seriously. Barbara Schaefer offered an aesthetic space and her neighbours were involved in something art-like. Their actions do not need to be defined as "art" and these actions will never be part of a "professional" art show. Nevertheless people undeniably acted together in an improbable and aesthetic way. For the participants who are normally not involved in art, these actions were worthwhile and made sense.

Here are some notes by Barbara Schaefer:

> A 20 × 20 cm canvas was art-quoted by my professor. It was ripped and torn. Later it was given to someone else as artistic supplement. The canvas' journey was conducted with the following steps: look at it – take it – do something with it – show it ('frame' or 'pedestal'?). After that we had to pass it over to another member of the seminar. What followed was an all over painting, Suprematist reductions, a happening – someone threw eggs at the canvas, someone burnt it, and before it was my turn, it was covered in concrete. Something like a piece of a sidewalk was passed over to me. I had been curious what shape the object would take from week to week and now I was curious what my contribution could be. [...] Is it an object or a kind of state? It's a 'thing' and it's a game with rules. Take it, do something, show it, pass it over. My project had the following setting: a sunny day in June 2002. A garden in the country, a mixed group of people, the canvas covered in concrete, a question for the people, a camera, a ladder and some paper bags. The question: *Here is something that looks somehow like 'art'. What is your opinion about that? Would you like to arrange it so that I can take a picture?* Another game got started. Doing with no purpose. Ideas that lead to other ideas. The cracking of the concrete brought new possibilities. Nobody wanted to make sense. And so we made sense. Not only me as the photographer changed their point of view a couple of times. Stop Making Sense.

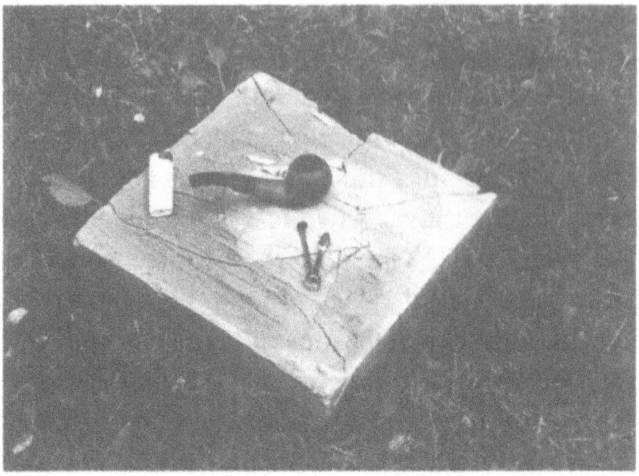

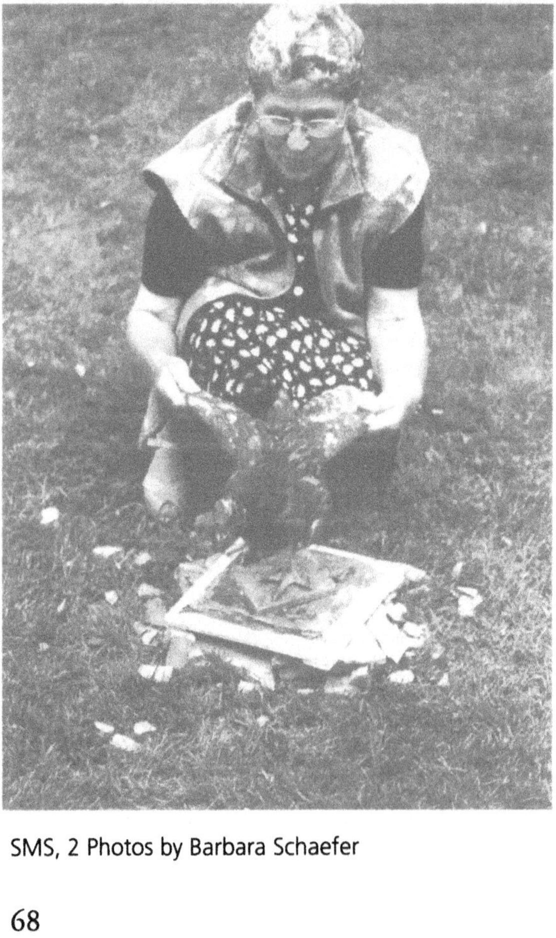

SMS, 2 Photos by Barbara Schaefer

This is an example of the confusing multiplicity of work with aesthetic operations. It is work with the intention of evolving an artistic or aesthetic mentality. It also questions the art system as a whole: Is there an "art" which does not belong to the art system but which is evolving in an elementary and communicative way somewhere else?

8. New Media Perspectives

The change wrought on the production of images by new technologies has launched a new inquiry into the understanding and the social function of images. Contemporary theories of the image try to go beyond defining "image" with linguistic categories such as "depiction", "message" or "meaning". Nowadays the hitherto neglected *use* of images has become the focus of research.

Developments in contemporary art are witness to this change in the understanding of the image. The current production of art deals with new forms of images and also questions the use of images. One example of this tendency is the so-called "net art" which uses the Internet and other technologies as the media, material and space of aesthetic strategies. Art and media education that claim to be contemporary must accept new challenges and investigate the specific constellation of image use in order to develop appropriate strategies for mediation.

Before the digital image was invented, art education could assume – as in a museum – that a confrontation between the aesthetic object and the viewer was the standard constellation for the process of learning. In this durable constellation the pupil was thought to be more receptive than productive. Nowadays such a reduction is unable to cope with a fast changing art world and the new kinds of images being produced. For this reason it is urgent for contemporary art and media education to research the new images and their changing use in order to venture new didactic concepts.

The new digital potential implies a different basic constellation of author/artefact, since an endless variety of rearrangements of the "original" image is possible. The "subject" as author is transformed into new, collective forms of aesthetic production.

With these changes on the level of production, changes in perception and the creative appropriation of the world also emerge. Contemporary visual forms like video-clips and desktop publishing are witness to this development that is deeply rooted in the practice of everyday life. Institutional teaching has already changed very much under the influence of these techniques, and new forms of image usage are part of daily methods of presentation and communication. Even "Powerpoint" and its many dull and time-consuming visualizations have unfortunately played an important role here.

Among the changes wrought on art and media education, we can focus on the potential of image usage which provoke us in the digital age. For research into the use of images the daily experience of children and youths should be combined in empirical research with results proliferated by the pictorial sciences. At my institution, the University of Lueneburg, we are working in our department on the following questions:

1. How did children's and young people's use of images change with the introduction of new technologies? What kind of image technologies do they use in their daily lives?
2. What kind of self-referential methods are possible in this use of images and what formal means are applied here?
3. How do young people develop skills for using images (like computer software) and how do they learn principles of composition and design? What means are considered by the "authors" as adequate and why?
4. Which forms and compositions are typical for the digital image? What creative potential does the transfer from analogue to digital images have and vice versa?

The transfer from analogue to digital images is an important element of research since it can clarify the creative potential that such transfers imply. With the help of the graphic software *Photoshop* for example, which young people and even children can handle quite well as we discovered in our research, analogue images, once digitalized, can be developed further by pupils. They can change an element or the complete structure of an image, and after they have decided on a result they can work on a series, or exchange the image via the Internet. This kind of work with an image is a response to the situation that *any image is a means for another image.*

Over the last three years, my colleague Julia Rabe Kröger has studied the use of images by children at a primary school. Here I would like to quote some of her notes at length to present the research and also to show possible aesthetic operations.

9. Operation "Use your Daily Image" (by JULIA RABE-KRÖGER)

"In the following description I refer to a school project that took place at the University of Lueneburg over two schooldays in autumn 2002. My goal was to find an approach to analyzing ways of using analogue and digital images, and especially the transfer of one into the other. At the same time the intention of the project was to find a method of using images based on digital technologies and their inherent qualities such as recycling, sampling or exchanging. In the project schoolchildren of a fourth grade primary-class worked together on the task of transferring selected analogue images into digital ones, and then using these to produce a series.

First, the boys and girls reflected on ways of using images, and started a collection of images used daily in the classroom. The image selection was regulated by two categories: the children were asked to bring either their favourite images, or images they considered curious. The collection grew quickly and brought various forms of images together such as holiday photos, Pokémon and Digimon gamecards, pencil drawings, newspaper prints, sticker collections, invitations, postcards with horses or landscape themes, and scribbling-pad prints. After talking about the images and the children's habits of using them the second step of the project took place in the university's computer room 'edulab'.

As something they frequently looked at and handled, the images were very familiar to the children. For this reason the next task – digitalizing the images with the scanner and viewing them on the screen – was surprising for the children and resulted in a number of problems and questions about this transfer procedure. What happened to the image in the scanner and why was the image on the screen much more attractive? Observing the digital data flow and comparing analogue and digital images were methods of the analysis.

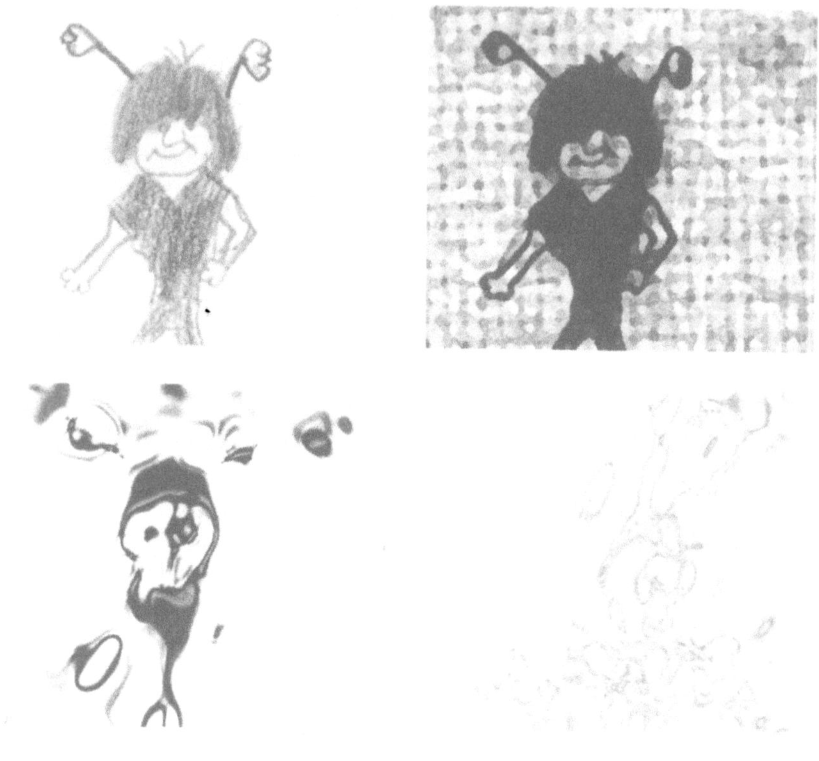

"Use your daily image", 4 Photos by JRK

After scanning the children titled and saved the digital images as graphic documents in a common directory since in the 'edulab' all workstations are connected. This network made it possible to exchange images, and the importance of authorship became obsolete. In this phase of the project the children spent a lot of time viewing all the images on the screen and talking about them.

In the end the children worked on a task, producing a series of images using graphic software. In this process the boys and girls chose one of the digital images in the directory and began to modify it into different types again and again. In experimental ways the many possibilities and functions of graphic software were applied by the children, so the production of an extensive series of images resulted very quickly.

The project provided an overview of how children digitalize images and use them in different ways. It also demonstrated the experience of a particular visual medium, drawing on associations with other media and other aspects of life informed by visual images.

Considering the use of images does not mean isolating a medium or form of image, but looking for several different, various and specific ways of using all forms of images. In the age of digital technologies the transfer of one form into another offers various possibilities."

10. Herbert Read's Thesis

I presume art education in the twenty-first century will evolve by dealing with all the different communicative and material forms and strategies of contemporary art and combining new technologies with earlier techniques. With regard to the legitimacy of art education we should mention Herbert Read's words from the first pages of his memorable book "Education through Art". He starts with the thesis that "art should be the basis of education". He wrote this in the 1940s, but I have the impression that we are only beginning to realize the connotations of this remark. I believe that teaching art means basically the mediation of an art mentality.

Nowadays art has increasingly become a kind of attractor that enables communication, where the artist or the mediator is an interface enabling the exchange of different forms of experience and perception. Art has become – as Nicolas Bourriaud said – a zone importing methods and concepts. In this sense the difference between art and mediation is no longer clear. Perhaps Herbert Read already foresaw that mediation could be art and art could be mediation. I hope that "aesthetic operations" can help to advance this diffusion.

Literature

Baraldi, Claudio / Corsi, Giancarlo / Esposito, Elena (eds.): *GLU. Glossar zu Niklas Luhmanns Theorie sozialer Systeme*, Frankfurt/Main 1997.

Bourriaud, Nicolas: *Das ästhetische Paradigma*. In: Schmidgen, Henning (ed.): *Ästhetik und Maschinismus*, Berlin 1995.

de Certeau, Michel: *Die Kunst des Handelns, Berlin 1988.*

Oliva, Achille Bonito: *Eingebildete Dialoge*, Berlin 1992.

Kamper, Dietmar: *Zwischen der Logik des Selben und der Wahrnehmung des Anderen.* In: *KUNST + UNTERRICHT*; Heft 176, October 1993.

Maset, Pierangelo: *Praxis Kunst Pädagogik. Ästhetische Operationen in der Kunstvermittlung*, Lüneburg 2002.

Lingner, Michael / Maset / Pierangelo / Sowa, Hubert: *ästhetisches dasein*, Hamburg 1999.

Luhmann, Niklas: *Die Kunst der Gesellschaft*, Frankfurt/Main 1996.

Selle, Gert: *Das Eine oder das Andere. Über eine minimalistische Didaktik der ästhetischen Irritation*, in: *BDK-Mitteilungen*, Heft 3/2003.

Art Education within a New Medium[1]

TORSTEN MEYER

The following is an attempt to think about what has often been called "the integration of computers into Art Education" (or similar) in Germany. For an example I will reflect on the model-project *sense&cyber* that was happening between 2000 and 2003. The project took place in four schools of art in Lower Saxony (Aurich, Hanover, Meppen and Oldenburg) and was sponsored by the German Bund-Länder-Kommission (BLK). The whole BLK-program, sponsoring lots of projects like this all over Germany, was labeled "Kulturelle Bildung im Medienzeitalter – KuBiM" (Cultural Education in the Media Age). I and three other scientists of the University of Hamburg[2] had been employed to have a look at what happened in the project from a scientific point of view. All in all around 30 people were involved in the project *sense&cyber*. They tried to explore what they can do with computers in their art schools. The main interest was to get to know if those more sensual things some people associate with art may be in any way compatible with those cyber-things some people associate only with digital media.

While I was gathering the first serious thoughts of what in retrospect I would like to say about the model-project *sense&cyber* an article showed up in my mailbox, entitled: "Bad Times for Art Education."[3] The author – Ulrich Schötker – criticizes an early attempt to make *Documenta11* tangible in a didactic sense, to process it, maybe rethink it, so that it fits into the existing framework of art education.

1 I'd like to thank Juliane Oepen for her patience while translating this text, which has earlier been published in German under: Meyer, Torsten (2003). "Kunstpädagogik im Neuen Medium." In: Lemke, Claudia; Meyer, Torsten et al. (Ed.): *sense&cyber. Kunst, Medien, Pädagogik.* Bielefeld: transcript, 241–264.

2 Claudia Lemke, Stephan Münte-Goussar and Prof. Dr. Karl-Josef Pazzini.

3 Schötker, Ulrich (2003). "Schlechte Zeiten für den Kunstunterricht. Anmerkungen zur Documenta11 und mögliche Zugänge". In: *BDK-Mitteilungen*, 1/2003, 7–11.

This criticism has accompanied me during the retrospection of the model-project *sense&cyber*. I was forced to see parallels, which – according to Schötker's suggestions – stand in relation of art education to its subject, which seems to be transforming somehow through *Documenta11*. The very thing Ulrich Schötker bears in mind when considering the integration of the past *Documenta* into art education is near what I'm trying to bear in mind when considering the integration of so-called "new media" into art education. At least a structural similarity can be found, maybe even more than that.

For now I only want to hint at that. I will go into detail later: I would suggest that the so-called "new media" not be reduced to a kind of new "devices" or "gadgets". Instead we should see them in the context of basic conditions: temporal, but possibly in interferences causally correlating new cultural, social, economic, political basic conditions, which can be summarized under the new heading "globalization". These "new basic conditions" I anticipate and say: This "new medium" was the subject of the *Documenta11, platform 1 to 5*.

To clarify where and why it becomes problematic to integrate a "new medium" into the art class or art school, for the time being I will explain in a paraphrase what exactly Ulrich Schötker criticized in the first attempts to "didacticize" the previous *Documenta*. For now I will keep attempts of integrating "new media" into art education in the back of my mind. At the same time I keep in mind that the project *Documenta11* – all *platforms* included – occurred at nearly the same time as the project *sense&cyber*. And I also keep in mind that in Kassel a discussion took place about the discursive field which in our case is more or less well captured in the key word of the title of the BLK- outline program "Media Age" – even though differently intended than in the context of art schools.

Art

I knew the author of the aforementioned article. He and a colleague had guided a group of students and teachers of the University of Hamburg through the *Documenta11_platform5* in the summer of 2002. He was one of the specially trained *Documenta*-guides who have been assumed to have a very hot wire to the creators of the *Documenta* and would know about any secret of the exposed art and the curator's conception. The first subheading of his article defines the problem caused at the conveying of the exposed arts' secrets and the curators' conception: "Globali-what? Mediati-what?"[4] I imagined Schötker standing in front of a barely motivated class of ninth graders and explaining that according to the concept of the *Documenta11* the cumulative effects and processes can be understood as mediatizations and representations namely in the context of space and time where globalization could get rid off big distances while time could be at best experienced as uneven ... – "Globali-what? Mediati-what?" is how the students might have reacted, understanding little if not nothing at all.

But Schötker doesn't address the students with his criticism. He addresses their teachers. And their teachers and university lecturers. They would have some difficulties to integrate this *Documenta*, this world exhibition of contemporary art, into their conception of the world, possibly also into their conception of the art educational world.

Color

I had to laugh quite hard when I read about Schötker's experiences as a *Documenta*-guide:

> [I] was irritated when a teacher interrupted my explanations of the works of Doris Salcedo. He didn't let me talk about the relation of the works to the situation in Colombia but wanted the works to be juxtaposed with van Gogh's chair representations. The theme of his current teaching unit in the ninth grade simply would be 'chairs'. [...] As soon as I saw the students who had to draw Yinka Shonibare's Rococo clothes I couldn't keep myself from intervening: "Don't do it. It doesn't amount to anything!"[5]

4 "Globali-Wie? Mediati-Was?"; see ibid.
5 Ibid., 10

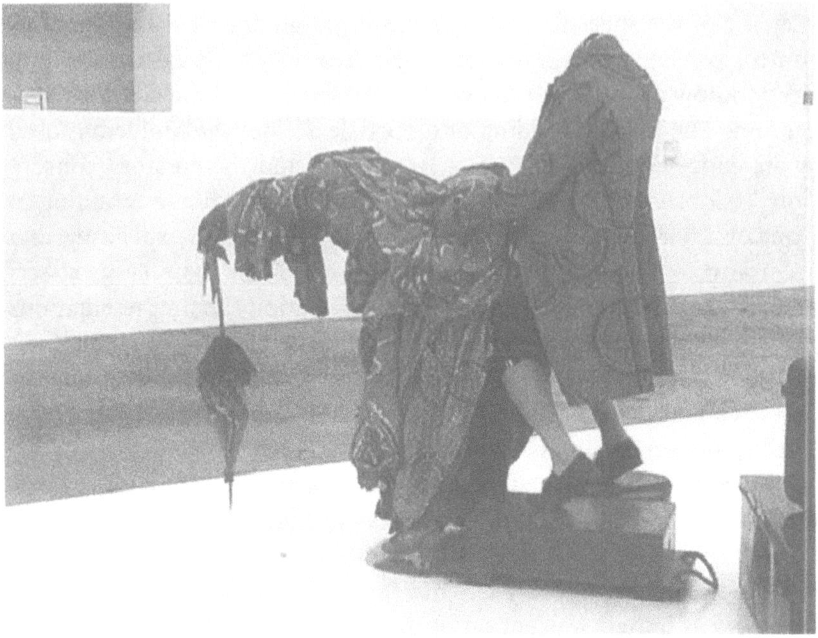

Yinka Shonibare: Drapery (Gallantry and Criminal Conversation, Documenta11_platform5)

It is so very abstruse that it could almost be intentional instead: One instructs the students with such obvious nonsense that they can't help but notice that something must be fundamentally wrong. Just imagine: the 16- or 17-year-olds are sitting there in front of these headless copulating puppets in their crazy costumes and concentrating on their well-sharpened pencils ... It can only be a question of time until they break into loud laughter, a laughter that will inhabit the whole Shonibare-installation, that will ring out into the corridors, fill the Binding-brewery, shake up the whole *Documenta* and maybe resound even further ...

I am thinking of the laughter that shook Michel Foucault when he read the mistakes of category of a "Certain Chinese Encyclopedia" by Borges which caused him to think about our "Order of Things" (and their categorical mistakes from a Borgesian-Chinese point of view) and to record his thoughts in a book with that very title.

Foucault writes that this laughter would be of a kind that stirs up all familiarity of our thinking, the thinking of our times and space, which disrupts all classified surfaces and all plans.

"A Certain Chinese Encyclopedia" (Jorge Luis Borges)[6]
a) those that belong to the Emperor,
b) embalmed ones,
c) those that are trained,
d) suckling pigs,
e) mermaids,
f) fabulous ones,
g) stray dogs,
h) those included in the present classification,
i) those that tremble as if they were mad,
j) innumerable ones,
k) those drawn with a very fine camelhair brush,
l) others,
m) those that have just broken a flower vase,
n) those that from a long way off look like flies.

On the occasion of Ulrich Schötker's articles I'm tempted to suspect that *Documenta11* or the art that has been displayed there or the way it was displayed there or all of this together could stir up the familiarity of art educational thinking (maybe of certain traditions only).

Form[7]

But isn't it a bit insidious ... I'm thinking about the monochromic color areas of the Atlas Group: "Secrets in the Open Sea". Out of habit I arrived at Barnett Newmann: Who is afraid of dark, light and mid-blue? ... if it wasn't for the "zips" ... not vertically from bottom up as in

6 See: Foucault, Michel (1966). *The Order of Things. Archaeology of the Human Sciences.* New York: Routledge.

7 Illustration: Walid Raad: The Atlas Group Archive: Files Type FD: The Secrets File: Secrets in the Open Sea (sample Plates), http://www.theatlasgroup.org (26.2.2003).

Newmann's work but bottom right, very small in the corner: blurred black-and-white-group portraits of women and men who – as one finds out if one is guided or reads the attached texts – have been found dead in the Mediterranean Sea between 1975 and 1990. Zip! Gotcha! Ambush: The "images" were only eye-catchers …

I imagined my old teacher: On the occasion of the "Secrets in the Open Sea" he brought to the students his affectionately cared for treasure – Josef Albers' "Interaction of Color" – to present them with a fundamental introduction to color reception (and then a head-shaking Ulrich Schötker comes along … "Don't do it. It doesn't amount to anything!"). Sorry about this, I'm exaggerating. That imagination is abstruse.

Just as abstruse, though, is what this Atlas Group tries to make us think or rather what the artist Walid Raad tries to make us think. He wants to make us believe an "Atlas Group" would exist, namely as a "foundation to research and document the contemporary history of Lebanon".[8]

The Atlas Group would have created an archive of so-called "files" which would be carefully analyzed and archived and at times would be made accessible to the public – e.g. here at the *Documenta11* but also in communication centers, theatres and schools – to shed light onto some unexamined dimensions of the Lebanese civil wars between 1975 and 1991.

Among these "files" different types exist: Type A: authorized files; Type FD: found files; Type AGP: Atlas Group productions. The blue color areas of the "Secrets in the Open Sea" belong to the Type FD. They supposedly had been found buried 32 meters deep under the rubble of the "commercial district" in Beirut. The Atlas Group would have sent 10 of the original 29 photo-prints in different shades of blue for "technical analyses" (as they say) to "laboratories in France and the US," and there those little black-and-white pictures would have been "recov-

8 See http://www.theatlasgroup.org (26.02.2003).

ered". And then the Atlas Group would have succeeded at identifying all the depicted people as those found in the sea during the times of the civil wars.

Composition

I actually believed it for a moment when told by my Documenta-guide. Despite or – I'm not sure anymore in retrospect – because of the car-bomb-collages I had just passed without guidance or explanation. But then I saw the "horse-race-files" and – across from it – the 8mm-films of a certain "Dr. Fadl Fakhouri". Dr. Fadl Fakhouri, a Lebanese historian, would have always walked around with two 8mm-cameras and would have shot a frame with one of them each time he thought the civil war was over and one with the other camera when he came by a doctor or dentist plate.

Is that imaginable? Or is it imaginable that Dr. Fadl Fakhouri – if he exists or existed – went to the horse race on Sundays with his colleagues from the club of leading Lebanese historians where they entertained themselves with bets? While within the week they would close professionally historical "bets" on how the civil war might end or what would be left of it in history?

Hmm ... if recording history was an unquestionably objective matter with no opinions on how important or unimportant and therefore worth mentioning or not an event or document is then maybe it would be imaginable that they – no matter whether Marxist or Islamist, Nationalist or Socialist – entertained themselves with bets.

But the recording of history is not a very easy science that objectively measures the clearly important and in retrospect explaining part, separates it from the unimportant and then neutrally documents it. They didn't bet which horse might be first. The matter is more complicated and more demanding to a considerable degree methodologically than the layman may think. They bet on how many mille-seconds before or after the finishing line the photographer would have pushed the button for the photo finish.

Documentation[9]

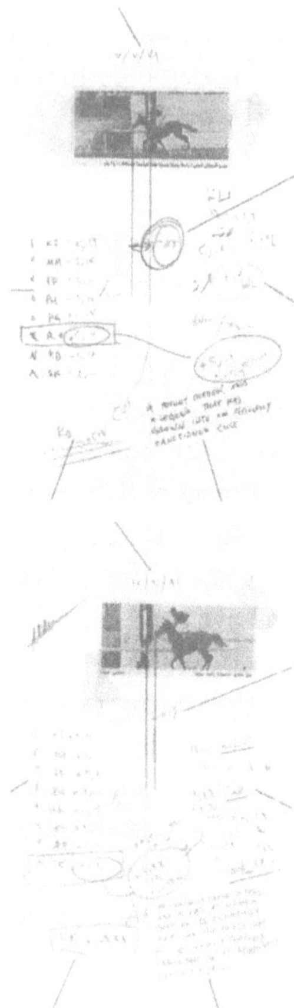

On the day after the race a photograph of the distance between the horse's snout and the finishing line – which was to be converted into mille-seconds – had been published in the daily newspaper "Al-Nahar". Along with it was posted all relevant information – as is a habit of leading historians – for details of date, length and distance of the race, average speed of the horses and even the initials of the Historians who bet on the horses or photographers and their estimated times, a short characterization of each winning historian ... All this can be found in the notebooks of "Dr. Fadl Fakhouri" and therefore in the "Atlas Group Archive". Oh, and this horse-race-story which belongs to the "files" of Type A, "authorized files," was entitled "Missing Lebanese Wars".

What's that? What is happening beyond a possible consternation, which as multicultural do-gooders we all spontaneously produce when we hear about such injustice and cruelties (such as people found dead in the sea while historians bet on horses)? Is this art? Is this documentation? If so, documentation of what? Is this recording of history? Is this criticism on the recording of history? Are these the "cultural studies" which Ulrich Schötker tries to open our hearts for? Is that a "cultural discourse"? Is that mediatization? Or communication-design? Is it a joke? Is it politics? And most of all: Does all of this fit into the larger context of the field which is entitled "art" and a linkage to education?

9 Illustration: Walid Raad: The Atlas Group Archive: Files Type A: The Fadl Fakhouri Files: Notebook Volume 72: Missing Lebanese Wars, http://www.theatlasgroup.org (26.02.2003).

Is the field too small? Or is this "art" too big? With regards to the Documenta shouldn't the subject-field of art education be enormously enlarged? Shouldn't sociology, political science, history and the science of history, cultural sciences, communication sciences, maybe the whole area of the so-called "New Humanities," be integrated into the curriculum to grant access to this art exhibited at the *Documenta11*? Shouldn't our work be radically interdisciplinary in the art educational field? Is this art not an interdisciplinary project in itself? And – assuming these subjunctives could come true – shouldn't the linkage which connects art, this art, and education be defined differently now?

Medium

Looking at the model-project *sense&cyber* we move around within the same medium. We – meaning the involved scientists – move around in the terrain that Walid Raad just stirred up. We pursue the recording of history or histories or stories and at the same time – as a methodological reflection incorporated in the interface of the project presentation on DVD – the criticism of it.

And on top of that we – meaning everybody involved in the project – move around within a similar horizon of questions as the ones just mentioned. On the occasion of the model-project *sense&cyber* similar questions arise with a slightly changed list of foreign sciences and a slightly different twist to it. The questions are similar because *sense&cyber* wasn't about integrating "new devices" into art school and to then continue – newly equipped – doing what has always been done before. Just as the *Documenta* wasn't about discussing questions of color and form (which supposedly have always been discussed in the field of art), now discussed on the basis of drapery on supposedly African clothes or Lebanese historians' notebooks.

And – last but not least – we move around in the same medium in a sense of a discursive – meaning thematic, social, communicational and communication technological – background. The reflection on the methods used by the science of recording history as the representation of what has happened can – and e.g. Walid Raads' works at the *Docu-*

menta11 show that – be put in layman's words. At least since Modern Art – long before a realization in the sciences – the "Crisis of Representation" has been debated in the white cubes. Instigated by the "new medium" of photography and its (supposedly) unprecedented truthful way of representation art lost its interest in visible reality and instead focused on the means of presentation – color, brush, canvas, frame. Magritte's pipe – which was the subject of an introductory lecture for the model-project *sense&cyber* – may serve as the perfect example for formally pointing out the questionability of representations. Walid Raad (and along with him a number of other artists appearing at the *Documenta11!*) addresses questions of presentation, re-presentation, imagination, substitution, mediatization and in a less formal but more subtle way – maybe instigated again by a "new medium".

Even though his "Atlas Group Archive" is accessible over the WWW,[10] surely nobody would claim Walid Raad as a "media artist" or call his art "media art" or his means or "media" of representation "new media".

Still, the playful use of his fragments which are at times camouflaged as documentary material, at other times as hints to the internal art discussions, leave no doubt about his amazing skillfulness in handling the current (re-)presentation techniques of the so-called "Media Age".

The Media

The model-project *sense&cyber* has been designed to examine – as could be and indeed has been expressed – "new media". But it can only be said in analogy to "the sun is rising" (even though we know that according to the latest research that is exactly not the case. Instead planet earth rotates in a way that suggests to its inhabitants that the sun is rising).

It may sound a little "sophisticated" but the more I'm occupied with "the media" and especially the "new media" being accompanied by artists like Walid Raad, the more clearly I see that the plural use of the word is extremely playing down. Talking about "media" suggests an idea of superficiality. Something that one could also keep away from,

10 http://www.theatlasgroup.org (26.02.2003).

something one doesn't switch on for instance. Something one doesn't switch on for longer than an hour per day maximum and at best with parental guidance for the optimal development and avoidance of long term consequences etc. And talking about "media" implies that there is a danger or a tendency of falsification and that – at least theoretically – it could be omitted so that what is in danger of falsification would be accessible directly and free of any manipulation.

I would suggest avoiding the plural use and to instead think of the "medium" as singular. The "medium" in a singular sense can't be understood as a "device" which can be used or not, which can be switched on or off and that therefore can be brought to art school or not.

The "medium" in a singular sense would be understood – just as in a physical or chemical context – as a "carrier" or a "substance" inside which certain processes take place: air as a carrier for sound waves in acoustics, for instance, or "medium" as a substance like in Chemistry where chemical processes take place. I think of this media term (with relevance for pedagogy) in the same sense that we talk about fishes as living in a "medium" called water. With one differentiation, of course, since in an educational context "medium" is being seen as a carrier and substance for mental and social processes rather than chemical or physical ones.

When dealing with the challenges of defining what the catchphrase "Media Age" means, I therefore prefer to talk about the new media in a singular sense: For a few years "those [new] gadgets" have existed. They are connected with each other by means of a huge net. The development of this World-Wide-Web of interconnected "devices" in offices, classrooms, bedrooms, children's rooms, universities and art schools coincides chronologically and causally with a bunch of economic, political, social and cultural highly explosive phenomena that can be accommodated under the umbrella-term "globalization".

Maybe it is a coincidence that the initials of the German term *Welt-weit-Werden* (worldwidization) appear as www. The World-Wide-Web is only one among several phenomena of this "globalization". But maybe there is a foresighted translator with imagination behind all this: Jacques Derrida insists on keeping the French term "mondialization" instead of "globalization" even in the German translation of his "L'Université sans condition." And that's why somebody later added

Weltweit-Werden (the worldization, the worldwidization of the world) behind the word "mondialization" for better identification.

Derrida wrote that he would keep the French word due to the idea of conveying its close relation to a "world" [monde, Welt, mundus] which is "neither cosmos, nor globe, nor universe". He wants to relate to a "world" [monde, Welt, mundus] which – at least etymologically – derives from and is connected to "man" (the German word "Welt" as well as the English "world" derives from the word "weralt" which is put together by the Germanic word for "man, human being" and an Indo-German root with the meaning "mankind, time").[11]

This WWW, the *Weltweit-Werden* (worldwidization) and its technical basis, the world-wide-web, these together could be called a "new medium". And this "new medium", the *Weltweit-Werden* (worldwidization), the technological, communicative, economic, cultural, social, political whole will be – as far we can anticipate now – something like the plural of what we are used to think of as "the whole" – if we take seriously the idea of a multicultural-pluralistic, postcolonial-heterogeneous, diverse-democratic and communication technological telematically structured "world society". The *Documenta11* gave us a sneak-preview-impression of that.

This is what the model-project *sense&cyber* has been about (at least indirectly). The outline question – "Cultural Education in the Media Age" – could be rearticulated correspondingly: Cultural Education – here: Art education – within a "new medium," what does that mean?

This Device

During the first discussions about "new media" entering schools Hartmut von Hentig warned us that it wasn't just about providing "new devices" for schools. Maybe it was rather – according to the media term suggested before – about schools entering a "new medium": "Can we really assume that this device could be brought into school – as a new

11 Drosdodowski, Günther (^{2}1998). *Duden Etymologie. Herkunftswörterbuch der deutschen Sprache.* Mannheim/Leipzig/Wien/Zürich: Dudenverlag.

subject and a new tool for education, without there being any consequences for the whole, for the "curriculum of the occident", for our conception of education and culture?"[12]

The rhetorical question of this "great old man of pedagogy" sounds like a very protective understanding of education; it's almost – I'm employing a barely current quote of the US Secretary of Defense – "old-European". But under close and trial-like serious examination there emerges a long ignored and unanswered, maybe not even seriously perceived, question. Furthermore this question displays the entry of "new media" in schools (or art schools) in a context of quite important significance. This isn't about whether we use laptops and beamers instead of overhead-projectors and erasable pens. It's not only about whether we can also draw pictures with a mouse. It's not only about the use of a different "device", a different tool for didactic purposes or image production which doesn't touch upon the question if and how the production of images would be beneficial for education – fundamental and independent of their "media".

I looked at the project *sense&cyber* in the sense of an attempt for a response or maybe just in the sense of loud and clear formulation of the question: Can we really assume that we can bring "this device" into art schools – without there being any repercussions? Without there being any consequences for our conception of "education and culture"? For our conception of cultural education?

Consequences

There is quite a lot to "this device". If one brings it into art school, then one brings quite a few other things into art school along with it: the necessity to be able to operate "this device" or to know or get to know people who can operate it. They probably have to be brought into art school as well. And there is quite an easily underestimated logistic effort associated with it, e.g. that if necessary the use of space has to be reorganized, because "this device" can't be accommodated in

12 Hentig, Hartmut von (1996). "Die Flucht aus dem Denken ins Wissen". In: *Medien + Erziehung*, Nr. 40, 327–330, 330.

the studio or workshop area next to the other old "devices" for the production of images without risking potential physical or at least optical damage.

Both the reorganization of space and new, other, additional "expertise" can have an impact on the course of long established and, through decades of experience, optimized art educational practice, which is based on a conception of cultural education. It may also be based on what Hartmut von Hentig calls "our conception of culture and education," what he calls "the whole", the "curriculum of the occident".

All art schools participating in the project were involved in this – each differently according to the history of the institution, infrastructure of the surroundings and expectation of the art school visitors. The art school *Klex* in Oldenburg was especially experimenting with different concepts of spatial and timely organization and with different "experts" – so-called "specialists" – who technically supported the educational work.

Mistakes of Category

Whenever a new medium is being introduced there usually is a phase when it is employed just like the old known media. Photography at first competed with traditional art, and cinema in the beginning was received – corresponding with the habits of the recipients but also the producers – as something similar to theatre (even today we still have a curtain in front of the cinema screen).

The newness of the respectively new medium is being discovered only slowly because the use of the new medium as old medium might have included some traps, e.g. because an HTML-"page" gets displayed in a landscape format on the screen while it was imagined to rather look like a typewriter page produced in an upright way. Or for instance because the World-Wide-Web doesn't resemble a library since there are neither librarians nor catalogues (a structure of the whole). Only slowly are new possibilities explored in an experimental way and only slowly does a specific new aesthetic of the new medium evolve and specific new ways and possibilities of presentation become interesting.

The phase of *assimilation*, meaning the attitude towards the new which treats this new something as an occurrence of something known (e.g. a toddler who sorts everything that has four legs and moves into the category "bow-wow" or an art teacher who occupies his students with Yinka Shonibares' interesting drapery) seems to be not yet overcome in regards to the "new media".

This is why the question of *accommodation* – abstract: the form of dealing with a new thing which leads to changes in the internal mental system (creation of new categories which for instance allow for a differentiation between dogs and cows) – may come too early. Maybe ...

The model project *sense&cyber* revealed a few traps that show how a careless assimilation of "this device" as a sole tool for image production is not possible (anymore) – without further questions being brought up. It made clear that bringing "this device" into school or art school to try some digital smudging is comparable – also considering the logistical efforts – to a class trip to the *Documenta* with the goal to study interesting drapery there.

Mistakes of category that allow "media" to be confused with "tools" are probably necessary in the assimilation phase of respectively "new media". We can learn from mistakes. We stumbled over a few. Hartmut von Hentig's rhetorical question is hereby – at least superficially – answered: No, we can't bring "this device" into art school without any repercussions. It does have consequences. We don't know yet which ones exactly but we have seen the traps. We have heard "bow-wow" uttered as "moo."

Design-Machine

One could have let it be. One could have held on to the result that there is now a "device" next to the others in the art school which resembles a "bow-wow" (image production tool), acts like it but utters "moo" at times. One could have documented through which organizational or didactic tricks one can achieve an effective easy-to-handle "bow-wow" and how the sometimes occurring "moo" can be stopped.

But linked to "this device" there are some additional things. In a quite literal sense the World-Wide-Web is linked to it.

In a way, this would be a reduction to a certain linked up "device" which would be quite welcomed or regarded as useful by all users in the art schools. But this reduction contributes to a more fitting categorization of the new (of the "moo") of the "new media." "This device" brings – even if only potentially – the WWW along with it, the World-Wide-Web as well as the *Weltweit-Werden* (Worldwidization).

The art school *miraculum* in Aurich has experimented with linkage in length. The new "device" was admittedly used to create pictures, movies and animations, but the main focus was on communicative and social processes. The different attempts at networking and "regional internet portals" for children, teenagers and educational multiplicators should be understood as works of communication structures and as social and institutional interlocking.

The "new media" were mainly used for conceptional and, in a more narrow sense, for interdisciplinary purpose in Aurich. They were also used as tools for working in the area of visual arts but most of all underneath as tools for working on communication structures.

Concerning the project *network miraculum* the formulation of bringing the "new media" into art school doesn't fit. It would be more appropriate to say: The art school was brought into the "new medium". And admittedly with great success, at least in the case of the relatively special infrastructure of the city of Aurich that we defined as the "Center of the Periphery".

Designable Machine

Something is still linked to "this device". Linked to it or associated with it is a way of radically formalized and formalizing thinking – known at some art schools as "male logic" – which turns "this device" into a "universal machine".

One can do anything with "this device". One can write texts, construct work pieces, visualize hidden organs of the body, produce videos, compose music, manage folders, surf the internet – and also create images. But no matter what one chooses to do, behind the surface of the software application this means: Organizing and sorting through data. Single values of databases are altered. The data of these databases can be interpreted as "text" – meaning a defined sequence of ASCII-code ("characters") – as "image" – meaning as a table of color values assigned to the dots of a Cartesian co-ordinate system – they can appear on the monitor or the printer; or the timed rhythmical sequences of numbers can be interpreted as defined frequencies via a digital-analogue-converter and through an analogue speaker poured out as "music". Normally the *user* doesn't get to see the database structures. They are hidden behind the interfaces of the software application.

The art school *KunstWerk* in Hanover was occupied with looking behind these surfaces in the context of a CD-ROM-production called "Sehreise über das Mehr" (sounds like "sea voyage across the ocean" but is written as "See-Travel across the More"). The "See-Travel behind the Surfaces" which the two art educationalists undertook in a (partly guided) test on themselves revealed that the supposedly Design-Machine was designable itself.

This can be paradigmatically deducted from the "text/color transformator". With the help of this self made "tool" the type of data that is *actually* "meant to be" ASCII-code will be interpreted as "image".

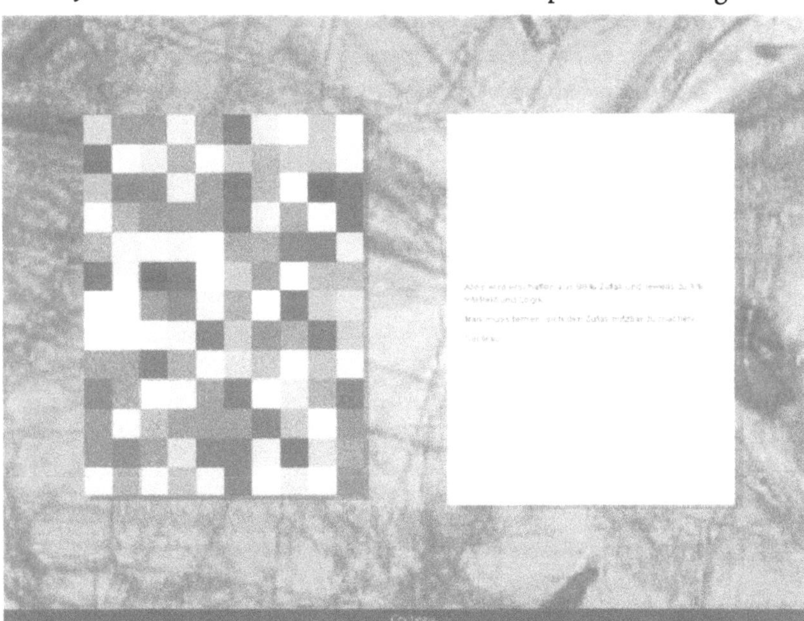

Screenshot "text/color transformator", CD-ROM "Sehreise über das Mehr" (*KunstWerk*, Hanover): The characters in the text on the right are interpreted as colors on the left.

For the radically formalized and formalizing thinking associated with "this device" – admittedly characterizing – it doesn't matter whether a data block was *meant* to be "image" or "text". It has no opinion. It doesn't know of any opinion. Such is its principle.

Symbolic Form

The "text/color transformator" may look like a cute game that might seem relatively see – through and no longer interesting, also because the "images" produced via "text-misinterpretation" aren't good images. It shows, though, what is new according the "new medium".

This is mirrored in a different way in "Hypermedia-Ethnographics". This is what we decided to call the method of scientific documentation. In short this refers to an experiment which portrayed the – for the 20th century – spectacularly productive problems with authority and authenticity of representation, entitled "Crisis of Representation". We found these new possibilities of representation behind the surfaces of the new "devices". Reduced to one sentence one could say: Our history of the project *sense&cyber* is a database.

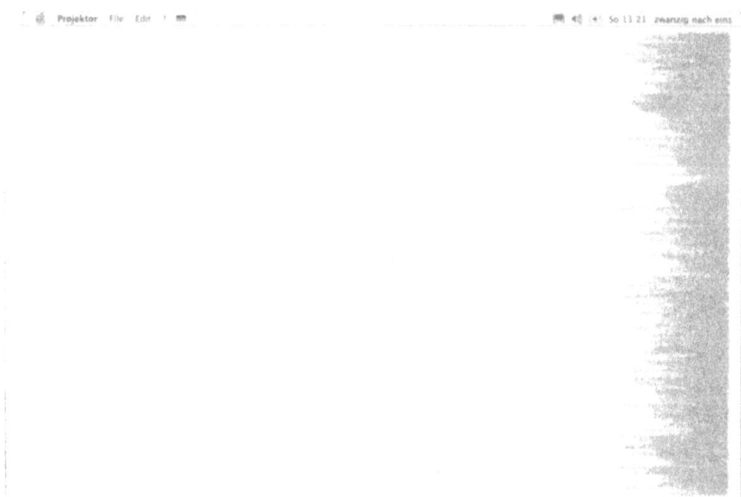

Our history of the project *sense&cyber*. Around 600 documents with no special point of view chosen. (Screenshot of DVD-Interface)

And one should stumble over this sentence – "our history of the project *sense&cyber* is a database": A database can't be a narration like a history would be. It is determined in the character of a database not to be a narration – neither story nor history. A database has no beginning or end. It has no subject, no "opinion", no "story", definitely no "moral", not even an order that could be recognized on the surfaces – neither a defined sequence of data or of hereby represented events nor a sequence of words or sentences that could represent events. Everything that defines a narration – whether as story or history – is missing. Everything that could define the "work of the author" is missing.

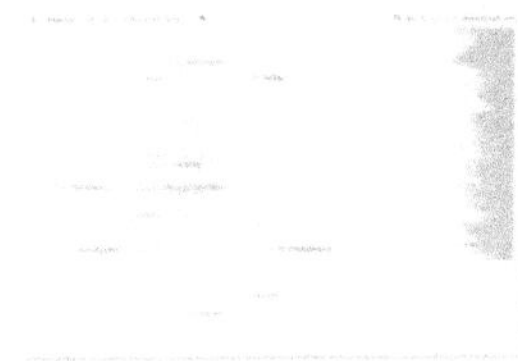

What happened in the project *sense & cyber* – art school *Klex'* point of view.

What happened ... – sorted by keywords.

What happened ... – where? Sorted by geographical order.

I'm referring to an essay by Lev Manovich entitled "Database as a Symbolic Form". Manovich puts "the database as a symbolic form of the computer age" against the symbolic form of the so-called "modern age" (Neuzeit) that had been – according to German art historian Erwin Panofsky[13] – the linear perspective. Instead of "Symbolic Form" one could say "medium" according to my earlier explanation:

> Indeed, if after the death of God (Nietzsche), the end of grand Narratives of Enlightenment (Lyotard) and the arrival of the Web (Tim Berners-Lee) the world appears to us as an endless and unstructured collection of images, texts, and other data records, it is only appropriate that we will be moved to model it as a data-base.[14]

There is no "author" anymore (God is dead, Roland Barthes' "Author"[15] as well); there is (therefore) no more common ground – even if

13 Panofsky, Erwin (1927). *Die Perspektive als 'symbolische Form'.* Oberer, H.; Verheyen, E. (Ed.). Berlin: Spiess.

14 Manovich, Lev (1998). *Database as a Symbolic Form.* See http://www.manovich.net/docs/database.rtf (16.5.2004).

15 Barthes, Roland (1989). "The death of the author". In: Lodge, David (Ed.): *Modern Criticism and Theory.* London: Longman.

only imagined – between reader and author or contemplator and painter. But this would have been the condition that enables the principle of the linear perspective to work. There is (therefore) no more "story", no more "railing" that one could hold onto – as for instance in the stories of enlightenment – there is no red thread. The thread got – we already know this from a lot of postmodern debates – ripped. Ariadne strangled herself. She was tired of waiting. Theseus won't come back. He is still erring through the labyrinth: "He runs and sprints, staggers and dances through the corridors, tunnels, cellars, caves, crossroads, abysses, thunder and lightning."[16]

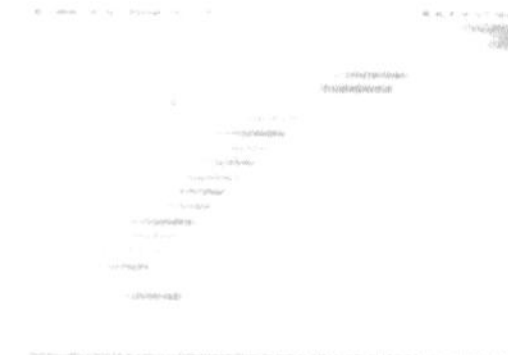

What happened ... – when? Sorted chronologically.

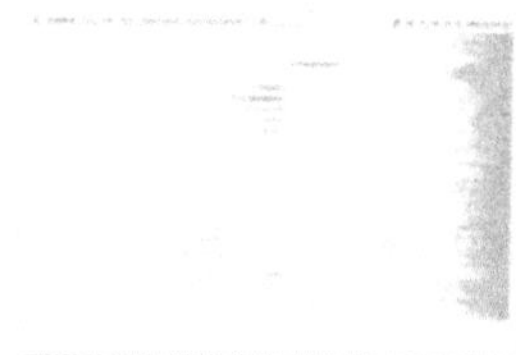

What happened ... – scientists' point of view.

And the corresponding media-technological reaction to the ripped thread and Theseus erring through the labyrinth is the database.

Education[17]

When I reread Michel Foucault's altered fable of Ariadne and Theseus on the occasion of the principle of database I saw Theseus as an art educator erring through the corridors of the Kasseler Binding-brewery. He runs, sprints, dances and staggers – I'm exaggerating – in the search of the kind of art which still can come close to the imagination of what he thinks is the reason or subject of his educational work. But the thread got ripped ...

This is definitely extremely exaggerated. And the class that Ulrich Schötker found in Kassel where students had to dedicate themselves to

16 Foucault, Michel (1977). "Der Ariadnefaden ist gerissen". In: Deleuze, Gilles; Foucault, Michel: *Der Faden ist gerissen*. Berlin: Merve, 7–12, 7.

17 In German I prefer the word "Bildung" which is different from "education". Associated with "Bildung" there is "Bild", meaning "image". "Bildung" is something between "formation" and "imagination".

Yinka Shonibare's interesting drapery is only a quite extreme exception. But it should be noted that it becomes more difficult when it comes to the relationship of art education to its subject. Or in other words, it remains difficult when it comes to the relationship of art education to its subjects. In any event, if art education is being understood as a specific form of application of art, a specific form of examination of always singular works of always singular individuals, then it is a specific characteristic of art education: It is dealing with the structure of this problem over and over again. In the beginning of this text I quoted Ulrich Schötker with "Bad Times for Art Education", referring to an attempt to "didacticize" *Documenta11*. Bad times for art education, meaning draining and unfamiliar times, as well – my prognosis – in the face of "new media". Admittedly the cooperation projects of the art school *Klex* have shown that – in direct comparison – a lot more was possible in art schools than in art classes at regular schools due to the comfortable infrastructural background regarding time, space, staff, equipment but also a stronger orientation towards project work. But looking behind the surfaces – which turns the new "device" into a designable machine and therefore turns the creator into the sovereign of his creations (again) – and looking into the structures of database and maybe in another sense looking into the "database" as a Symbolic Form remained a privilege only granted to art school founders and even among these only to a few.

It should be the perfect opportunity to instigate an argument about the implicit claim mentioned here that only looking behind the surfaces would turn "this device" into a designable machine – I know that from much experience. In an argument like this, however, this should be taken into consideration: first, what should be understood by *examination* of "new media," and second, how far an examination of whichever kind is being assumed to be education through art.

Media Competence

The terms "media competence" and "aesthetic competence" appeared in relatively close order in a catalogue of questions which the model-project *sense&cyber* started out with. The first one was even, at the beginning of the project, a hip term of an admittedly shimmering quality which was a door-opener for potential project sponsors in the field of education. But under close examination it's substantially relatively void. It never became quite clear what it really stands for. The smallest common denominator could be more exactly defined as "instrumental media competence." This refers to an operating competence, a skill to use "this device" according to its intended purpose. People who are "instrumentally media competent" can send emails, use the Internet search engines, manage text editing, and import images from a digital camera or a scanner.

There isn't much to discuss here at all. One should know how to handle our still new communication technology "device". It should therefore naturally be part of a repertoire for art class at regular schools as well as at art schools. Most of the logistical problems are – I suspect – of temporary nature. In the (near) future they will be pragmatically solved and one could concentrate again on "aesthetic competences" in a sense of "successful" productions of images, films, collages etc.

Another glance at the *Documenta11* shows that in the field of professional image production such an attitude towards "new media" has been established in a very unspectacular way. Professional artists naturally use "new media" as new and partly efficient tools – wherever it seems to make sense from an economical work approach. However, one can't necessarily tell this by looking at the products, nor are they exhibited with a special label such as "media art".

From my point of view the process of learning a pragmatic way of dealing with "new media" can be described as *examination* of "new media" only in a phase of habituation. Besides automatically becoming "instrumentally media-competent" I can't point out any qualitative difference in regards to the educational effects of image production using "new" tools or "old" tools. The tools for production are just more "up to date" but nothing more than that.

Aesthetic Competence

It's a different matter when "aesthetic competence" is being understood as a skill to deal with questions of presentation, imagination, substitution (re-)presentation, presence, performance etc. in an experimentally reflecting way. Then new options play an important role as well as necessities of (re-)presentability (Darstellbarkeit), the escalation of the "crisis of representation" and the "new medium" as discursive basic conditions. Then "aesthetic competence" has to be declared as the determining contribution to a participating qualification, a "ticket" into the "new medium" so to speak. It is a participating qualification for a multicultural-pluralistic, postcolonial-heterogeneous, diverse-democratic and in communication technology telematically structured "world society". The linkage connecting art and education hereby acquires a new function and a new highly relevant meaning.

It is not the "new media" or the "Media Age" which deserve credit for comprehending aesthetics as a fundamental question for presentation and (re-)presentability (Darstellbarkeit) and to correspondingly support art education as a possibility and skill in this area. At the latest, this topic has emerged with the "crisis of representation" in Classic Modernity. A kind of art education that is understood as one among many specific forms of the application of art, the addressation of art (also applying contemporary art) can't be surprised by the claim that we suddenly fell from the sky into a "media society". In all seriousness everything which has been called "media society" was always (and only) being held together by the use of technical "devices" functioning as communicative and communional mediators which are probably called "media" since they have to be plugged to a power socket.

Such understanding of art education could pave the way for an *examination* of "new media" – understood as a preparation to something what children and teenagers of the so-called "Media Age" will have to deal with – even if no new "devices" were used. The art school *Koppelschleuse* in Meppen followed this logic in the first part of its project plan. Thinking about "ZauberSpaces" *(sounds near to "cyberspaces" but means "magic spaces")* was intended to make the "magic" of playing with *signifier and signified* – allegedly only reserved to "new media" – presentable and easy to handle with older tools such as brush and paint.

A Substitute for the Internet

The Slovenian net.artist Vuc Cosic captured this starting-point – which doesn't have to imply any direct repercussions on art educational practice (though on its art educational foundation) – in a rather extreme formulation: "Art was only a substitute for the internet".[18]

If this is a recommendation to art educators it sounds a little strange: Art was only a substitute … but that doesn't mean that we don't need art anymore now that we have the Internet. It reveals though that art changed nearly simultaneously with the introduction of the Internet so that it leaves the impression that the description remains and there are more Biennales now and so on, but this isn't the art of the beginning of the 20th century anymore. Instead, maybe art can be understood as a training camp for the production and repair of helplessness and confusion when it comes to the diverse and plural options of symbolization and mediatization that are being imposed on us by our communicative and communional means and mediators.

There is no previously known or easy to handle method for the reception of the Internet – as one example of the symbolization and mediatization within the "new medium", within the *Weltweit-Werden* (Worldwidization). There is no recipe. That doesn't mean that we have to feel helpless or that there *couldn't* be a method or that we can't make one up.[19]

When it comes to the examination of art – no matter if at the *Documenta11* or, in a completely different context, in the project *sense&cyber* – one can learn to invent methods: Methods which show that it's possible to find a way even if the goal can't be reached. Starting at art and looking at singular works and processes one can train methods of reception and methods of production: Many different methods in many diverse materials. Many different methods such as painting, writing, composing, programming, cartographing, experimenting … in many diverse

18 Cosic, Vuc; Baumgärtel, Tilman (1997). "Kunst war nur ein Ersatz für das Internet. Interview mit Vuc Cosic". In: *Telepolis, Magazin der Netzkultur*. See also http://www.telepolis.de/deutsch/special/ku/6157/1.html.

19 See: Pazzini, Karl-Josef (2000). "Kunst existiert nicht. Es sei denn als angewandte". In: *Thesis. Tatort Kunsterziehung*, Nr. 2, 8–17.

materials such as colors, words, notes, numbers ... among others in so-called "new media".[20]

Experiences with Material

To think of the "new media" in this way – as *material* and not as tools – is a thought that needs habituation for the moment. In converse conclusion this could mean that a clay sculpture can be understood as a "user interface" since it provides (among other things) a point of intersection between the viewer and the material. It needs habituation, but one could still try to think that way.

Along the same lines can be understood what art educator Anne Möllers of the art school *KunstWerk* in Hanover describes as an investigation of possibilities offered by this new "device". First experiments with the computer at art school had been "experiences with material" comparable to those being made in a first encounter with the material clay for instance. Without any concrete creational intention an experimentally exploring *examination* can still take place. Although she was talking about exploring and experimenting "clicks" within the application software (which pre-configures the "material" already to a relatively large extent – one can't produce sounds with *Photoshop* or images with *SoundEdit*), the term "experiences with material" can be quite successfully transferred to e.g. the afore-mentioned "color/text transformator". Here the experimentation happened on the level of the program code which pre-scribes (or pro-grams) the display or use of the data stored in the databases behind the users' interfaces.

The "experiences with material" of this kind may lead to the suspicion that the database – which also means the "symbolic form", the "medium" of the "computer age" – is "itself" (here meaning without programmed user intersection) an amorphous entity comparable to a lump of clay; an unstructured collection, an archive without catalogue, a labyrinth without Ariadne's thread, a "medium" of loosely linked up

20 See also: Meyer, Torsten (2002). *Interfaces, Medien, Bildung. Paradigmen einer pädagogischen Medientheorie.* Bielefeld: transcript, 239 ff.

possibilities of meaning. Only the pre-scription (or pro-gramming) of the codes can pour the meaningless data into the one ("text") or other ("image") form. And this pre-scription (or pro-gramming) could always be another. The start interface of the CD-ROM "Seereise über das Mehr" pro-grammed at the art school *KunstWerk* is quite a good visualization of the database principle. Countless different documents symbolized as icons are floating through a "medium" – seemingly a coincidence which had to be programmed though – which vaguely resembles water: The "Mehr" (the More/the ocean).

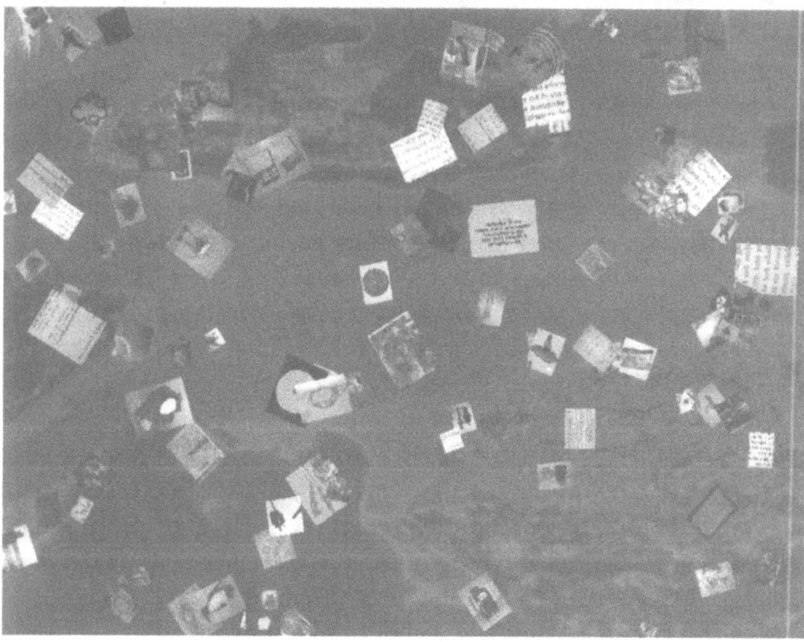

Screenshot start-interface, CD-ROM "Sehreise über das Mehr" (*KunstWerk*, Hanover).

The "operating system" of the DVD we pro-grammed in Hamburg makes use of different codes and different metaphors. This database – or *data-material* of the project events – only gains structure and form when questions to sort, filter or search are being *formulated*. One can also try to compare this to making pottery: The mass of information is being kneaded, then shaped by special tools. Instead of a modeling tool we have used for example a "simple query language" (SQL), a program language for the communication with or the shaping of databases. For the details we have invented special tools: Algorithms in PHP or – in this case – lingo or java which we use to formulate and pre-scribe how, where and which information clusters should be presented or – in other words – in which form the "lump of material" should apply. In contrast to a clay sculpture, which is fired in the oven and is therefore permanently fixed, the database stays malleable. This is its principle: It is a potential of form. It has no specific form but it can be rendered into any possible form – like a lump of clay (see previous screenshots).

Thinking within the Medium

The experimenting investigation of ways and methods of (re-)presentation – both producing and receiving – is part of the genuine work field of art education. To gather "experiences with material" on the level of program codes though is still (maybe until now) unusual and strange for art educators. It seems to be something for information technologists. From an art educator's perspective one has to move relatively far into quite unfamiliar terrain to understand the computer as a designable machine (for the design of information). But maybe information technology has to be understood as a "(re-)presenting play", as an art of performance somehow …

The model project *sense&cyber* has shown that not all art educators are capable of that and want that and that it isn't something that art school students or parents would ask for. But it also showed that it is possible – at least under the laboratory conditions of the model-project and with a temporarily uncertain result for educational practice – and that it could be realized with great success. The art educators of the art school *KunstWerk* have begun – as they said – "to think within the medium".

To engage with Yinka Shonibare's installation it is necessary not only to examine the surfaces of the "images" of the *Documenta11* but also their conception, context and their "new medium" – including the "Globali-What" and the "Mediati-What". It then becomes a casual phenomenon that the drapery of the Rococo clothes appears "picturesque", that the monochrome color areas of the "Secrets in the Open Sea" fascinate the mind and that the recorded history of "Dr. Fadl Fakhouri" is somehow *beautiful* in its conception. Though in a continuously irritating, instigating one …

It remains exciting.

Thinking digitally in art education: A historical review of its origins in the 1980s and development in the 1990s

MARTINA PAATELA-NIEMINEN

Abstract

Computers were introduced to the degree program at the School of Art Education in the University of Art and Design, Helsinki, in 1985, when second-year students were required to take a two-credit compulsory information technology course (for more information about the background of the course, see ATK-poliittinen ohjelma 1980; Teknologiakomitean mietintö 1980; TOP 1986; Paatela-Nieminen 1985). In 1988, the course comprised three credits and was already included in the first year curriculum. This article describes, through a series of examples, the early history of the information technology course and its application in the School of Art Education from 1985 to 1998 as well as highlights the more significant advanced subject study courses, projects and research from 1985 to 2000 in which I have been involved.

Although art, art education and art pedagogy have been emphasised when computer-assisted instructional strategies were introduced to the classroom, the major differences in using computer graphics systems in art education have involved perspectives on what, how, when, where and to whom to apply new media. Computer systems and their role in the area of art education have developed rapidly in recent years. The 1980s, the 1990s and the new millennium have seen a different emphasis on using new media in art education. However, greater emphasis should involve providing students with a cognitive, aesthetic, process-oriented and practical approach to thinking digitally in art education rather than merely creating digital images. In this article I examine how information technology has been taught as well as what content the course has included in applying IT to art education. I identify three areas that have all comprised the early history of digital art education in the School of Art Education at the University of Art and Design, Helsinki: 1) Computer graphics as artistic expression, 2) Computer software as a tool for creating art, and 3) Computer-based learning in art education. These three areas combine elements from computer graphics and art, computer systems (including software as a medium) and computer-based art education. I then summarise the ideas about the course development in the last section as well as identify new opportunities in digital art education.

Computer graphics as artistic expression

Art is the keystone in art education. In the 1980s, microcomputer art was a fairly new area of expression that possessed its own aesthetics. Computer graphics represent a different form in which artists generate fascinating geometries and patterns using the computer system both as a means for creating as well as displaying their work.

Our first information technology course in 1985 involved the study of computer graphics to understand what new potential it stood to offer art education. It was important to identify the unique characteristics of computer graphics to understand both the aesthetics and the new imagery of this medium (for more information, see Newman & Sproull 1981; Wilson S. 1986). We studied works of computer art from videos published by ACM SIGGRAPH. Although these three-dimensional fantasy scenes were all created with huge, expensive computer systems, they nevertheless showed the future potential of microcomputer graphics. I also showed examples of the creative use of small computers and microcomputers in the arts (for more on this, see the Proceedings 1985, 1986). That sections of images could be electronically cut, pasted and copied was entirely new. Saving the images on disks offered the designer greater visual freedom, since the work could be continued endlessly. A digital image could also be changed from one- or two-dimensional to three-dimensional images and reintroduced into new contexts. The technique of changing a transparent surface to a covering texture could also alter the nature of an image. According to Dale Peterson (1983), precision, iteration, transformation and serendipity became those qualities that artists began to use in their work (pp. 60–67). These qualities in particular appeared in the work of artists who used digitality as a means of fabrication, when programmed algorithms offered the artist a tremendous variety of solutions (for more information, see Wilson M. 1986, Kerlow & Rosebush 1986; Lewell 1985 and Cynthia Goodman 1987; ACM Siggraph 1989).

Early on, I learned of conflict between programmed computer art and images created with a simple paint system. In 1988, I met several artists in the First International Symposium on Electronic Art in Utrecht, and later visited several art schools and universities in the USA. Charles Churi from Ohio State University, for example, taught computer art. He programmed his own works of art by himself and encouraged his students by offering courses on programming. In those days, artists often worked with programmers who computerised their visual ideas. Lillian Schwartz, for example, worked with algorithms that changed her works of art into computer-generated images. Additionally, some artists used software, but presented their work of art through another medium. Joan Truckenbrod from The Art Institute of Chicago combined a video camera with a computer to create image synthesis, thus rendering her images more personal (for more information, see Truckenbrod 1988). Darcy Gerbarg showed me how she used an electronic paint-system when creating her work. Following the process, however, she took a photo of the screen and projected slides onto canvas where she had her final work painted. Artists preferred to use computing systems as a new medium that demanded to be used in new ways consistent with the intrinsic character of these systems. It seemed that no artist would use ready-made software unless it was programmed for further artistic use or expressed through another medium.

Programming certainly offered solutions for computer art in those days. It also offered new potential for teaching. In my class, for example, we applied a simple BASIC listing to still images to create an interesting "animation", a fascinating project given the circumstances at that time. Our classroom equipment included four Apple IIe microcomputers, two with colour screens and two with black and white screens, running Koala Micro Illustrator software, which offered eight colours. With 12 students per class, each student created three images with a joystick using the Koala program, and tied them together with a BASIC listing which displayed the series of images one after another. The images were displayed and seemed to materialise magically, pixel by pixel. In 1985, I received this list from The School of Visual Arts in New York, where I saw how students learned to create animations. Below is an example of the New York City skyline created by Antti Lokka, whose series combines several pictures that change colours in an interesting manner: the skyline transforms from a realistic scene (fig. 1) to an expressive composition (fig. 2) and finally to an abstract city (fig. 3).

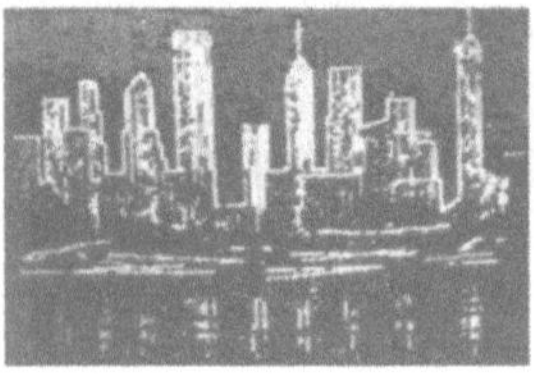

(fig. 1)

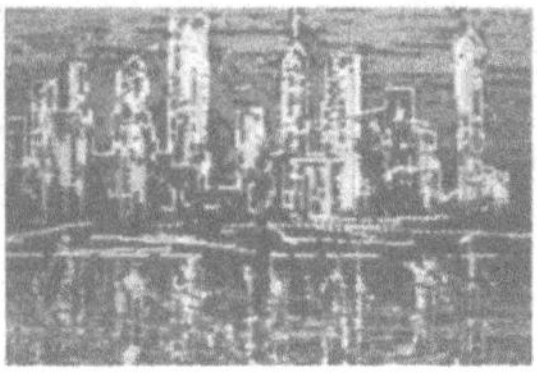

(fig. 2)

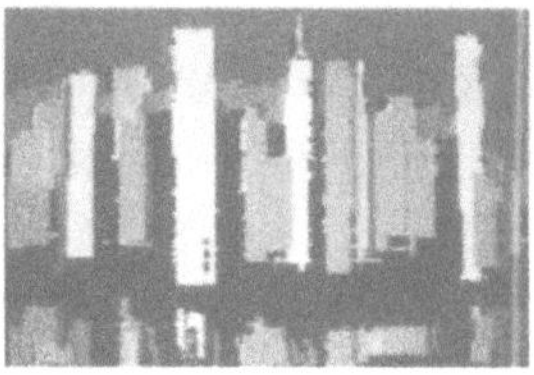

(fig. 3)

After visiting the USA in 1985, I became curious to see what kind of microcomputer art existed in Finland. The students in our information technology course and The Student Union of the University of Helsinki organised the first Open Computer Art Exhibition in Finland at the gallery of The Old Student House in Helsinki from 17–25 May 1986. This exhibition was called the Bite Festivals (for more information, see Romppanen 1986; Paatela-Nieminen 1986a, Bittifestivaalit 1986), and any work of art created with a microcomputer was acceptable. Our class used its newly acquired software, Dazzle Draw (which offered 16 colours), to design a poster for the exhibition. Juha Saari's poster was selected for printing (fig. 4, lower left); the image shows a warm and delicate hand against a blue cloud. The headline indicates computer art. Information about the exhibition date and location appears on the left. Juha Saari's caricature of Max, created with Koala Micro Illustrator software, appears on the right (fig. 5, below).

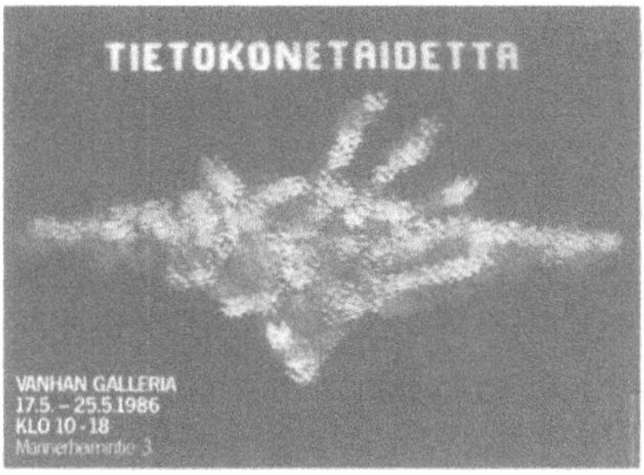

(fig. 4)

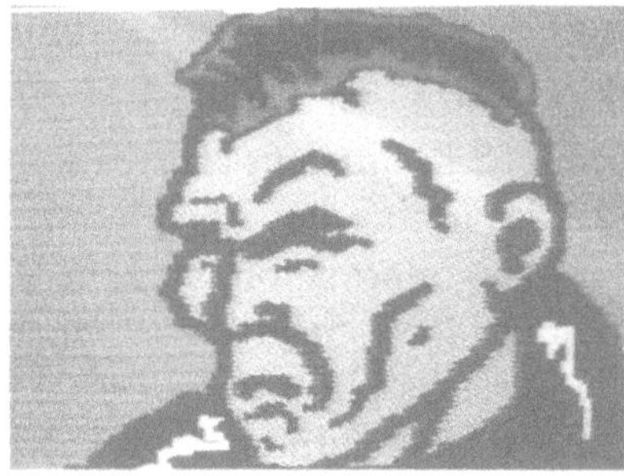

(fig. 5)

The exhibition included artwork from elementary school pupils to art education students, as well as programmed algorithm art shown on television screens, and computer art by Finnish computer artists such as Erkki Kurenniemi and Markku Metsämäki. This exhibition showed both new and traditional trends in digital images. To illustrate a new solution, students Tuula Rajamäki and Sirkka Hirvelä electronically drew a cave painting of an ox, had it printed in sections using the program Zoom Grafix, assembled them to form two sides of a huge ox, and finally painted them (for more details, see Numminen 1986). One side of the ox was painted electric blue (fig. 6) and the other painted brown (fig. 7) as in cave paintings. These two sides were then joined, and the ox was hung in the middle of the gallery, interestingly dividing the space.

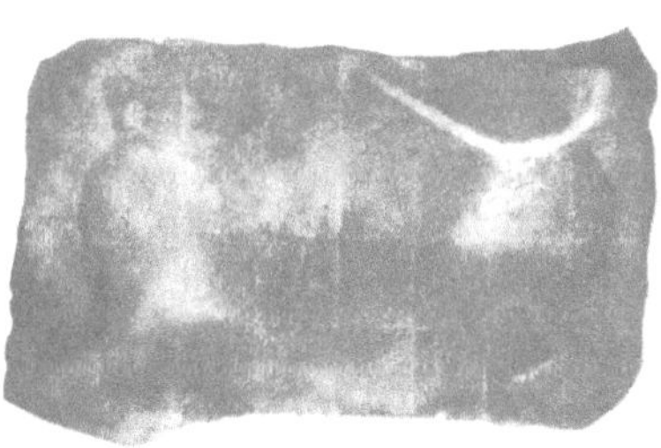

(fig. 6)

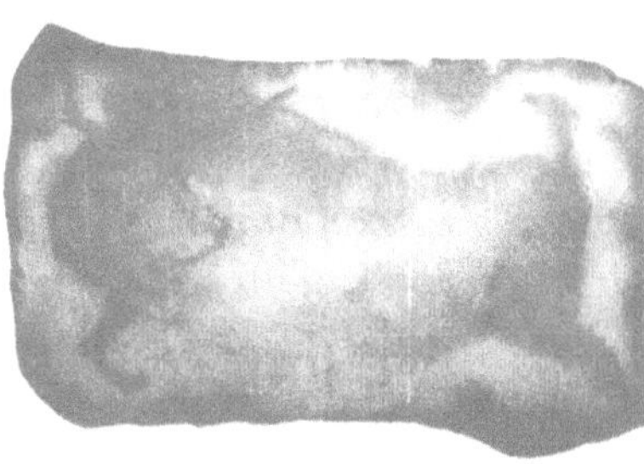

(fig. 7)

Later, The Finnish Artificial Symposium, Step.86, which ran from 20-22 August 1986 in Otaniemi, Espoo, showed some of the art education students' works. Although computer art represented one part of the information technology course, the first year in particular offered a glimpse of the fantastical potential of digital art, its digital and dimensional form and its different aesthetics.

After visiting the Siggraph conference in Anaheim, California in 1993 (for more information, see Linehan 1993; New Media 1993; Druin & Solomon 1993, Siggraph 1993) and ISEA in Helsinki in 1994 (Tarkka 1994; Paatela-Nieminen 1994), I felt eager to experience what students could achieve with computer technology. As a new advanced subject study course, MA students could participate in a massive Lemminkäinen hypermedia study project. The project objective was to invite students to design installations in co-operation with students from different fields of study. Students from several universities in Helsinki participated in the project: Sibelius Academy (Department of Music), The University of Art and Design (School of Art Education) and The University of Technology (Departments of Computer Science and Architecture). Several teachers and staff from these institutions assisted in guiding the co-operative project. We held countless meetings during 1993–1995, the fruit of which saw the presentation of the students' installations at the Ateneum Art Museum, Finnish National Gallery. The project also sought to offer the opportunity to study classical Finnish art from the collections of the Finnish National Gallery and to combine them with hypermedia installations, and high tech sounds and images. The classical Finnish art was displayed differently within these five installations: The Wanderer, Parergon, Click, the Cartoon Factory and Observer 95. The Wanderer interpreted a classical epic legend from a contemporary perspective. Parergon showed the famous Fighting Capercaillies and their numerous reproductions. The Cartoon Factory explored composition through a process of hands-on experimentation. Click was an interactive whorehouse of private confessions. And Observer 95 monitored an eye on events happening both in and outside the museum. A new program called Lemmikki was used to develop many of these projects and enabled the artist to create multimedia presentations that could be controlled using a variety of sensors or shape-recognition systems. One could link peripherals to the system and the choice of controls could be expanded to offer additional alternatives to the mouse. (Pettersson 1995) Although programming still represented an important part of it, this digital art exhibition showed how computer art had developed rapidly (for more on the course material used, see Laurel 1993, Papert 1993, Velthoven & Seijdel 1996, Vince 1992 and Turkle 1984).

Today's media culture, however, differs significantly from the microcomputer art that existed in the past. Instead of fractal dreams, the virtual world of fantasy and imagination is now at hand. Additionally, the media-saturated younger generations are born immersed in this new media that is both popular and appealing. Imagination seems to be both the artist's creative force as well as his or her artistic limit. We may ask how creative the artist can be, or if limits to the artist's imagination indeed exist. Alternative cultural forms as well as critical media literacy should exist alongside today's numerous fantasy worlds. According to Douglas Kellner (1995), we should be able to discriminate between the best and worst media culture. Clearly, there exists a need for critical media literacy, which demands several strategies of cultural pedagogy (p. 335).

Computer software as a tool for creating art

The second area involves the computer as a medium in art education, the history of which dates from the 1980s. In 1985, I met Margaret DiBlasio, Head of the Art Education Program, and Professor Kerry Freedman at the University of Minnesota. DiBlasio had already written an interesting article in 1983 in which she introduced the computer as a medium for producing art and computer teaching about art to discipline-based art education (DBAE). DiBlasio (1983) combined different plains of cognition (acquire, reinforce, integrate, test) and the content of art education (art facts, art skills, established concepts of art, frontier concepts of art and aesthetic values) to the use of technology (tutorial, drill and practice, dialogue, problem solving, simulation, games, inquiry). In DiBlasio's article, she writes that a well-designed program is an opportunity in the art class. According to her, various software applications should be available to motivate different students. The experience of instructionally meaningful and integrated computer programs in art may convert some of the students to advocates of art instruction. Students may also realise that pursuing the inquiry process in art is stimulating, although not everything needs to be computerised. The challenge is in the balance of what is made possible and what is educationally desirable in certain learning situations. DiBlasio also noticed that students who could not draw could learn visual thinking by producing pictures on a computer (pp. 39–47).

The School of Art Education gradually embraced the challenge of using the computer as a tool in art education. Computer system basics were taught at the very beginning of the IT-course in the School of Art Education. Little by little, the need to teach basic computer skills systematically decreased during the 1990s; such skills were already taught in schools and eventually became altogether unnecessary in the context of this course. One important trend in using computers in art education class was to use them as a medium for producing images; this trend also grew popular in schools (see Ahonen 1986, Lehtinen 1985, Rantanen 1984; Konttinen et al. 1986). The information technology course had few tools to meet the needs of students. The first program taught as a tool was the Apple Works program, which was later replaced by Microsoft Word for word processing. Writing and editing skills are required in almost all courses and particularly when images and text are related to each other. At the very beginning (in 1985) students wrote essays about the role of new technology in art education in schools (for more on this theme see Asikainen & Rautasalo 1985, Paatela-Nieminen 1986b, Paatela-Nieminen 1986c, Paatela-Nieminen 1988a). Starting from 1987, the writing task was later replaced by writing seminar reports.

The next and most important tool in the course was used for teaching the principles of computer graphics in relation to the art education curriculum. One could study the basics of design and visual composition by learning to understand how a picture works. Different painting and drawing programs were used. Johan Vikström, for instance, studied different drawing styles (fig. 8), Marja Rajamäki studied perspective (fig. 9), Tuire Leppälä studied movement by repeating elements (fig. 10) and Niina Luukkala studied free and tied rhythm (fig. 11) by using a Super Paint program. Their examples appear below.

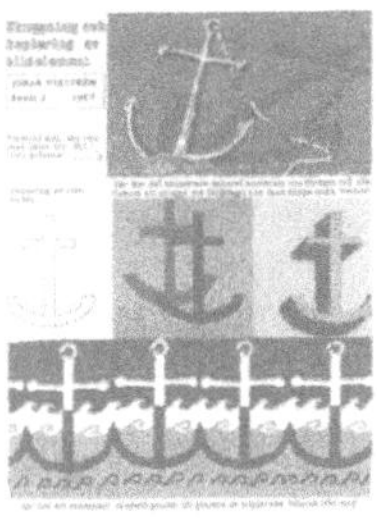

(fig. 8)

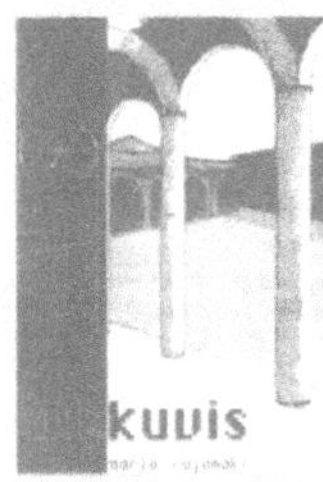

(fig. 9)

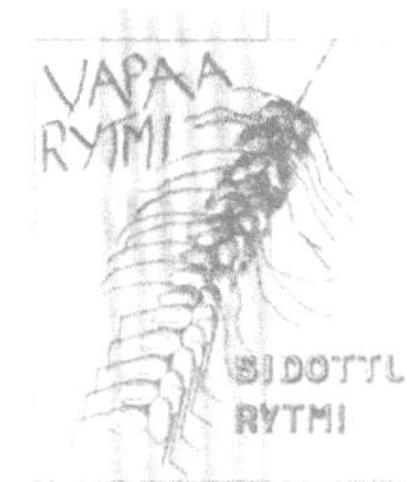

(fig. 10)

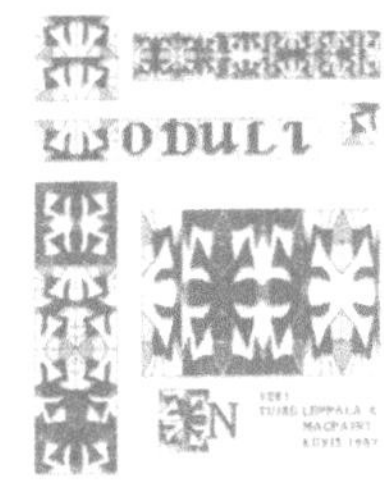

(fig. 11)

This task was associated with a Visual Design course in the School of Art Education taught in 1987 by lecturer Elsa Ytti. Students were to analyse the composition of classical Finnish works of art. In the information technology course, students digitised one work of art for a more profound study. They digitally investigated the composition of the chosen work of art as well as the principles of its composition by making small changes to the digitised image with the paint program. Changing the size, direction and placement of elements in the work of art, for example, help students visualise and understand the meaning of the compositional elements (Paatela-Nieminen 1988b). The computer system as a tool seems a natural choice of medium in such tasks. Depending on the software, one can truly study the issue in-depth. In the mid 1990s teachers switched to Photoshop software, which not only improved the quality of the digitised pictures but also offered new potential for studying the work of art. The results could also appear in the form of a digitised picture, animation or multimedia.

Students also studied tools for three- and four-dimensional graphics since software offered new potential and tools for studying space and time. In the course, we used the MAC 3D program for investigating space and objects. Although the program had potential for studying space, the program was much too slow to be used in practice in those days. As an example, Pasi Vainionpää studied "impossible space" with the program (fig. 12), and Iiris Salovaara created a bird two- and three-dimensionally in the same picture (fig. 13).

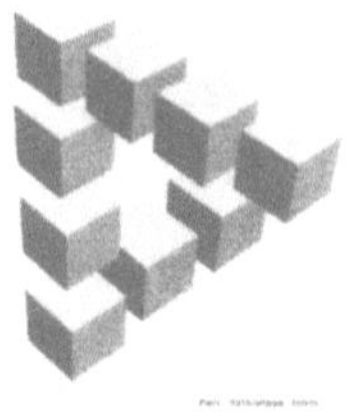

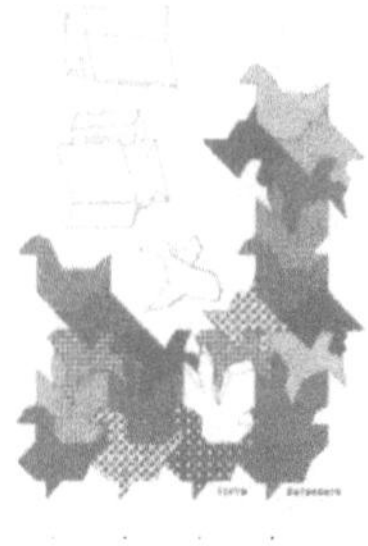

(fig. 12) (fig. 13)

We also created animations to familiarise ourselves with four-dimensional graphics. After the KOALA & BASIC transformations, we had used an animation program called Animate. Students used Apple IIe computers and the Animate program to create the background, characters and some effects. Created in 1987, Marja Rajamäki's animation "Blownaway" which recounts the story of a young girl and a balloons, represents such an example. In Rajamäki's animation, the girl is running happily with a balloon in her hand (see left corner of fig. 14, below). When the girl runs into the middle of the forest, however, the balloon begins to lift her up, and finally, she is blown away altogether (fig. 15). Because the colours are very impressionistic, they appear in the main role of her animation. Her use of contrast and shading in the black and white version, however, is also very interesting.

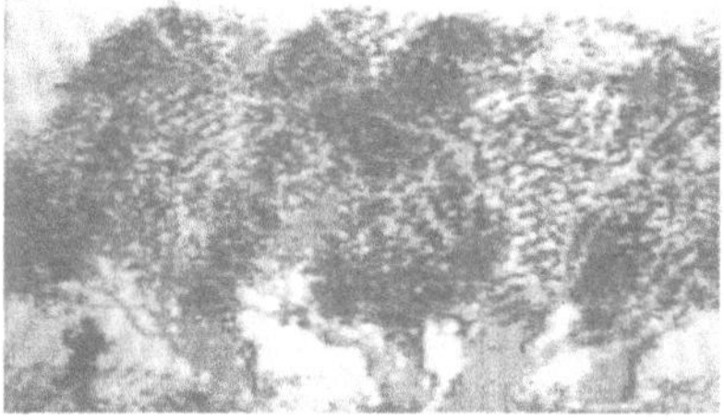

(fig.14)

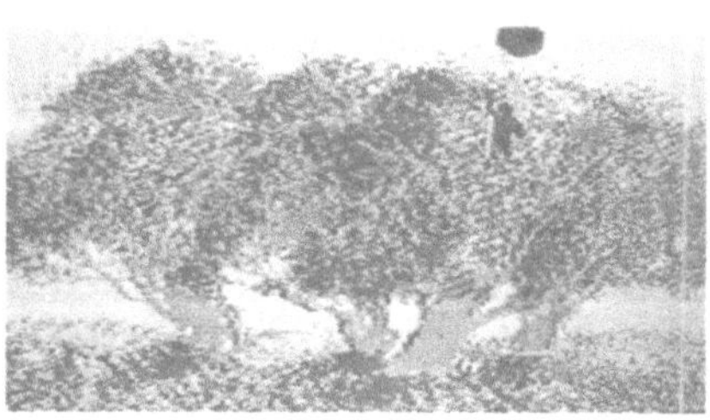

(fig.15)

In practice teaching was well balanced. Four Apple IIe and four Macintosh 512K computers were available for use in the classroom at the same time. While one group wrote an essay with Apple Works, the other group studied three-dimensional space with the Mac 3D program. Alternatively, while one group studied a picture composition analysis from a work of art with Super Paint on a Macintosh 512K, the others created animation first with Koala, and later with Animate programs on an Apple IIe.

In the spring term 1988, new Macintosh Plus computers were purchased to replace half of the existing computers, allowing for use of a more demanding software for animation. The Animate program was replaced by the Video Works II program, later known as Macromedia Director, which is often used in multimedia projects. In 1988, Raisa Neva-Aho used the Video Works software to create one example of such work in her animation entitled "A Bitch" (fig. 16, below). She incorporated several different viewpoints and close-ups of her main character as well as her sound character. Her series has 12 images placed in two rows that are to be read from top to bottom.

In 1989, our computer class received nine Macintosh computers. Although we had different computer models, we could finally give up the Apple IIe computers, which made teaching more pleasurable. In the 1990s, computer equipment became faster and better, and we even received similar models of computers in the class. Besides new and improved hardware, advances in software development also influenced teaching. 3D and animation programs were given up in teaching. On the one hand, this development narrowed the computer graphics area and restricted opportunities to experiment with different tools in various areas of art education, such as three-dimensional space and time. On the other hand, this change offered more time for the profound study of graphic design. Graphic design became a new subject area. When studying the composition of Finnish art work, visual design analysis was still taught using raster and vector graphics with Super Paint, later Photoshop and FreeHand programs. Because graphic design aimed at relating pictures and text, one of the tasks was to design a leaflet with ReadySetGo desktop publishing software. This program was later changed to PageMaker. Initially, my class co-operated with the Department of Graphic Design as well, but in 1996 the task was connected to a photography course taught by lecturer Tarja Trygg at the School of Art Education. Students came to my class with their photographs. After studying graphic design in relation to the software, students designed a leaflet by combining their photos, text and other graphic elements. The example below of a leaflet created by Moosa Myllykangas illustrates three different perspectives of the same work (fig. 17).

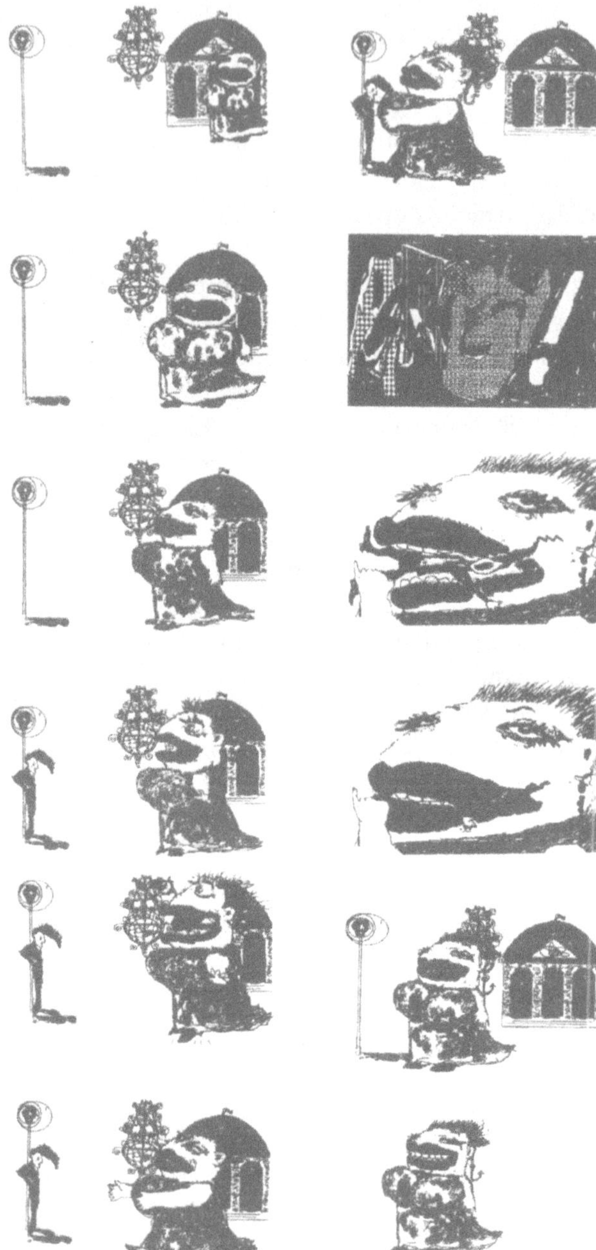

(fig. 16)

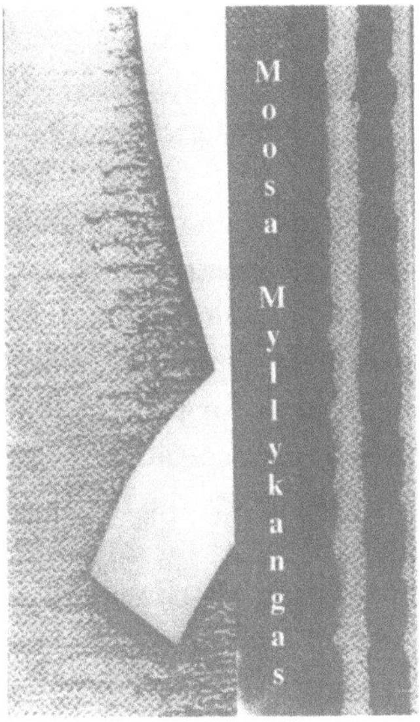

(fig. 17

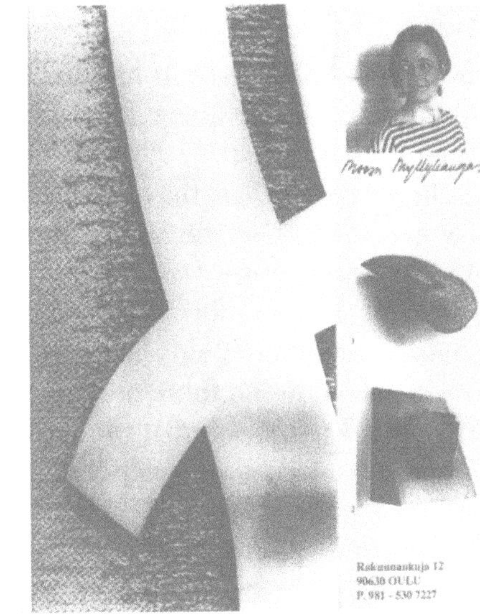

(fig.17)

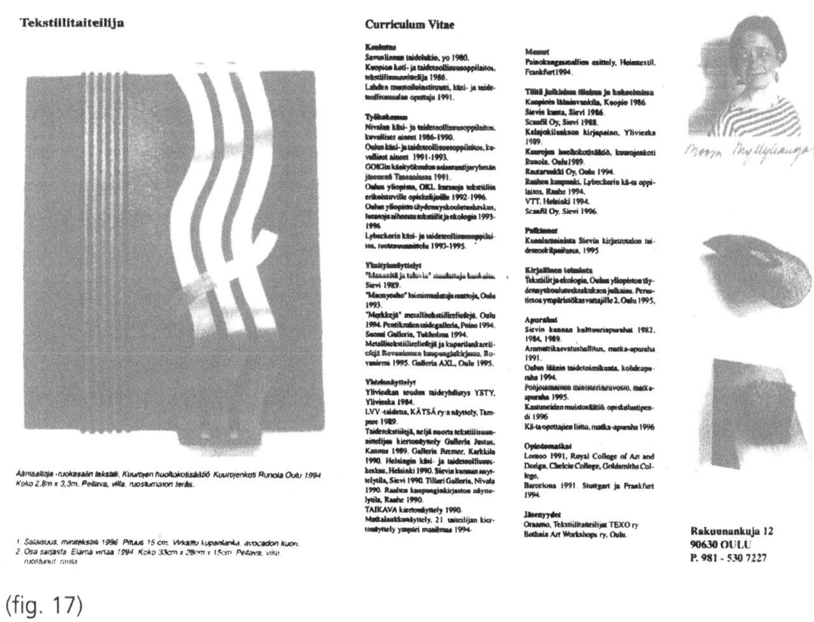

Tekstiilitaiteilija

Ääniaaltoja -ruokasalin tekstiili. Kuurojen huoltokotisäätiö Kuurojenkoti Runola Oulu 1994 Koko 2,8m x 3,3m. Pellava, villa, ruostumaton teräs.

1. Salaisuus, minitekstiili 1996 Pituus 15 cm. Virkattu kuparilanka, avocadon kuori.
2. Osa salaista. Elämä virtaa 1994. Koko 33cm x 28cm x 15cm. Pellava, villa, ruostunut rauta

Curriculum Vitae

Koulutus
Savonlinnan taidelukio, yo 1980.
Kuopion koti- ja taideteollisuusoppilaitos, tekstiilisuunnittelija 1986.
Lahden muotoiluinstituutti, käsi- ja taideteollisuusalan opettaja 1991.

Työkokemus
Nivalan käsi- ja taideteollisuusoppilaitos, kuvalliset aineet 1986-1990.
Oulun käsi- ja taideteollisuusoppilaitos, kuvalliset aineet 1991-1993.
GOKGin käsityökoulun asiantuntijaryhmän jäsenenä Tansaniassa 1991.
Oulun yliopisto, OKL kursseja tekstiiliin erikoistuville opiskelijoille 1992-1996.
Oulun yliopisto täydennyskoulutuskeskus, luentoja aiheesta tekstiilit ja ekologia 1993-1996.
Lybeckerin käsi- ja taideteollisuusoppilaitos, tuotesuunnittelu 1993-1995.

Yksityisnäyttelyt
"Mennneitä ja tulevia" muotoiltuja kankaita, Sievi 1989.
"Maonyosho" koimintamalatuja mattoja, Oulu 1993.
"Merkkejä" metallitekstiilireliefejä, Oulu 1994. Pentikmäen taidegalleria, Poiso 1994. Suomi Galleria, Tukholma 1994.
Metallitekstiilireliefejä ja kuparilankareliefejä Rovaniemen kaupunginkirjasto, Rovaniemi 1995. Galleria AXL, Oulu 1995.

Yhteisnäyttelyt
Ylivieskan seudun taideyhdistys YSTY, Ylivieska 1984.
LVV -taidetta, KÄTSÄ ry:n näyttely, Tampere 1989.
Taidetekstiilejä, neljä nuorta tekstiilisuunnittelijan kiertonäyttely Galleria Justus, Kannus 1989. Galleria Bremer, Karkkila 1990. Helsingin käsi- ja taideteollisuuskeskus, Helsinki 1990. Sievin kunnan näyttelytila, Sievi 1990. Tiiliari Galleria, Nivala 1990. Raahen kaupunginkirjaston näyttelytila, Raahe 1990.
TAIKAVA kiertonäyttely 1990.
Matkalaukkunäyttely, 21 taiteilijan kiertonäyttely ympäri maailmaa 1994-

Messut
Painokangasmallien esittely, Heimtextil, Frankfurt 1994.

Töitä julkisissa tiloissa ja kokoelmissa
Kuopion lääninvankila, Kuopio 1986.
Sievin kunta, Sievi 1986.
Scanfil Oy, Sievi 1988.
Kalajokilaakson kirjapaino, Ylivieska 1989.
Kuurojen huoltokotisäätiö, kuurojenkoti Runola, Oulu 1989.
Rautaruukki Oy, Oulu 1994.
Raahen kaupunki, Lybeckerin kä-ta oppilaitos, Raahe 1994.
VTT, Helsinki 1994.
Scanfil Oy, Sievi 1996.

Palkinnot
Kunniamaininta Sievin kirjastotalon taideteoskilpailussa, 1995

Kirjallinen toiminta
Tekstiilit ja ekologia, Oulun yliopiston täydennyskoulutuskeskuksen julkaisu. Perustietoa ympäristökasvattajille 2, Oulu 1995.

Apurahat
Sievin kunnan kulttuuriapurahat 1982, 1984, 1989.
Ammattikasvatushallitus, matka-apuraha 1991.
Oulun läänin taidetoimikunta, kohdeapuraha 1994.
Pohjoismainen ministerineuvosto, matka-apuraha 1995.
Kaatuneiden muistosäätiö, opiskelustipendi 1996
Kä-ta opettajien liitto, matka-apuraha 1996

Opintomatkat
Lontoo 1991, Royal College of Art and Design, Chelsea College, Goldsmiths College.
Barcelona 1991. Stuttgart ja Frankfurt 1994.

Jäsenyydet
Ornamo, Tekstiilitaiteilijat TEXO ry
Bothnia Art Workshops ry, Oulu.

Rakuunankuja 12
90630 OULU
P. 981 - 530 7227

(fig. 17)

The Font Folio software could also be used with PageMaker, so students could choose from hundreds of fonts. This demanded subject-specific knowledge about fonts per se. Our course material incorporated studies by Leivo 1991 and Sumiloff 1996.

In the mid-1990s, the information technology course had to change again. Although some areas of computer graphics had already been given up, the basic course was too short to be sufficiently thorough. Also, programs offered more than could be taught during this short basic course because programs had developed specific tools for professional use. This requires a more profound knowledge of that specific area of expertise. In fact, some of the software used today meets the needs of professional artists, designers and photographers.

Some schools also used these same programs. Many art educators in Finland used microcomputer systems with special hardware and software as tools at schools. I also collaborated with other teachers from the Nordic countries (especially Umeå and Stockholm in Sweden) and the Nordic Academy for Advanced Study (NORFA), where we began developing the role of computers in art education curricula for different school levels in the Nordic countries (for more, see Lärarens läräre 1993). The subject of digital art education was examined in the IT-workshop arranged in 1998 by the Nordic Network of Research in Visual Arts Education.

The visual imagery of the new media appears to originate both from traditional art as well as from innovative computer graphics, which take on a form of their own. In some sense, the structure of different programs tends to determine the form of the imagery and the thought processes. The quality of the microcomputer system, however, also influences the form of the imagery. The quality of the imagery also depends on the skilful use of and familiarity with the tools that influence the sophistication of the form created. When thinking about the thought processes and critique, Freedman (Efland, Freedman, Stuhr 1996) writes that the sophisticated paint system software may even promote divergent thought processes and critical skills (p. 52). Consequently, it is important to combine several areas when teaching "digital tools" in art education: the subject area in question, combined with the nature of computer graphics, the application of the skilful use of software tools and the target group. Because new technology is in constant change, one must often ask what is educationally desirable in a particular learning situation, and then design the course to meet those needs.

Computer-based learning in art education

The third area involves computer-aided instruction (CAI) and learning (CAL) using a special program or environment; CAI and CAL were used mostly in the advanced study projects for MA students. Teachers participate in the development of computer environments ranging from systems that guide children's every step to those which encourage children to develop their own paths of learning. I had the opportunity to participate in a field trip to the USA in 1986 with a group of teachers from Herttoniemi primary school where we were all taught LOGO programming. LOGO actually taught me a cognitive perspective on teaching new technology. We visited M. I. T. and Microworlds Learning Inc. and observed LEGO-LOGO learning environments (for more, see Heikkilä 1985). Seymour Papert (1982) invented LOGO and applied his theory to Jean Piaget's model of children as builders of their own intellectual structures (p. 7). Papert believed that when a child teaches a computer, programs LOGO, s/he is actually thinking about her/his own thinking and learning about models of learning. Instead of being right or wrong, learning becomes self-directed and active where the computer becomes a heuristic object with which to think. In addition, one also learns about oneself as a learner. Jean Piaget and Marvin Minsky have both been interested in the laws that govern the learner rather than what is learned (ibid. p. 158). Minsky (1988) developed Papert's principles of learning. According to these principles, a crucial step is not just to learn a new skill but also to acquire administrative ways of using what one already knows (p. 102). Also, Cynthia Solomon (1987) has studied powerful computer environments.

While visiting the Bank Street College of Education in New York, our group observed an interesting computer environment called the Voyage of the MIMI (for more on this theme, see the Voyage of MIMI 1985). This is a powerful example of a project that combines a television series, workbooks and learning material. Students learned about whales and ecosystems with maps, navigation tools and LOGO computing. Both LOGO and MIMI offered opportunities for perception and visual thinking. Papert, Minsky and Rudolf Arnheim identify the knowledge and methods needed for conscious perception. According to Arnheim (1969), the arts are often neglected because they are based on perception rather than thought. Nevertheless, Arnheim notes that thinking is essential to perception and cognition, and art is the most powerful means of strengthening perception (p. 3). LOGO has been used in some schools in Finland. In fact, our group used it for three years (for more information, see Korhonen, Korpinen, Lakkala 1987).

I also learned of other learning methods and environments. In 1986, I was invited to join a group of teachers and researchers from Finland's National Board of Education. We were taught the Grimstad method, which is originally a Canadian teaching method developed by Kel Crossley and Les Green (for more on this see Crossley and Green 1987). After learning the Grimstad method, we applied it at Jyväskylä Summer University. We taught several different groups of teachers to visualise their concept of what constitutes traditional course material by applying the Grimstad method. The objective was to visualise the idea of the course material in the form of a metaphor. This could be adapted later to the main page or "market square" of computer-aided courseware. The Grimstad method offered thinking tools for a teacher to design lessons. Through this method, teachers could design courseware that would be not only digitised, but also well conceived and practical for activating the students' role in learning. The Grimstad method is known in several Finnish schools. In 1989, I supervised the MA theses of art education students Tuire Leppälä and Leila Hanhimäki, who applied the Grimstad method to Josef Albers' colour theory (for more information, see Hanhimäki & Leppälä 1989). With their CAI program, one could develop perception through Albers' tasks on colour. The pedagogical thought process was studied. They also benefited from a programmer who used different tools such as Hyper Card, Video Builder, Course of Action and Super Card. In our department, there was also one more powerful computer Macintosh II computer that allowed for easier software programming.

In 1989, the Grimstad method was also applied in an advanced IT study course for MA students. The method was, however, taught differently. Three of us teachers taught the Grimstad method from the viewpoint of Veli-Pekka Lifländer (for more information see Lifländer 1989). Lifländer had developed the method further, especially from the didactical point of view, and had combined this method with Yrjö Engenström's ideas of teaching to create an interesting learning model. (see Lifländer 1989; Paatela-Nieminen 1990). Students Anu Nyberg and Maria Weckman wrote their MA theses during this course, which is a CAI program designed especially for the Ateneum Art Museum, Finnish National Gallery, that describes symbolism in Finnish art (for more details, see Nyberg & Weckman 1992).

From 1998 to 1990, the Grimstad method was also applied in another advanced subject study course for MA students that focused on children's culture. In this class, students were interested in designing and programming a multimedia program. They used Macromedia Director software. After studying different learning environments, they drafted a visual plan of the content of the learning environment. They then drew or photographed all of the necessary images and icons before programming the whole environment. The project involved three teachers proficient in the following areas of expertise: child and teen culture, multimedia-based learning environments and LINGO programming. Students learned to use LINGO scripts in their own multimedia environments and thus program their own ideas. Students also used a Future Learning Environment (FLE) developed in the Media Lab of the University of Art and Design. Our idea was to study programming in the learning environment and test the first prototype of FLE in learning, which seemed to offer great potential for group learning (Paatela-Nieminen 1999). "The group's works are based on the social constructivist theory that sees learning as participation in social processes of knowledge construction FLE" (http://fle3.uiah.fi). Several works of art as well as an MA thesis were completed in this course. Riitta Ajanki and Nina Paajanen were visiting teachers in an art school in Kenya for two months. They photographed and filmed videos of a Kenyan secondary school. As part of their thesis, they created a multimedia demo on the original voices and opinions of the Kenyan people from a cross-cultural viewpoint (for more information, see Ajanki & Paajanen 2000).

To summarise, I have combined three different viewpoints: computer art, digital tools and teaching/learning environments in the IT courses. I sought to study the potential of the new media, the aesthetics and form of the new imagery, the potential of the digital tools, and the new media's potential for teaching and learning in the School of Art Education, UIAH. Especially at the very beginning, in 1985, it was necessary to maintain a broad view of new media potential given the limited opportunities to create images. For this reason, instruction focused on those principles that could be adapted for further use. For example, two-, three- and four-dimensional graphics possess certain functions not bound to specific programs. Later, and especially in the 1990s, the course changed. Several teachers, new programs and new trends were eagerly experienced. Information technology was learned, taught and expressed from the point of art education. However, due to the different educational background of the teachers the content of the course varied from an art education emphasis to a more technical orientation. From 1995 on, other courses and projects were undertaken in the School of Art education. One project worth noting is lecturer Pirkko Pohjakallio's CAI project on art education history (for more information, see Pohjakallio 1998). Besides enthusiasm, critical approaches also abound. One of the main criticisms in the 1980s frowned upon the use of computers in artistic creation for fear of losing the delicacy of the pencil and the hand-drawn line. Others feared the loss of true reality to virtual reality. Today such images wield even more power and thus compel us to understand and decode them.

The challenge of the intertextual method in investigating intermedial relations

From today's perspective of art education, the power of images has increased greatly in our society, and especially in digital culture. Digital software makes it even easier to use images, such as works of art or other pictures, as a basis for, or as a part of, our own production. Images are sometimes literally reinvented from other images. Such borrowing is not limited to visual loans; we borrow music and literature as well. These textual loans represent vast cultural and post-modern accumulations. I became interested in understanding and interpreting these accumulations, which compelled me to develop a theory for post-modern art education. I wrote my licentiate thesis on an intertextual method (Paatela-Nieminen 1996; Rastas 1997, Paatela-Nieminen 1998), which I investigated further in my doctoral thesis (Paatela-Nieminen 2000, Haikarainen 2001; Paatela-Nieminen 2003). In these studies I have developed an intertextual method for art education research and practice, and have tested the method in practise in several courses since 2001.

Intertextuality can be used subjectively, open-endedly and interculturally, while at the same time maintain a strong, clear method behind the interpretation that structures the reading process. One can explore texts subjectively through a plurality of readings. I take the term text to mean visual and verbal. Intertextual reading is challenging because, in the interpretative process, one moves through the depths of texts and across different cultures and media. Learning is motivated because the reader her/himself becomes the researcher who constructs her/his own path or story. The method also has potential for intersubjective interpretation. Students can, for example, study together, intersubjectively, areas of art through an e-learning program, share the results, and build together an intertextual space. Intertextuality is a method for current art education which considers the relations and differences between cultures, subjects, and media. In the intertextual approach, for example, the researcher is interested not only in a work of art per se, but also in its several intercultural, intersubjective and intermedial relations.

References

ACM SIGGRAPH <http://www.siggraph.org/>. 1.3.2004.

ACM SIGGRAPH/89. Computer art in context. *Leonardo. Supplemental issue. Journal of the international society for the arts, sciences and technology.* Oxford, New York, Beijing: Pergamon Press.

Ahonen, Anu (1986). Tietotekniikka muuttaa koulua [Information technology is changing schools.] *Tietotekniikka. Tietojenkäsittelyn ja toimistoautomaation ammattilehti* No 6–7/1986, 14–21.

Arnheim, Rudolf (1969). *Visual thinking.* Berkeley, Los Angeles, London: University of California Press.

Asikainen, Eila & Rautasalo, Kirsti (1985). *Tietokoneen käyttö kuvaamataidon opetuksessa. Kokeiluja ja kokemuksia* [Using microcomputers in art education.] Jyväskylän yliopisto: Kasvatustieteiden tutkimuslaitos.

ATK-poliittinen ohjelma (1980). Komiteanmietintö 1980:51. [ADP political agenda.] Helsinki: [Valtioneuvosto].

Bittifestivaalit – näyttely Vanhan Galleriassa. Valmiiden muotojen varojat. [Ready made shapes – No thanks.] *Helsingin Sanomat HS, kuukausiliite,* toukokuu 1/1986, 14.

Crossley, Kel & Green, Les (1987). *Lessonware. Käytännönopas opetusohjelmien laatimiseen.* WSOY kurssikirjat. Porvoo, Helsinki, Juva: Werner Söderström.

DiBlasio, Margaret (1983). If and where to plug in the computer: A conceptual framework for computer assisted art instruction. *Studies in art education. A journal of issues and research in art education,* Vol 25. Number 1, pp. 39–47.

Druin, Allison & Solomon, Cynthia (1993). *Course 27 notes. MM: Designing multimedia environments for children. SIGGRAPH 93.* 20th International conference on computer graphics and interactive techniques. California, Anaheim: Association for Computing Machinery.

Efland, Arthur & Freedman, Kerry & Stuhr, Patricia (1996). *Postmodern art education: an approach to curriculum.* Virginia: The National Art Education Association.

FLE learning environment <http://fle3.uiah.fi/group/>. 1.5.2004.

Goodman, Cynthia (1987). *Digital visions. Computers and art.* New York: Harry N. Abrams.

Haikarainen, Paula (2001). Intertekstuaalisuuden ihmemaassa [In the Wonderland of Intertextuality.] *Arttu* 1/2001, 32–33.

Heikkilä, Markku (1985). Tietokonemullistus Herttoniemen ala-asteella [Computer revolution at Herttoniemi primary school.] *Kouluikkuna* N:o 2, 4–5.

Kellner, Douglas (1995). *Media culture. Cultural studies, identity and politics between the modern and the postmodern.* London, New York: Routledge.

Kerlow, Isaac & Rosebush, Judson (1986). *Computer graphics for designers and artists.* New York: Van Nostrand Reinhold.

Konttinen, Raimo & Asikainen, Eila & Kivinen, Antti & Korhonen, Hannu & Leijala, Jyrki (1986). *Tietokone koulutyön välineenä.* [The computer as a tool in school.] Sarja B, Nro 87. Helsinki: Suomen Itsenäisyyden Juhlavuoden 1967 Rahasto SITRA.

Korhonen, Mia & Korpinen, Heikki & Lakkala, Minna (1987). *Hei, me teemme sen! Tietokonekerhon perustamis-, toiminta- ja koulutusopas.* [How to establish a computer club for children.] Helsinki: Herttoniemen ala-asteen tietokonekerhon tuki ry.

Laurel, Brenda (1993). *Computers as theatre.* Reading, Massachusetts, Menlo Park etc.: Addison-Wesley.

Lehtinen, Jukka (1985). *Tietokone opetusvälineenä. [Computer as a tool for* teaching.] Julkaisusarja B, 38. Helsinki: Valtion Koulutuskeskus.
Leivo, Osmo (1991). *Mikrojulkaisukirja.* [Publishing by microcomputer.] [Helsinki:] Tecnopress.
Lewell, John (1985). *Computer graphics. A survey of current techniques and applications.* New York: Van Nostrand Reinhold.
Lifländer, Veli-Pekka (1989). *Tietokoneavusteisen opetuksen kehittäminen.* [Developing CAI.] Helsingin kauppakorkeakoulun julkaisuja D-112. Helsinki: Helsingin kauppakorkeakoulu.
Linehan, Thomas (ed.) (1993). *Computer graphics. Visual proceedings.* Annual conference series, 1993. New York: ACM SIGGRAPH, The Association of Computing Machinery.
Minsky, Marvin (1988). *The society of mind.* Touchstone edition. New York, London, Toronto, Sydney, Tokyo: Simon & Schuster.
Newman, William & Sproull, Robert (1981). *Principles of interactive computer graphics.* Second edition. International student edition. Auckland, Bogota, Guatemala, Hamburg etc.: McGraw-Hill.
New media showcase. The digital sourcebook (1993). New York: American Showcase.
Numminen, Pekka (1986). Kuvantekijän uusi apulainen [The artist's new maid.] *Sähköviesti* 3/1986, 22–23.
Paatela-Nieminen, Martina (1986a). Tietokonetaidenäyttely Vanhan Galleriassa [Computer art exhibition.] *Stylus* 3/86, 8–9.
Paatela-Nieminen, Martina (1986b). Tietokoneen tulevat kuvaamataidon opetukseen. [Microcomputers are coming to art education.] *Stylus* 3/86, 4–5.
Paatela-Nieminen, Martina (1986c). Tietokoneen mahdollisuudet kuvaamataidon opetuksessa. Kuvallista ajattelua voidaan kehittää. [Using computers is art education. Developing visual thinking.] *Apple koulu-uutiset. Koululehti,* No 1/86,12–13.
Paatela-Nieminen, Martina (1988a). Computers in art education. *Graphic design of CDE '88. Arttu.* Extra issue of the bulletin of the University of Industrial Arts. Helsinki: University of Industrial Arts.
Paatela-Nieminen, Martina (1988b). Computers in art education. *Stylus* 3/88, 25–26.
Paatela-Nieminen, Martina (1990). Tietotekniikka taidekasvatusta kehittämään [Developing art education with information technology.] *Stylus* 1/90, 24–25.
Paatela-Nieminen, Martina (1994). Elektronisen taiteen uudet suunnat [New trends in electronic art.] *Stylus* 4/94, 70–73.
Paatela-Nieminen, Martina (1998). Intertextuality and Multimedia in Visual Arts Research. In Lars Lindström (ed.), *Nordic visual arts research. A theoretical and methodological Review* 1998, pp. 56–62. Stockholm Library of Curriculum Studies, Vol 2. Stockholm Institute of Education Press.

Paatela-Nieminen, Martina (1999). Uudet oppimisympäristöt ja multimedia [Multimedia in new learning environments.] *Arttu* 1/99, 22–23.

Paatela-Nieminen, Martina (2000). *On the threshold of Intercultural Alices. Intertextual research on the illustrations of the English Alice in Wonderland and the German Alice im Wunderland in intermedia research in the field of art education.* Publication series A 29. Doctoral dissertation. (CD). Helsinki: University of Art and Design.

Paatela-Nieminen, Martina (2003). Intertextual and intercultural Alices in Wonderland. In: Prabha Sahasrabudhhe (Ed.) *International conversations through art: The 31st InSEA world congress. August 2002. New York Proceedings.* Center for International Art Education. New York: Teachers College, Columbia University.

Papert, Seymour (1982). *Mindstorms. Children, computers and powerful ideas.* Brighton: Harvester Press.

Papert, Seymour (1993). *The children's machine. Rethinking school in the age of the computer.* New York: Basic Books.

Peterson, Dale (1983). *Genesis II. Creation and recreation with computers.* Reston, Virginia: Reston Publishing.

Pettersson, Susanna (1995). *Lemminkäinen.* Helsinki: The Finnish National Gallery.

Pohjakallio, Pirkko 1998. New and old: multimedia as a tool for providing interpretation and meaning: Reflections on the Finnish art education history project. *Journal of Art & Design Education.* Vol 17. Number 3. 1998.

Proceedings. 5th symposium on small computers in the arts (1985). October 5–8, 1985. Philadelphia, Pennsylvania. Massachusetts: IEEE Computer Society Press.

Proceedings. 6th symposium on small computers in the arts (1986). October 10–12, 1986. Philadelphia, Pennsylvania. Massachusetts: IEEE Computer Society Press.

Rantanen, Jukka (1984). *Tietokonepohjainen oppimateriaali. Markkinat ja tuotanto.* [CAI programs in schools.] Sarja B, 77. Helsinki: Suomen itsenäisyyden juhlavuoden 1967 rahasto.

Rastas, Perttu (1997). Multimedian tiet ovat kaikki yhtä hyviä. [Multimedia's choices are equally good.] *Arttu* 3/97, 25.

Romppanen, Päivi (1986). Tippuuko maali pensselistä oleellisesti eri tavoin kuin väribitti tietokoneen muistista? [Using bits or paints – is there a difference in painting.] *VTAY. Tietoväki* 2/1986, 8–10.

Siggraph 93. Final program. Introducing multimedia 93. 1–6. August. Anaheim, California: Association for Computing Machinery.

Solomon, Cynthia (1987). *Computer environments for children: a reflection on theories of learning and education.* 2nd printing. Cambridge, Massachusetts, London: MIT Press.

Sumiloff, Lasse (1996). *Graafisen suunnittelijan teknologia.* [Technology for graphic designers.] Helsinki: Opetushallitus.

Tarkka, Minna (ed.) [1994]. ISEA '94. *The fifth international symposium on electronic art catalogue.* Publication series of the University of Art and Design Helsinki UIAH B 40. Helsinki: University of Art and Design.

Teknologiakomitean mietintö [Technology committee report.] (1980). Komiteanmietintö 1980:55 Helsinki: [Valtioneuvosto].

TOP (1986). *Tietotekniikan integroiminen kouluopetukseen: taustaa ja etenemisstrategia. Tietokone opetuksessa -projekti.* [Integrating information technology into teaching in schools.] Helsinki: Ammattikasvatushallitus, Kouluhallitus.

Truckenbrod, Joan (1988). *Creative computer imaging.* New Jersey: Prentice Hall.

Turkle, Sherry (1984). *The second self. Computers and human spirit.* New York: Simon & Schuster.

Velthoven, Willem & Seijdel, Jorinde (1996). *Multimedia graphics.* London: Thames and Hudson.

Vince, John (1992). *Computer graphics.* London: Design Council.

Voyage of the MIMI. The Bank Street College project in science and mathematics. (1985). Bank Street College of Education. New York, Mexico City, London, Sydney, Tokyo: Holt, Rinehart and Winston.

Wilson, Mark (1986). *Drawing with computers.* New York: Perigee Books.

Wilson, Stephen (1986). *Using computers to create art.* New Jersey: Prentice-Hall.

Unpublished works

Ajanki, Riitta & Paajanen, Nina (2000). Mind Bar – Kohtaamisia kenialaisessa kylässä. [Mind Bar – Meetings in the Kenyan village.] Master's thesis. Helsinki: University of Art and Design, School of Art Education.

Hanhimäki, Leila & Leppälä, Tuire (1989). "Väriharhat" – opetusohjelma: Tietokoneavusteinen opetusohjelma värien vuorovaikutuksesta lukion väriopin opetukseen. [Alber's colour theory for high school in the form of a CAI program.] Master's thesis. Helsinki: University of Art and Design, School of Art Education.

Lärarens lärare i bild år 2000 [The teacher's teacher in art education.] 5–8 Oktober (1993) Helsingborg. En konferensresume. Dataprogramgruppens rapportserie. Rapport nr. 10. Manuscript. Copenhagen: Nordisk ministerråd.

Nyberg, Anu & Weckman Maria (1992). Ahvenen ruoto – Symbolismi suomalaisessa kuvataiteessa 1890–1900 [Symbolism in Finnsh art.] Master's thesis. Helsinki: University of Art and Design, School of Art Education.

Paatela-Nieminen, Martina (1985). ATK:n käyttö taidekasvatuksessa [ADP in art education.] Master's thesis. Helsinki: University of Art and Design, School of Art Education.

Paatela-Nieminen, Martina (1996) Intertekstuaalinen tutkimus englantilaisista Alice in Wonderland -kuvituksista vuosilta 1984–1994 ja Alices in Wonderlands – multimedia [Intertextual study on Alice in Wonderland illustrations in the form of a multimedia.] Licentiate thesis. Helsinki: University of Art and Design, School of Art Education.

Media Pedagogy and Interdisciplinary Artistic Education – Analogies and Synergy Effects[1]

IWAN PASUCHIN

The following article unfolds the analogies in methods and goal settings between media pedagogy and artistic education in Germany and the reciprocal synergy effects. The conclusion gears towards the vision of a close cooperation between the two pedagogical fields in a future joint function. The perspective is limited to Germany (and German-speaking publications) due to the fact that media pedagogy there, contrary to Anglo-American countries, holds a very long tradition and for many decades various attempts have been pursued towards cooperation in the above-mentioned areas.

The central field of research evolves from the premise that in the present multi-media saturated world, a strict separation between artistic-pedagogic areas is becoming less possible, producing the effect that all creative fields (art, music, literature, dance, etc.) progressively become considered as one interdisciplinary entity[2].

1 The article is based on the thesis from the author entitled "Künstlerische Medienbildung – Ansätze zu einer Didaktik der Künste und ihrer Medien" (Artistic Media Education – Approach to a Didactic for Arts and their Media), which is to be published in early 2005.

2 To simplify the article, reference to artistic pedagogy will principally be extracted from visual component conceptions in relation to and compared with music pedagogy.

1. A Comparison between the Historical Development of Media Pedagogy and Artistic Pedagogy in Germany

In comparing the development of media pedagogy and artistic pedagogy in Germany from the reform pedagogy until the early 1970s, numerous significant analogies are evident. In the critical phases of media pedagogy history, artistic pedagogy played a decisive role in the respective developments. Numerous researchers (e.g. Hüther; Podehl 1997, 119; Tulodziecki 2000, 22; Kübler 1994, 60) claim that the origin of media pedagogy in the beginning of the 20th century (which dealt foremost with film media), was a result of the *Art Education Movement* (Kunsterziehungsbewegung) within the reform pedagogy. Contrary to the so-called *"Bewahrpädagogik"* (Protection Pedagogy), which aimed at defending against a media offer which was classified as corrupt (and in part, exerted much influence until the end of the 60s), the Art Education Movement conveyed a "direction toward 'good' and 'valuable' medium, in connection with education in art appreciation and judgement ability" (Hüther; Podehl 1997, 119). An inseparable synthesis between media and aesthetic education is visible in the conceptions of the reputable teachers and researchers, referred to as the pioneers of media pedagogic. In the 1930s, one of these, Adolf Reichwein, using the research from Berthold Otto, developed the conception of *Critical Visual Education* (kritische Seherziehung), the goal of which was to enable students to observe and use media in a reflective manner, whereby the recipients were granted the ability to decode film contents. One of the working methods included experimenting and testing media production (mainly with the help from photographers) to obtain independent media design knowledge (cf. Schorb 1995, 29f.; 1994, 162f.).

Another significant point in the history of the two pedagogical fields was the reform discussion in art education in the early 1970s. According to Baacke, it gave an important incentive towards the final separation from the "protective pedagogical" tendencies within German media pedagogy (cf. Baacke 1995, 34ff.; cf. Vollbrecht 2001, 46ff.). The central point here was the conception of *Visual Communication* (visuelle Kommunikation) which granted optical mass media such as photography, film, television, magazines, advertisements, comics, etc. a significant role in art education, and thereby intensified the focus on media pedagogical issues (cf. Ehmer 1971, 7f.). At the same time music pedagogy also initiated similar conceptions entitled *Audio Perception Education* (auditive Wahrnehmungserziehung) and *Audio Communication* (auditive Kommunikation) whereby the definition of art was quite broad and every form of music, including "acoustic events" was accepted as part of the curriculum (cf. Frisus et al. 1972, 0.9) – the increase in employment possibilities of "technical mediators" in class played a central role within this conception (cf. Helmholz 1996, 31).

In the historical development, both fields reveal not only analogies but also sources of numerous mutual misunderstandings and prejudices. For example the conception of Visual Communication, based on "ideology criticism" (Ideologiekritik) of Adorno, Horkeimer etc., can be described as extremely "anti artistic" relating to traditional art (such as painting, sculpture, etc.). One of the most significant representatives of this movement, Heino R. Moeller, even went so far as to demand the deliberate "discrimination of art as an instrument of authority" as "the most important educational goal for lessons in art education" (cf. Moeller 1971, 23). Due to the fact that these conceptions were closely involved with media pedagogical objectives, one of the consequences of the detachment in the subsequent artistic-pedagogic movements included less consideration of media educational perspectives. As one of the results of this process adequately developed media pedagogical conceptions and didactic models exist neither in (visual) art pedagogy nor in music pedagogy up to now (cf. Kirschenmann 2003, 7; Münch 2003, 32).

2. Media Competence Discourse

The "genesis" of modern day German media pedagogy is Dieter Baacke's 1973 augural dissertation entitled, *Communication and Competence – The Foundation of a Didactic of Communication and its Media* (Kommunikation und Kompetenz – Grundlegung einer Didaktik der Kommunikation und ihrer Medien) introducing his conception of *Communicative Competence*. Today, the term *Media Competence* (even though Baacke used the term only after 1996) is used by German media pedagogues referring to this publication (cf. e.g. Groeben 2002, 11; Fromme 2002, 158; Moser 2000, 213; Vollbrecht; Mädgefrau 1998, 267), hence the reason the conception of Communicative Competence will briefly be introduced. The basics of this conception (and that of the media competence discourse) allow the following "superior competence conceptions" classification: communicative, social, and action competence (kommunikative-, soziale- und Handlungskompetenz – cf. Groeben 2002, 11f.).

2.1 Origins of the Media Competence Discourse

Baacke's *communicative* approach, his *Basic Axiom of Communicative Competence* (Grundaxiom der kommunikativen Kompetenz) originated mainly from the theories of the linguist Chomsky. Chomsky's main theory maintained that due to a universal system of rules which everyone is born with and need not learn, everyone has the potential to generate an infinite amount of sentences and hence express any amount of thoughts. Chomsky termed this the creative aspect of language use (according to Baacke 1973, 100). Subsequently, Baacke concludes that man is capable of using individual creativity and competence to generate new knowledge without "pedagogic intervention" – without depending on imitating foreign behaviour or external stimulation (cf. ibid, 100ff.). Hence, Baacke demanded (long before the term "constructivism" gained importance in learning theory) a pedagogical understanding of learning as a mutual constructing process between teachers and students, whereby the usual hierarchy situation is lifted for *symmetrical* communication because only in this way can "each participant develop their communicative competence" (Baacke 1973, 332). This wording refers to the central meaning of the term "competence" in modern pedagogy: Regardless how problematic this term appears, it has the decisive advantage to suggest (if not to enforce) the utilization of related terms in language use (and comprehension) in the pedagogical context, which correspond to the recent postulates of learning theory. Competence (in the sense of a natural ability that each person possesses or individually acquires) cannot be taught, nor can a person be "raised to competency". Even publications which explicitly disassociate themselves from Chomsky's competence understanding as an innate, universal ability, only speak about the promotion, improvement, and expansion of competence (cf. e.g. Hurrelmann 2002, 111).

For the *social* approach, Baacke proceeded from Habermas' *Interaction Theory*. Habermas developed his pragmatic communication theory often mentioned as *authority free discourse* (herrschaftsfreier Diskurs) to prove the possibility of authority free communication as a prerequisite for the universal emancipation of man (cf. Habermas 1971, 101 ff.). Proceeding from the bond between socialization and sociological theoretical perspectives, Habermas postulated that "the structures of cognitive, social, and moral development can be derived from the general levels of communicative competence" (Sutter; Charlton 2002, 134). This aspect of the conception of Communicative Competence results, at first glance, in a contradiction of two approaches: On the one hand, the "radical democratic" approach (cf. Baacke; Röll 1995, 16) – the acknowledgement of the innate or rather socially acquired competences toward an independent lifestyle for each and every one and the effort to reach an "authority free discourse" between teacher and student; on the other hand, simultaneously the strong bond of the social and moral aspects with the cognitive aspects of media competence (cf. also Tulodziecki 1992, 59; Gapski 2001, 14). For media pedagogical practice, the consequences are that the ethic, democratic, and similar dimensions of communicative, respectively, media competence, which go beyond the basic skills and abilities of man for a personal life style plan, must not only be supported but also conveyed by intense pedagogical intervention and, accordingly, the learning process must be "accompanied and directed by external ethic-moral factors." (Schorb 1997, 68) These two approaches are compatible, as Baacke continually stressed that media competence cannot be "subjectively-individualistically diminished" but must be looked upon as a "planned objective of an ultra individual social level" (cf. Baacke 1997, 27; 99) – that means every person, regardless of his/her liberties, has a responsibility to society. This aspect is currently described as "critical reflection" (kritische Reflexivität) (cf. Schorb 1997, 67).

In the approach to *action competence*, Baacke commenced mainly from the *action-oriented pedagogy* based on the theories of John Dewey. Most important for Baacke was the activity aspect: An acting person has control over himself/herself and what occurs. Action is therefore intentional and in contrast to "behaviour" shows itself through a dimension of independence towards the situation (Baacke 1997, 55). Action is not understood as conduct within a predestined or social process adopted behavioural pattern, but implies a "behavioural independence" (Baacke 1973, 262). This makes it clear why the term *emancipation* took such a central position in Baacke's augural dissertation (for example, the complete second half was entitled *Communication: Competence and Emancipation* – Kommunikation: Kompetenz und Emanzipation): Emancipation for Baacke "strives for self realization of the individual: adapting someone else's authority as one's own." (ibid. 313) To Baacke, emancipation in a pedagogic context means not only teaching the student independence, but also to create the social preconditions which enables the "self realization of the individual"; therefore, education is always political (cf. 314). It is self-explanatory that such thought constructions lead to demand for a reform of the educational system (cf. 363). Baacke's recommendations regarding this "new pedagogy" resemble the postulate of the current (radical) constructivistic learning theory: It is a definite decision for democratic educational structures; the autocratic management in the school should even be renounced, if one expects higher learning effectiveness regarding the "subject" (302). In the long run, people learn much better when they have "the opportunity to deal freely and independently with tasks they choose themselves." (325)

The conception of Communicative Competence was summarized by Schorb et al. (1980, 622) into the following three components, which can also be combined with the "superior competence conceptions" (cf. Groeben 2002, 11 f.):

Superior conceptions	**Components of the Communicative Competence conception** (according to Schorb et al.)	
communicative competence	communicative component	Ability to an adequate and reflective experience management and representation
social competence	analytical component	Ability to reflect the "blocking connections" of the mass media and realize possibilities to overcome them
action competence	creative component	Ability to find alternatives with regard to the ruling communication structures and push through personal collective interests

Table 1

2.2 Current Media Competence Discourse

The term "Media Competence" stems from the federal German education policy discourse of the 1980s. At that time fears settled in that the young working force was not qualified enough compared to other industrial nations and that they were competitively at a disadvantage. The business community demanded to "shape up" the youth for the working world by teaching them how to professionally deal with technical applications. The psychological dimensions of the learning process were neglected and social and political implications in the technology development were grossly ignored (cf. Ackermann 1992; Brehm-Klotz 1997; Schorb 1995, 51). For this reason, the media pedagogy struggled against accepting this terminology (cf. Binder 1992, 21). But by the mid 1990s, the term "media competence" was so deeply imbedded in the general vocabulary that the academic media theory was compelled to execute a "pedagogical turnaround" (Gawert 1996, 2). In 1996, Baacke introduced his own differentiations to the pedagogical dimensions of "media competency" in his article *Media Competence Network (Medienkompetenz als Netzwerk)*. He concluded his article with the following words: "A concept is booming – we should seize the opportunity." (Baacke 1996, 10)

The media pedagogical opportunity of this term was the possibility to take this concept and reinstall it into the original conception of Communicative Competence (as it was practically non-existent to the public) – the description of this initial conception encompassed more than half of Baacke's "network-essay" (1996, 4–8). The most important difference between the two conceptions is: Communicative Competence treated mainly general, day-to-day aspects of competence; Media Competence concentrates on the promotion of skills to "master the media development" (cf. ibid, 8; Schorb 1997, 65). For this reason Media Competence is an "actualization and simultaneously an actual reduction of the conception of Communicative Competence." (Schorb 1997, 63)

The question, what has to be actually understood by the term "media competence", leads to a vehement discourse in the German media pedagogy. Moser, for example, criticizes that Baacke's opinions are too focussed on the "old media" and the ideologies from the 70s, rather than on new technology (chiefly, the computer). Consequently, Moser develops his own didactic model where he expresses the absolute importance of technological competence as a necessity to be able to handle media (from the remote control to computer programs) properly (Moser 2000, 215f.). Accordingly, first and foremost – media competence is the understanding of routine technical abilities and the corresponding fundamental knowledge as the "basic qualifications in the information society" (cf. Mandl; Reimann-Roithmeier 1997, 80). Media pedagogues such as Bernd Schorb view with detachment theories of that kind because they believe that the world is so saturated with media (technology) that it is practically impossible for an individual to accumulate the necessary detailed knowledge (Schorb 1997, 66). In his opinion it is much more important to accumulate "structural knowledge" (Strukturwissen), in order to be able to cross-reference information, and "orientation knowledge" (Orientierungswissen) using historical, ethical, and political views and facts to evaluate the phenomena of information and communication technology (ibid.). Based on such postulates numerous media pedagogues, first and foremost Baacke (1996, 8), but also Aufenanger (2001, 119f.), Tulodziecki (2000, 25f.), and Pöttinger (2002, 88), stress the cognitive, social, ethical, and moral abilities, as most important in dealing with the media and demand one to strongly pursue critical-reflective abilities in view of media constructed realities (cf. Schorb 1997, 76f.). A third group of media pedagogues differentiate themselves from this standpoint of media competence as being too rationalistically diminished and criticize the "neglect of the emotional *media competence* components." (Groeben 2002, 17; cf. Luca 2001) In their opinion media pedagogy pays insufficient attention to "aesthetic experiences beyond a discursive practice." (Mikos 2000, 2) Recently this leads to an "increasing importance of aesthetic-based media pedagogical conceptions" (Paus-Haase 2001, 91). On the other hand such approaches are already present in "established" media competence models. For example Baacke's media competence model contains the dimension of "creative media design" that emphasizes aesthetic aspects. They are described as "going-over-the-boundaries-of-routine-communication" (1996, 8). Stefan Aufanger imparts his media competence model with an "aesthetic dimension" (2001, 120) and even Bernd Schorb stresses that creativity and fantasy are imperative in designing something innovative in order "to overcome the codified rules of reality." (Schorb 1997, 71)

These diverse approaches to the term media competence need not be regarded as contradictory but can also be interpreted as differing facets of a concept especially valuable through its pedagogical versatility. Based on the conception of Communicative Competence and the "superior competence concepts" it is possible to summarize the presented dimensions of media competence and to formulate the objectives of media pedagogy as follows (compare also Pöttinger 2002, 88; 96):

Aspects of Media Competence	Objectives of Media Pedagogy
communicative	Promoting personal competences of each individual, to understand media contents, to express oneself coherently with help from media technology, and to use media productively for personal (day-to-day) interests
social	Imparting "ultra individual" abilities to use media considering social, democratic, and ethical aspects and knowledge in relation to structures, formal designs, and possible effects resulting from media
action	Directing towards an active and creative modelling of the individual lifestyle and engaging in social developments with the aid of media technology

Table 2

2.3 Pedagogical and Didactical Consequences of Media Competence Discourse

Principally, *communicative competences* are perceived as personal competences of each individual in association with media (technology). Basically, each individual possesses this "user-know-how", and acquires this capability by causal demonstration and advising, and through "learning-by-doing" and "learning-by-experience" (Kübler 1999, 35). Consequently, "a very momentous opening [...] in relation to informal teaching methods" takes place in current media pedagogy (Fromme 2002, 166). Fromme also speaks of learning with new media within the education system as "a possibility to broaden the learner's self-organized, *autodidactic* learning." (ibid, 165) This does not conclude that media pedagogy can be reduced to offering information access for mediating basic communicative competences because independent learning in a hyper-media environment requires effective search, evaluation, and learning strategies (ibid). The pedagogy cannot leave students possessing weak strategy abilities alone with their learning requirements, questions, and problems (cf. Müller 2000, 29), but must develop methods to promote capabilities toward efficient self-control in the learning processes (cf. e.g. Ziegler et al. 2003 *Self-regulated Learning and the Internet* – Selbstreguliertes Lernen und Internet). On the other hand, it is a fact that people of all ages not only can, but also increasingly have to learn "lifelong" within multi-media educational environments. This opens a vast working field for media pedagogues because it is proven that only a few of the existing products in this area can be utilized efficiently for self-regulated learning; hence there is a great need for future development (cf. e.g. Astleitner 2002, 148 *The Quality of Learning in the Internet* – Qualität des Lernens im Internet; compare also Astleitner 2001).

As previously addressed, *social competences* are closely related to critical reflection which must be conveyed by intense pedagogical intervention. Apart from imparting information regarding complex historical, cultural, and social relationships and teaching of discursive abilities (defining, deducing, debating etc.), also collaborative learning forms (collective problem solving) and open learning environments (to increase the independence and responsibility of the student) are seen as concrete pedagogical possibilities to convey social competences not only in the classical form of teaching but also in a more or less virtual learning environments (cf. Astleitner 2002, 88; Tulodziecki 1997, 54). Regarding social competences the pedagogues developing multi-media learning environments are confronted with a special challenge since many are of the opinion that the individualization of learning situations through media can lead to an estrangement of essential social learning processes (cf. Aufenanger 2001, 116; Brehm-Klotz 1997, 150).

The possibility to promote *action competences* is most likely to occur with the establishment of practice-oriented opportunities for integral creative learning experiences with the media. In practice, these lead to regarding the task of action-oriented media pedagogy primarily as creating possibilities to support and carry out creative media projects, subsequently, active (alternative creative) media work has developed "not only into the most important option but as well into the ideal way [Königsweg] of media pedagogy" (Kübler 2002, 176; cf. Thiele 1999, 63). This also explains the above mentioned increased significance of aesthetic media pedagogy conceptions. At this point, media pedagogic and artistic education widely correspond because "creative media work" usually means nothing else than the production of medial or multimedial art projects including primarily (video-) films, but also songs, performances and interactive CDs, DVD-ROMs, respectively, net projects. The topics are usually developed from an everyday situation, an event from the participant's life or from a current political problem (cf. Baacke et al. 1999). In the recent past, regarding media pedagogical projects the reflection aspect is increasingly stressed: With every newly acquired experience and piece of information, its relevance, placement, and context should become clear to the students in order to enable them to transform it into knowledge and results for their own actions (cf. Aufenanger 1999).

The singular aspects of media competence discourse can be assigned the following concrete Tasks of media pedagogy:

Competences	Tasks of Media Pedagogy
communicative	Pointing out the strategies toward efficient self-organisation of learning processes and developing of multi-media environments for self-regulated learning
social	Informing about complex historical, cultural, and social relationships; instilling discursive abilities; developing collaborative and open multi-media learning environments
action	Establishing practice-oriented opportunities for integral creative learning experiences with the aid of media technology; transferring into action-oriented knowledge through reflection of the newly acquired information

Table 3

3. Analogies between the Media Competence Conception and the Conception of Artistic Education

Not only within the media pedagogic discourses but also within the discourses of artistic education in Germany, a much-heated controversy has arisen over the last years and decades in regard to the concept "competence". A representation of this discourse would overwhelm the limits of this article and therefore, some exemplary aspects will be shown by means of the conception of *Artistic Education* (Künstlerische Bildung) as published in the anthology *Perspectives of the Artistic Education* (Ed. by Carl-Peter Buschkühle 2003).

The conception of Artistic Education is based on the visual art pedagogy but can be adopted into any of the art fields as it is based on the *Extended Art Concept* (erweiterter Kunstbegriff) of Joseph Beuys and the *Philosophy of the Art of Life* (Philosophie der Lebenskunst). Therefore it is highly interdisciplinary and open to many venues, not only art. Andreas Steffens describes the understanding of art in these surroundings as follows: "The important thing about art is not art; important is, what happens until it has been developed, what is manifested in its creation, in whatever form, [...]." (2003, 68)

3.1 Theoretical Background of Artistic Education Conceptions

Numerous parallels are already recognizable in the theoretical foundation of the conception of Artistic Education and the theoretical base of the media competence discourse. Joseph Beuys, referred to by many authors in this publication, can be described as a "radical democrat" in reference to artistic-pedagogical conceptions since to him, every individual is an artist. Referring back to the media pedagogical competence discourse, one can assume that every individual can also be described as "art competent". That also means a responsibility to one's own abilities: "We can only be what we really are when we make use of all of our capabilities." (Steffens 2003, 61) This does not mean that every individual is obligated to produce works of art in the traditional form. Following Beuys the conception of Artistic Education assumes a very broad definition to the term "artistic" – it is defined as the "fortune of an individual to express his own identity and his integral relationship to the world and time." (Regel 2003, 137) Ultimately, it deals with the ability to promote creativity in various life situations – in daily life, at work, and above all, forming the individual life style and relations within social groups (cf. ibid, 138; Beuys' "social sculpture" concept).

Hence, it is understandable why the *Philosophy of the Art of Life* (Philosophie der Lebenskunst) plays such an important role in the conception of Artistic Education (cf. 2003, 47ff.): This philosophy is described by Wilhelm Schmid as "a reflection of the base and possible forms of a consciously lead life." (Schmid 2003, 47) The art of life is the continuous forming of one's life and ego, whereby life depicts the material and art the design process (cf. ibid.). Schmid also introduces the conception of *Intelligence Education* (Klugheitserziehung), that means enabling an individual to take on responsibility to form his/her own life within a complex society. The basis of this type of "intelligence" is *sensitivity* on three levels: First of all, the *sensual* perception "of what is there", in other words, differentiating intense sensitive experiences from facts and situations. Then, the *structural* perception "of what is 'actually' there", hence, the cognitive conclusion of the general conditions and structural attributes of what has been perceived (as an example, Schmid takes the understanding of medial power structures). And lastly, the *virtual* perception, which concentrates on the developing of fantasy and power of imagination in order to "let life have a choice", and "not lock oneself into the prevailing reality [...], but rather get a glance at the future's horizon [...]." (ibid, 49) An education which enables a conscious art of life and living together must, according to Schmid, contain the following three types of knowledge: *knowledge of signs* – having a command of the informal world of signs such as language, writing, and numbers; *meta-knowledge* – the ability to retrieve and evaluate information; and above all, *creative thinking* – setting free creative abilities to develop and transform individual ideas in relation to life experiences, whereby, according to Schmid, these possibilities can be especially promoted through active interaction with the arts. (cf. ibid, 51)

The conception of the Art of Life, according to Schmid, can be summarized and assigned to the mentioned aspects of the media competence in the following manner:

Competences	Art of Life Conception (according to Schmid)	
	Types of Perception (Sensitivity)	*required knowledge*
communicative	*sensual* = perception "of what there is"; differentiate experience from facts and situations	knowledge of signs
social	*structural* = perception "of what is 'actually' there"; cognitive conclusion of the conditions and structural attributes of what has been perceived	meta-knowledge
action	*virtual* = expansion of fantasy and imagination in order to develop action alternatives	creative thinking

Table 4

3.2 Objectives of Artistic Education in Relation to Aspects of Media Competence

Proceeding from such considerations, Buschkühle defines the objective of the conception of Artistic Education as an "education and upbringing of a person to become an artist" in the sense that an individual "due to his mental agility, is capable to form himself and his life in an independent and responsible way" (Buschkühle 2003, 36). According to Buschkühle, the receptive and active occupation with art implies educational objectives, highly relevant for society as a whole. His summary of these educational objectives can be combined with the previously described aspects of media competence discourse:

Communicative Competences: The first two of five "socially relevant educational objectives" according to Buschkühle are the individual's ability to find one's own position and the mental agility respective to orientation ability. These aspects can be linked with the promotion of communicative competence because Buschkühle postulates that working with art – receptive or productive – requires not only the acquisition of knowledge but also its transformation into personal statements. Artistic work is always creative work with new, unknown, and unusual tasks; therefore occupation with art teaches individuals the ability to formulate and explain one's position. Buschkühle also believes that a particularity of artistic sensitivity and thinking is the integral perception of each object: "Sensuality, sensation, cognition, and imagination are activated simultaneously and interdependently influence, inspire, but also conflict with one another." That is why the receptive and productive occupation with art promotes the "agility of mental abilities" and hence, the entire variety of the mental capacities. Moreover, because it forces to find individual positions and formulate independent statements it trains the orientation abilities in view of the new, the unusual, and the controversial (cf. Buschkühle 2003, 39).

Social Competences: The third and fourth objectives of artistic education are described by Buschkühle as the teaching of responsibility of each individual and the ability for democratic communication. According to Buschkühle, the shaping of an individual art project demands the assuming of responsibility for its development and success. Analogous to media pedagogical postulates, Buschkühle stresses that social responsibility can be taught especially in group and team work: The occupation with art in groups, where individuals are required to explain and defend their opinions and creations and also critically analyse the work and opinions of others, trains a critical-constructive deportment, and teaches how to sensitively express relevant criticism and how to accept and deal with such criticism. (Buschkühle 2003, 39f)

Action Competences: The final educational objective of artistic education, according to Buschkühle, is the mobilization of individuals' initiatives. The parallels to media pedagogical action-orientation are obvious: Art education should promote not only critical cognition but also the formulation of individual messages and representations and in this way, help to detect potential consequences of actions or developments and train the visionary imagination as an ability to create alternatives. The creation of art projects developed out of situations from the lives of the students and from current political problems supports the discussion of, and participation in, social developments and leads not only to the conscious forming of the individual's life, but also to the assuming of social responsibility (cf. Buschkühle 2003, 38 ff.). The comparison of the objectives of the artistic education with the aspects of media competence discourse can be summarized as follows:

Competences	Objectives of Artistic Education
communicative	Proceeding from the acquiring of artistic knowledge and the transformation of this knowledge into individual messages, promotion of capabilities to formulate and substantiate individual positions, to reach an integral understanding in relation to the new, the unusual, and the controversial, and to obtain a corresponding orientation ability
social	Proceeding from artistic work and the combined reflection of this work in learning teams, teaching of individual responsibility and ability to democratic communication – in other words, a critical-constructive stance towards oneself and others
action	Proceeding from the mobilization of the individual's initiatives within artistic production, increasing the awareness for potential consequences of actions or developments, and training of the visionary imagination for alternative actions in respect to one's own life as well as in social relations

Table 5

3.3 Methods of Artistic Education in Relation to Media Competence Aspects

Numerous parallels are visible between media pedagogy and artistic education in relation to methods necessary to reach the discussed objectives:

With regard to *communicative competences* (the basic abilities necessary to obtain artistic knowledge and skills), informal independent learning takes on an increasing role within the conception of Artistic Education. The fact that even small children create their own pictures and possess their own (artistic) language is perceived as the "basis and beginning of all art-educational efforts"; no individual therefore is "stupid in the artistic field." (cf. Stielow 2003, 148) Accepting these basic artistic competences of each individual, art educators stress the "(self-)educating chances for artistic individuals in broadly self-controlled artistic processes." (Kettel 2003, 159) Also the term *Aesthetic Research* (ästhetische Forschung), introduced in the discourse from Helga Kämpf-Jansen (2001), receives an increased importance in this context: The creative, independent occupation with art can, according to Kämpf-Jansen, be described as an aesthetic or artistic research project as it is a complex and extremely challenging process with open structures and an uncertain result (Kämpf-Jansen 2003, 266). Projects such as these are usually based on everyday situations and subjective interests of the learners, and making detours or going astray is seen as an important part of such a research. Therefore, a realization of these projects in linear processes of formal learning (such as the usual classroom situation) is rejected (cf. ibid 274f.). Describing artistic learning processes in the publication "Perspectives of Artistic Education" *(Perspektiven künstlerischer Bildung)* teachers are depicted as impulse givers and advisors but never as announcers of objective aesthetic truths; in some comments it is even rejected that teachers relay the artistic tasks during the lesson – the duty of the teacher is chiefly the "art of asking questions": "Not the questioning of the known, but rather probing the unknown is our primary task" (Zaake 2003, 298). Such ideas lead to the demand for a new orientation within art education in the sense of a radical individualization in the pedagogic orientation in regards to differences, uniqueness, and character development of the individual (Kettel 2003, 196).

With regards to *social competences*, the conception of Artistic Education (analogue to the rejection of the subjective-individualistic diminishing of the term competence in media pedagogy) demands an increasing consideration of the ethical implications of artistic pedagogy processes (cf. e.g. Sowa 2003, 213ff.) and grants high value to critical reflection. As previously described, the most important methods in promoting these abilities are seen in teamwork and discussion regarding the working results of the group (cf. Buschkühle 39f.). An additional method used to achieve this learning result includes intensifying the consciousness of the student for his/her development in a specific socio-historical cultural environment (cf. Stielow 2003, 149), which can be accomplished through the development of inter-cultural relations proceeding from information about (art) history contexts and work and text analyses (cf. Buschkühle 2003, 41). In the framework of the intellectual occupation with the arts, the following levels, according to Buschkühle are connected: "Personal experiences, political problems, individual dismay, and moral and ethical questions." (Buschkühle 2003, 43) Helga Kämpf-Jansen probes even farther in her construction of Aesthetic Research – the objective of this research process includes a change of awareness and the achieving of an expanded cognition; for this reason, it is impossible for her to exclude theoretical research from the previously described practical studies. Investigation, analyses, work with theme related scientific papers, and even the independent compilation of such papers is an inseparable part of the Aesthetic Research theory. In this way Aesthetic Research is "a conception of the connection between daily experiences, art or aesthetic experiences and scientific discourses." (Kämpf-Jansen 2003, 273)

In reference to the *action competences*, the methods within the conceptions of Artistic Education and Media Competence are practically identical: Even here, creative (artistic) project work appears to be the best way to promote these competences, because according to Buschkühle, this is the only way which provides enough time and space for intense personal occupation with the complex content and formal processes of art creation (cf. 2003, 42). In the process, a high importance is attached to interdisciplinary connections and cooperation between varying (school) subjects, whereby the combination of the different arts (fine arts, music, literature, theatre) is stressed as most obvious (Buschkühle 2003, 42f.; Regel 2003, 134). A transformation of insights and experiences in individual statements and definitions is possible only within cooperative artistic projects, whereby the separation of facts and personally acquired experiences is overcome and "the artistic" is allowed to influence other ("non-artistic") subjects (Buschkühle 2003, 42f.). Promoting these transfer effects is most important for the conception of Artistic Education because it does not deal primarily with experiences and knowledge, but rather with design, in a very broad sense: Artistic thinking grasps the element of perception, "in order to change it, to give it new forms and contexts, and to extract new meaning out of it." (ibid, 35) Thus the term (central for art) "design" means the creation of contexts and meaningful structures in order to express one's own self and one's personal relationship with the world (Regel 2003, 138).

The methods within this conception can be concatenated with the tasks of artistic education and assigned to the aspects of media competence as follows:

Competences	Tasks and Methods of Artistic Education
communicative	Promoting self-regulated artistic (learning) processes through radical individualization of the teaching situations – pedagogical orientation in regards to difference, uniqueness, and character development of the individual
social	Teaching critical reflection in relation to political, ethical, and social implications of artistic processes through collaborative team work, discussing the work results in the group and proceeding from information regarding (art) historical contexts and work and text analyses
action	Establishing possibilities for creative artistic project work beyond the boundaries of time and space; interdisciplinary cooperation especially within the art field; promoting transfer effects – changing the perceived objects in order to gain meaning

Table 6

4. Synergy Effects of Media Pedagogy and Artistic Education

When comparing the discussed conceptions of media pedagogy and art education (see Table 7), it becomes clear how intense the analogies between the pedagogical objectives and didactic methods are; in many areas they can almost be considered to be identical. As such, it is of course not *nparison between the Objectives and the Tasks and Methods of Media Pedagogy and Artistic Educatior*

EDUCATIONAL OBJECTIVES		TASKS AND METHODS	
dia Pedagogy	*Artistic Education*	*Media Pedagogy*	*Artistic Education*
moting personal compe- ces of each individual, to lerstand media contents, xpress oneself coherently h help from media tech- ogy, and to use media ductively for personal y-to-day) interests	Promoting capabilities to formulate and substantiate individual positions, to reach an integral understanding in relation to the new, the unusual, and the controversial, and to obtain a corresponding orientation ability	Pointing out the strategies toward efficient self-organisation of learning processes and developing of multi-media environments for self-regulated learning	Promoting self-regulated (learning) processes throu cal individualization of th ing situations – pedagogic tation in regards to differe uniqueness, and characte opment of the individual
parting "ultra individual" ities to use media consid- g social, democratic, and cal aspects and knowl- e in relation to structures, nal designs, and possible cts resulting from media	Teaching of individual responsibility and ability to democratic communication – in other words, a critical-constructive stance towards oneself and others	Informing about complex historical, cultural, and social relationships; instilling discursive abilities; developing collaborative and open multimedia environments	Teaching critical reflectio tion to political, ethical, a implications of artistic pr through collaborative tear discussing the work result group and proceeding fro mation regarding (art) his contexts and work and te
ecting towards an active creative modelling of the ividual lifestyle and engag- in social developments h the aid of media techno- y	Increasing the awareness for potential consequences of actions or developments, and training of the visionary imagination for alternative actions in respect to one's own life as well as in social relations	Establishing practice-oriented opportunities for integral creative learning experiences with the aid of media technology; transferring into action-oriented knowledge through reflection of the newly acquired information	Establishing possibilities f tive artistic project work b the boundaries of time an interdisciplinary cooperat pecially within the art fiel moting transfer effects – c the perceived objects in o gain meaning

a new discovery and has settled itself in practice for a long time: As previously explained active and creative media work which also includes an intense artistic occupation is perceived as the ideal way in media pedagogy. Baacke even wrote in one of his last articles that "'media competence' can only and exclusively be realized in project work" (1999, 35). At the same time, the occupation with media (technologies) plays an increasingly important role in the artistic pedagogy. In the reviewed publication "Perspectives of Artistic Education" alone, three articles deal primarily with media pedagogical topics in the context of art pedagogy (Serexhe 2003, 113ff.; Freiberg 2003, 345ff.; Spormann 2003, 369ff.). Serexhe argues in his article for an orientation of the fine arts education in the direction of an "Art and Media" subject, where students should learn to independently and critically deal with various types of image production and express themselves using diverse forms of media. Freiberg, one of the pioneers in this field, in 1998 already called for the development of a *Media-Art-Pedagogy* (Medien-Kunst-Pädagogik), whereby he proceeds from media art as being exemplary for the development of a new artistic pedagogy which couples media critical aspects with fun-loving experimental media use (cf. Freiberg 1998). Even for Buschkühle, the new media plays an important role for the realization of the objectives of the conception "Artistic Education": He postulates that the traditional and the new media stand in a mutual inspirational relationship in regard to artistic education[3] (Buschkühle 2003, 43). According to Buschkühle, the perceptions of reality today experience their creative transformation in virtual images such as video art, installations, or performances. The occupation with these reciprocal effects enables

> a critical relationship toward special properties of each particular media form, promotes the competence to deal with them independently, and teaches position abilities in the sense of development and reasoning of personal standpoints in regard to a topic and its medial influences. (ibid, 44)

The media also plays an increasingly important role in other areas of artistic pedagogy. In recent times a strong tendency within music peda-

3 In this case, "traditional" media means the ones which have already been a part of art production before the discovery of technical media (photography, film, etc.) – such as painting, sculpting, etc.

gogy to integrate media pedagogical topics has developed – which appears quite legitimate considering the high value of music in media consumption by the youth of today (cf. Münch 1999). A research project was realized at the University of Oldenburg between 2000 and 2002 entitled *Media Competence in Music Pedagogic Practice* (Medienkompetenz in der musikpädagogischen Praxis), with the aim to interpret the term "media competence" music-pedagogically, in order to settle on which media competences music teachers require (cf. Stroh 2002). Since 2002, the music universities in Würzburg and Magdenburg have been running a project model entitled *New Media as Tool, Music Instrument, and Topic in Music Instruction* (Neue Medien als Werkzeug, Musikinstrument als Thema in Musikunterricht), dealing with the development of didactic-methodical conceptions for the integration of new music technologies in music lessons. In the description of this project, Niels Knolle and Thomas Münch postulate that music technologies are practically unconditional music instruments and enable the access to practical and analytical occupation with music to all students (Knolle; Münch 2003, 32). Already in 1999, Thomas Münch wrote that music education which integrates media work offers manifold pedagogical chances, mainly because media work combines action, reflection, and critical reception in an ideal way and therefore allows project, action, and communication oriented forms of learning and teaching to be realized (cf. Münch 1999, 5).

The objectives of media pedagogy and the artistic education goal settings can be summarized as a pedagogy which connects the tasks of both fields – in other words the goal settings of an "Artistic Media Education":

Competences	**Goal settings of "Artistic Media Education"**
communicative	Promoting individual competences, to independently understand media content and aesthetic media messages, and to articulate one's own (also artistic) thoughts and conceptions with the aid of media technologies, respectively, to use the media for personal (creative, daily, and occupational) interests
social	Teaching "ultra-individual" knowledge regarding structures, forms, and possible effects of media (esp. in relation to the arts) with the aim to enable critical use with regards to ethical and democratic aspects, respectively, to instigate a corresponding usage through personal artistic work
action	Establishing of the possibilities for and structuring of creative (learning) experiences with the help of media where abilities for active artistic planning of an individual living environment and participating in social processes can be learned and tested

Table 8

5. Outlook with Respect to Possible Tasks of "Artistic Media Education"

Proceeding from this proposed model, an "Artistic Media Education" based on theory and practice of media pedagogy as well as artistic pedagogy can be found. This is not an attempt to introduce a new conception whereby the two specialized fields are dissolved and fused into one singular field. The research interest relates to the question of how two specialized fields, both of which seize such obvious analogies in their objectives and methods but seldom cooperate with one another, can profit from the knowledge of the other field. Finally, some ideas regarding possible future working fields will be introduced which claim no completeness, quite the contrary: These recommendations are intended to encourage additional thoughts and developments.

Working fields in relation to communicative competences: In artistic education (esp. at the university level) the education policy increasingly demands the use of E-learning – meaning that entire seminars or parts of them (for example, dealing with theoretical principles necessary for artistic production) are to be carried out in multi-media environments on the internet (web based learning). The development of such learning environments comprised one of the main working fields of media pedagogy, especially didactics, over the last years and decades, while the artistic pedagogy has practically no corresponding experiences. Consequently, artistic fields could profit immensely from the theoretical and empirical experience within media didactics. At the same time, media didactics could also acquire an important innovative thrust as a result of the involvement in the development of learning environments for creative and artistic education. The last few years have exhibited a stagnate situation due to an apparent irreconcilable gap between the media didactical theory and the educational practice: On the one hand, the results of theoretical learning research require a realization of constructivistic postulates leading to the development of open and collaborative teaching environments where each student should be able to choose his/her own method of study and assigned practical tasks from real life, which encourage the development of creative problem solving strategies. On the other hand, such learning environments are seldom required in practice due to the fact that the education in most subjects is still organized in an absolute linear way and based on the testing of given facts. Through a joint development of multi-media learning environments for creative and artistic learning, numerous chances present themselves for advancement in both areas in relation to the promotion of basic (communicative) competences.

Working fields in relation to social competences: The intense promotion of social and ethical competences based on imparting critical-reflective abilities is demanded by representatives from both areas. As previously mentioned, there is a growing scepticism within the media pedagogy, complaining that the orientation on media criticism is too intense and leads to a rationalistic diminishing and neglect of emotional and aesthetic aspects of media competence. In this respect, conceptual approaches, such as Freiberg's "Media-Art-Pedagogy" (Medien-Kunst-Pädagogik) claim exceptional consideration since in this media art based conception critical aspects are connected with fun-loving experimental media use. Simultaneously, with respect to the teaching of cognitive abilities in artistic education, research results from the media pedagogical field are quite significant – the communication, socialization, and reception research have developed media-theoretical foundations and analyzing tools that can be implemented into various situations within artistic education and which are irreplaceable in dealing with media related problem areas. There is also evidence here for the possibility and necessity for further development in close cooperation between media pedagogues and pedagogues in artistic fields.

Working fields in relation to action competences: The central task for cooperation between the mentioned areas is creative media project work. Previously, in the institutionalized form of artistic pedagogy, the inflexible structure of educational institutions made project work extremely difficult to realize; now this type of pedagogical approach is increasingly stipulated and promoted also by the educational policy. However, corresponding experiences are virtually missing within the institutional artistic education – these can be derived from the decade-long media pedagogical practices with media work outside educational institutions. Alternatively, media pedagogical project results often suffer criticism due to inadequate quality in regard to the handling of the utilized material and the formal design of production. Consequently, the artistic pedagogy has the opportunity to play an important role in developing a qualitative and sustainable "Artistic Media Education", if it manages to overcome the barriers of the respective singular areas and to intensify the development of interdisciplinary working forms.

Bibliography

Ackermann, Heike (1992): Informationstechnische Bildung im Spannungsfeld von Politik, Bildungsverwaltung und Pädagogik. Opladen: Leske + Budrich 1992.

Astleitner, Hermann (2001): Quality assurance as the next major goal for web-based distance education. In: M.R. Syed & V. Tareski (Eds.), Advances in educational technologies. Multimedia, WWW and distance education. New York: Wiley, p. 71–79.

Astleitner, Hermann (2002): Qualität des Lernens im Internet: Virtuelle Schulen und Universitäten auf dem Prüfstand. Frankfurt am Main; Berlin; Bern; Wien (u.a.): Lang.

Aufenanger, Stefan (1999): Medienpädagogische Projekte – Zielsetzungen und Aufgaben. In: Baacke, Dieter; Kornblum, Susanne; Lauffer, Jürgen; Mikos, Lothar; Thiele, Günter A. (Ed.): Handbuch Medien: Medienkompetenz. Modelle und Projekte. Bonn: Bundeszentrale für politische Bildung, p. 94–97.

Aufenanger, Stefan (2001): Multimedia und Medienkompetenz – Forderungen an das Bildungssystem. In: Aufenanger, Stefan; Schulz-Zander, Renate; Spanhel, Dieter (Ed.): Jahrbuch Medienpädagogik 1. Opladen: Leske + Budrich, p. 109–122.

Baacke, Dieter (1973): Kommunikation und Kompetenz. Grundlegung einer Didaktik der Kommunikation und ihrer Medien. München: Juventa.

Baacke, Dieter (1995): Zum pädagogischen Widerwillen gegen des Sehsinn. In: Baake, Dieter; Röll, Franz J. (Ed.): Weltbilder, Wahrnehmung, Wirklichkeit – der ästhetisch organisierte Lernprozess. Opladen: Lieske + Budrich, p. 25–47.

Baacke, Dieter (1996): Medienkompetenz als Netzwerk – Reichweite und Fokussierung eines Begriffs, der Konjunktur hat. In: medien praktisch 2/96, p. 4–10.

Baacke, Dieter (1997): Medienpädagogik – Grundlagen der Medienkommunikation. Tübingen: Niemeyer.

Baacke, Dieter (1999): Medienkompetenz als zentrales Operationsfeld von Projekten. In: Baacke, Dieter; Kornblum, Susanne; Lauffer, Jürgen; Mikos, Lothar; Thiele, Günter A. (Ed.): Handbuch Medien: Medienkompetenz. Modelle und Projekte. Bonn: Bundeszentrale für politische Bildung, p. 31–35.

Baacke, Dieter; Kornblum, Susanne; Lauffer, Jürgen; Mikos, Lothar; Thiele, Günter A. (Ed.) (1999): Handbuch Medien: Medienkompetenz. Modelle und Projekte. Bonn: Bundeszentrale für politische Bildung.

Baake, Dieter; Röll, Franz J. (Ed.) (1995): Weltbilder, Wahrnehmung, Wirklichkeit – der ästhetisch organisierte Lernprozess. Opladen: Lieske + Budrich.

Binder, Hartmut (1992): Zur Geschichte und Entwicklung schulischer Medienerziehung. In: Schill, Wolfgang; Tulodziecki, Gerhard; Wagner, Wolf-Rüdiger (Ed.): Medienpädagogisches Handeln in der Schule. Opladen: Leske + Budrich, p. 17–31.

Brehm-Klotz, Christiane (1997): Informationstechnische Bildung. In: Hüther, Jürgen; Schorb, Bernd; Brehm-Klotz, Christiane (Ed.): Grundbegriffe Medienpädagogik. München: KoPäd Verlag, p. 145–150.

Buschkühle, Carl-Peter (Ed.) (2003): Perspektiven Künstlerischer Bildung. Texte zum Symposium Künstlerische Bildung und die Schule der Zukunft. Köln: Salon-Verlag.

Buschkühle, Carl-Peter (2003): Konturen künstlerischer Bildung – Zur Einleitung. In: Buschkühle, Carl-Peter (Ed.): Perspektiven Künstlerischer Bildung. Texte zum Symposium Künstlerische Bildung und die Schule der Zukunft. Köln: Salon-Verlag, p. 19–44.

Ehmer, Hermann K. (Ed.) (1971): Visuelle Kommunikation. Beiträge zur Kritik der Bewusstseinsindustrie. Köln: DuMont.

Freiberg, Henning (1998): Medien-Kunst-Pädagogik Anstösse zum Umgang mit Neuen Medien im Fach Kunst. Vortrag vom 18.10.1998. In: http://www.kunstunterricht.de/material/.

Freiberg, Henning (2003): Gestalten mit neuen Medien als ein Beitrag zur Kunsterziehung im Fach Kunst. In: Buschkühle, Carl-Peter (Ed.): Perspektiven Künstlerischer Bildung. Texte zum Symposium Künstlerische Bildung und die Schule der Zukunft. Köln: Salon-Verlag, p. 345–368.

Frisus, Rudolf et al. ("Arbeitgemeinschaft Curriculum Musik") (1972): Sequenzen – Musik Sekundarstufe I. Beiträge und Modelle zum Musik-Curriculum. Elemente zur Unterrichtsplanung (Lehrerband). Stuttgart: Klett.

Fromme, Johannes (2002): Mediensozialisation und Medienpädagogik: zum Verhältnis von informellem und organisiertem Lernen mit Computer und Internet. In: Paus-Haase, Ingrid; Lempert, Claudia; Süss, Daniel (Ed.): Medienpädagogik in der Kommunikationswissenschaft – Positionen, Perspektiven, Potenziale. Wiesbaden: Westdeutscher Verlag, p. 155–168.

Gapski, Harald (2001): Medienkompetenz. Eine Bestandsaufnahme und Vorüberlegungen zu einem systemtheoretischen Rahmenkonzept. Wiesbaden: Westdeutscher Verlag.

Gawert, Johannes (1996): Im Trend. Konzept "Medienkompetenz" als Krisensymptom? In: medien praktisch 2/96, p. 2.

Groeben, Norbert (2002): Anforderungen an die theoretische Konzeptualisierung von Medienkompetenz. In: Groeben, Norbert; Hurrelmann, Bettina (Ed.): Medienkompetenz. Voraussetzungen, Dimensionen, Funktionen. Weinheim; München: Juventa, p. 11–22.

Habermas, Jürgen (1971): Vorbereitende Bemerkungen zu einer Theorie der kommunikativen Kompetenz. In: Habermas, Jürgen; Luhmann, Niklas (Ed.): Theorie der Gesellschaft oder Sozialtechnologie. Frankfurt am Main: Suhrkamp, p. 101–141.

Helmholz, Brigitta (1996): Musikdidaktische Konzeptionen in Deutschland nach 1945. Essen: Blaue Eule.

Hurrelmann, Bettina (2002a): Zur historischen und kulturellen Relativität des "gesellschaftlich handlungsfähigen Subjekts" als normativer Rahmenidee für Medienkompetenz. In: Groeben, Norbert; Hurrelmann, Bettina (Ed.): Medienkompetenz. Voraussetzungen, Dimensionen, Funktionen. Weinheim; München: Juventa, p. 111–126.

Hüther, Jürgen; Podehl, Bernd (1997): Geschichte der Medienpädagogik. In: Hüther, Jürgen; Schorb, Bernd; Brehm-Klotz, Christiane (Ed.): Grundbegriffe Medienpädagogik. München: KoPäd Verlag, p. 116–126.

Kämpf-Jansen, Helga (2001): Ästhetische Forschung. Wege durch Alltag, Kunst und Wissenschaft. Zu einem innovativen Konzept ästhetischer Bildung. Köln: Salon Verlag.

Kämpf-Jansen, Helga (2003): Ästhetische Forschung – zur Verknüpfung alltäglicher Erfahrungen, künstlerischer Strategien und wissenschaftlicher Diskurse in einem innovativen Konzept ästhetischer Bildung. In: Buschkühle, Carl-Peter (Ed.): Perspektiven Künstlerischer Bildung. Texte zum Symposium Künstlerische Bildung und die Schule der Zukunft. Köln: Salon-Verlag, p. 263–276.

Kettel, Joachim (2003): Kartografien des Selbst – Selbstorganisation und Künstlerische Bildung. In: Buschkühle, Carl-Peter (Ed.): Perspektiven Künstlerischer Bildung. Texte zum Symposium Künstlerische Bildung und die Schule der Zukunft. Köln: Salon-Verlag, p. 159–204.

Kirschenmann, Johannes (2003): Medienbildung in der Kunstpädagogik – Zu einer Didaktik der Komplementarität und Revalidierung. Weimar: VDG.

Knolle, Niels; Münch, Thomas (2003): Me[i]Mus – Neue Medien als Werkzeug, Musikinstrument und Thema im Musikunterricht. In: Bundesministerium für Bildung und Forschung; Zentrum für Kulturforschung (Ed.): Kulturelle Bildung im Medienzeitalter. Projekte – Praxis – Perspektiven. Bonn: ARCult Media, p. 32–33.

Kübler, Hans-Dieter (1994): Medienwissenschaft – Produktanalysen als Grundlage medienpädagogischen Urteilens und Handelns. In: Hiegemann, Susanne; Swoboda, Wolfgang H. (Ed.): Handbuch der Medienpädagogik. Opladen: Leske + Budrich, p. 59–99.

Kübler (1999): Medienkompetenz – Dimensionen eines Schlagworts. In: Schell, Fred; Stolzenburg, Elke; Theunert, Helga (Ed.): Medienkompetenz: Grundlagen und pädagogisches Handeln. München: KoPäd Verlag, p. 25–49.

Kübler, Hans-Dieter (2002): Modalitäten von Medienkompetenz. Von der Medienerziehung zum Wissensmanagement? In: forum medienethik, Medienkompetenz – Kritik einer populären Universalkonzeption, 1/2002, p. 18–28.

Luca, Renate (2001): Medien und Emotionen. Eine vernachlässigte Dimension in der Medienpädagogik. In: Aufenanger, Stefan; Schulz-Zander, Renate; Spanhel, Dieter (Ed.): Jahrbuch Medienpädagogik 1. Opladen: Leske + Budrich, p. 337–350.

Mandl, Heinz; Reinmann-Rothmeier, Gabi (1997): Medienpädagogik und -kompetenz: Was bedeutet das in einer Wissensgesellschaft und welche Lernkultur brauchen wir dafür? In: Deutscher Bundestag (Ed.): Medienkompetenz im Informationszeitalter. Enquete-Kommission Zukunft der Medien in Wirtschaft und Gesellschaft; Deutschlands Weg in die Informationsgesellschaft. Bonn: ZV Zeitungs-Verlag Service, p. 77–89.

Mikos, Lothar (2000): Ästhetische Erfahrung und visuelle Kompetenz: Zur Erweiterung der diskursiven Medienkompetenz um präsentative Elemente. In: http://www.medienpaed.com (1.09.2003).

Möller, Heino R. (1971): "Gegen den Kunstunterricht – Versuche einer Neuorientierung". Ravensburg: Otto Maier Verlag.

Moser, Heinz (2000^3): Einführung in die Medienpädagogik. Aufwachsen im Medienzeitalter. Opladen: Leske + Budrich.

Müller, Ulrich (2000): Weiterbildung – in Zukunft nur noch selbstorganisiert? Zur Integration selbst- und fremdorganisierten Lernens. In: Erwachsenenbildung 46 (1), p. 27–31.

Münch, Thomas (1999): Musik – Medien. Zur Entwicklung einer Medienkompetenz bei SchülerInnen der Sekundarstufe. In: Musik & Bildung 1/1999, p. 2–5.

Paus-Haase, Ingrid (2001): Vom Bewahren zum Wahrnehmen und Verstehen. Medienpädagogische Konzepte in unserem Informationszeitalter. In: Aufenanger, Stefan; Schulz-Zander, Renate; Spanhel, Dieter (Ed.): Jahrbuch Medienpädagogik 1. Opladen: Leske + Budrich, p. 85–107.

Pöttinger, Ida (2002^2): Lernziel Medienkompetenz. Theoretische Grundlagen und praktische Evaluation anhand eines Hörspielprojekts. München: KoPäd Verlag.

Regel, Günther (2003): Die zweite Moderne, die Schule und die Kunst – Konsequenzen für die künstlerische Bildung. In: Buschkühle, Carl-Peter (Ed.): Perspektiven Künstlerischer Bildung. Texte zum Symposium Künstlerische Bildung und die Schule der Zukunft. Köln: Salon-Verlag, p. 121–140.

Schmid, Wilhelm (2003): Schule der Lebenskunst. In: Buschkühle, Carl-Peter (Ed.): Perspektiven Künstlerischer Bildung. Texte zum Symposium Künstlerische Bildung und die Schule der Zukunft. Köln: Salon-Verlag, p. 47–58.

Schorb, Bernd (1994): Zwischen Reformpädagogik und Technozentrik – Über Kinoreformer und die "Keilhacker-Schule" zu einer handlungsorientierten Medienpädagogik. In: Hiegemann, Susanne; Swoboda, Wolfgang H. (Ed.): Handbuch der Medienpädagogik. Opladen: Leske + Budrich, p. 149–168.

Schorb, Bernd (1995): Medienalltag und Handeln. Medienpädagogik im Spiegel von Geschichte, Theorie und Praxis. Opladen: Leske + Budrich.

Schorb, Bernd (1997): Vermittlung von Medienkompetenz als Aufgabe der Medienpädagogik. In: Deutscher Bundestag (Ed.): Medienkompetenz im Informationszeitalter. Enquete-Kommission Zukunft der Medien in Wirtschaft und Gesellschaft; Deutschlands Weg in die Informationsgesellschaft. Bonn: ZV Zeitungs-Verlag Service, p. 63–75.

Schorb, Bernd; Mohn, Erich; Theunert, Helga (1980): Sozialisation durch (Massen-)Medien. In: Hurrelmann, Klaus; Ulich, Dieter (Ed.): Handbuch der Sozialisationsforschung. Weinheim und Basel: Beltz, p. 603–627.

Serexhe, Bernhard (2003): Neue Technologien verlangen neue Curricula. In: Buschkühle, Carl-Peter (Ed.): Perspektiven Künstlerischer Bildung. Texte zum Symposium Künstlerische Bildung und die Schule der Zukunft. Köln: Salon-Verlag, p. 113–118.

Sowa, Hubert (2003): Ethische Implikationen kunstpädagogischer Prozesse. Vorbemerkungen zu einer künftigen kunstpädagogischen Handlungstheorie. In: Buschkühle, Carl-Peter (Ed.): Perspektiven Künstlerischer Bildung. Texte zum Symposium Künstlerische Bildung und die Schule der Zukunft. Köln: Salon-Verlag, p. 213–235.

Spormann, Ulrich (2003): Kunstspartenübergreifende Gestaltung durch multimediale Technik: eine Herausforderung für die ästhetische und didaktische Konzeptentwicklung. In: Buschkühle, Carl-Peter (Ed.): Perspektiven Künstlerischer Bildung. Texte zum Symposium Künstlerische Bildung und die Schule der Zukunft. Köln: Salon-Verlag, p. 369–386.

Steffens, Andreas (2003): Kunst der Weltbildung. In: Buschkühle, Carl-Peter (Ed.): Perspektiven Künstlerischer Bildung. Texte zum Symposium Künstlerische Bildung und die Schule der Zukunft. Köln: Salon-Verlag, p. 369–386.

Stielow, Reimar (2003): Problemfelder und Schlüsselprobleme einer künstlerischen Kunstpädagogik in der Schule der Zukunft. In: Buschkühle, Carl-Peter (Ed.): Perspektiven Künstlerischer Bildung. Texte zum Symposium Künstlerische Bildung und die Schule der Zukunft. Köln: Salon-Verlag, p. 141–158.

Stroh, Martin W. (2002): Medienkompetenz als musikpädagogisches Leitbild? In: Praxis des Musikunterrichts 4/2002, p. 42–47.

Sutter, Tilmann; Charlton, Michael (2002): Medienkompetenz – einige Anmerkungen zum Kompetenzbegriff. In: Groeben, Norbert; Hurrelmann, Bettina (Ed.): Medienkompetenz. Voraussetzungen, Dimensionen, Funktionen. Weinheim; München: Juventa, p. 129–147.

Thiele, Günther A. (1999): Produktive Medienarbeit in der Schule – heute. In: Baacke, Dieter; Kornblum, Susanne; Lauffer, Jürgen; Mikos, Lothar; Thiele, Günter A. (Ed.): Handbuch Medien: Medienkompetenz. Modelle und Projekte. Bonn: Bundeszentrale für politische Bildung, p. 62–69.

Tulodziecki, Gerhard (1992): Mediennutzung als situations-, bedürfnis- und entwicklungsbezogene Handlung – Konsequenzen für die Medienerziehung. In: Schill, Wolfgang; Tulodziecki, Gerhard; Wagner, Wolf-Rüdiger (Ed.): Medienpädagogisches Handeln in der Schule. Opladen: Leske + Budrich, p. 59–72.

Tulodziecki, Gerhard (1997): Nutzung von Multimedia – ein Weg zur Verbesserung schulischen Lehrens und Lernens? In: Freese, Peter (Ed.): Neue Medien und Schule – Paderborner Universitätsreden. Paderborn: Niesel.

Tulodziecki, Gerhard (2000): Medienpädagogik in der Schule der Zukunft. In: Kleber, Hubert (Ed.): Spannungsfeld Medien und Erziehung – Medienpädagogische Perspektiven. München: KoPäd Verlag, p. 13–32.

Vollbrecht, Ralf (2001): Einführung in die Medienpädagogik. Weinheim und Basel: Beltz Verlag.

Vollbrecht, Ralf; Mägdefrau, Jutta (1998): Medienkompetenz als Bildungsaufgabe. In: Die Deutsche Schule 3/1998, p. 266–277.

Zaake, Gerd-Peter (2003): Handarbeit. Aufgabenhand. Verbindung von Kopf und Hand. In: Buschkühle, Carl-Peter (Ed.): Perspektiven Künstlerischer Bildung. Texte zum Symposium Künstlerische Bildung und die Schule der Zukunft. Köln: Salon-Verlag, p. 295–308.

Ziegler, Karin; Hofmann, Franz; Astleitner, Hermann (2003): Selbstreguliertes Lernen und Internet. Theoretische und empirische Grundlagen von Qualitätssicherungsmaßnahmen beim E-Learning. Frankfurt am Main: Lang.

Media, Suggestion, Suspicion

On obstacles in handling new media in the context of art education – An approach unfolded by means of psychoanalytic devices[1]

KARL-JOSEF PAZZINI

In the past, in the present, and probably in the future as well, the use of new media in pedagogical situations finds itself confronted with suspicion. This is far from being devoid of effects on pedagogical projects. While being vague and confused, the suspicion is time and again of considerable impact. It encompasses anything from fear of youth corruption, threat of imminent solitude, future stupidity, distraction and forgetfulness, to naïve belief in progress.

If, as a pedagogue, you do not notice and comprehend this, you are in trouble.

Why are the media suspect?

What the existence of the media – if nothing else before that – makes clear is that we have no direct, no immediate or unmediated, no constant already given relation to the world, neither to things nor to human beings.

On the other hand, a direct, nonmediated, immediate relation to oneself and to the world is that which produces the most anxiety. Death seems to be an instance of such an immediacy. And, in small doses, so is the orgasm.

1 This contribution is an elaborated version of my "Versuch über das Suggestive der Medien," *RISS. Zeitschrift für Psychoanalyse. Freud. Lacan*, 6. Jg., No. 52 (2001/III), 25–46.

Immediacy not only induces anxiety but also fascination: hence the frequent representation of dying, of death, and of killing in the media. Death seems to also effect a sense of relief. This admission used to be articulated more distinctly in earlier times. But it is now no longer compatible with the task of self-realization and self-actualization through continuous work, through the obligation towards pleasure. The longing for death is considered to be decadent, to be an attempt to escape and shirk from the task that obliges everybody and everything. This already starts with each little idleness.

Those media which are in frequent use and have been around for a long time no longer remind us of alienation as much, given that their existence appears familiar to us. We know what they can do; we have turned them into a kind of unnoticed prosthesis. In addition, the old media fit better to the bourgeois image of man, consisting as it does of uniqueness, of not being copyable, of irreplacability. They flatter the citizen as a mirror reflection.

At their time of introduction the more recent media are unfamiliar, and they seem to invite copying; they are simple, simply dichotomic, not complex enough. This is due to the canard about the zeroes and ones. The fact that this is not correct, neither with respect to production, for example, nor to reception, and no more so in terms of the semantic and the syntactic levels, can be seen from the efforts involved in handling these media, and from the complexity of their effects. One can also assume, therefore, that the opposition of "digital" and "analogue" is not what marks the difference in the media change. At least this is not with regard to the fundamental difficulties in handling these new media, as opposed to older new media. One doesn't speak of the individual medium "pencil" [*Bleistift*] as of something that would only have to do with lead [*Blei*], which is equally true for the gun bullet.

One task of art is certainly to make the known and the familiar become conspicuous. Therefore, working in an art-related way, close to art, must involve working with the known media in such a way as to make something appear conspicuously unfamiliar, so as to be produced in an unusual way, and as a result also be received – perhaps – in a correspondingly noteworthy and odd way. With regard to the new media, art deals with something that is per se conspicuous and unfamiliar, which is why it will initially be difficult for art to add any precision to something, while on the other hand it is spared from the burden of conventions.

Suggestion

> ... but also because it has since been discovered how great an economy of thought can be effected by the use of the catchword 'suggestion'. Nobody knows and nobody cares what suggestion is, where it comes from, or when it arises – it is enough that everything awkward in the region of psychology can be labelled 'suggestion'.
>
> Sigmund Freud[2]

No admittance to persons under age 18

It is said that media have uncalculable effects. One seems to know all about some of the effects, for how else would it be possible to attribute predicates such as "valuable" or, for that matter, "youth-endangering", to them?

Along the same lines, advertising companies seem to know about the effects of varying media presentations. They would otherwise not be capable of wanting to sell something. But they are just the ones who – in order to reach their goal by way of a seduction which is itself effected via some detours – bet on those effects that are precisely meant to *not* be entirely accessible to consciousness. This is what Vance Packard, by now a classic reporter of media and advertisement effects, asserts as early as in the title of his book, *The Hidden Persuaders*.[3]

2 Sigmund Freud, "Analysis of a phobia in a five year old boy," trans. James Strachey, *The Standard Edition of the Complete Psychological Works of Sigmund Freud*, vol. 10 (London: The Hogarth Press 1955–1964), 102. [Orig.: "Analyse der Phobie eines fünfjährigen Knaben" (1909). *Gesammelte Werke* (1906–1909), vol. VII. (Frankfurt am Main: Fischer 1972), 337.]

3 Vance Packard, *The Hidden Persuaders* (London: Random House 1957). Translator's note: The German subtitle added to *Die geheimen Verführer* (Düsseldorf: Econ 1958) is suggestive on this point: *Der Griff nach dem Unbewußten in Jedermann*, literally "grasping for the unconscious in everyone".

Advertising is not the only field driving at detours. Besides the manifest statement purported by the media there is a direct effect that is made to operate, of which the very fact of being a detour is the real effect. This effect is produced by a shortcut, in as much as it does not pass through the cumbersome and capacity-restricted control mechanism of conscious apperception.

Media are suggestive, as the story goes

To apply the catchword "suggestion" not only effects an "economy of thought" – as Freud writes – because it is difficult to determine the meaning of this word, but suggestion itself, i.e. the willingness to suggestion both on the passive and on the active side, is already an economy, a saving, that is, or sparing [*Ersparnis*], of working through. An economy does not always have to be condemned, nor can it always be avoided.

According to Freud, everything that is psychically awkward is called suggestion. What is it that is awkward in the psychic system? It is that which threatens to draw one into insanity, that which is disquieting, that which doesn't allow for any (conclusive) sense to be made out, in short: just that of which one neither knows exactly where it comes from nor where or to what it will lead.[4]

We are confronted with an uneasiness, with an awkwardness, arising as it does with each new media development. This awkwardness in turn spreads out in two directions: One is that every new medium is concurrent with the promise of ridding you of an old awkwardness. The new medium is said to be faster, more economical, easier to have command of, more deceptively authentic; in other words, it is supposed to have a tendency to be immediate. And in fact, each new medium, at least within a restricted domain and for a certain amount of time, makes you forget

4 See Karl-Josef Pazzini, "Über die Produktivität von Unsinn. Ex- und Implosionen des Imaginären," *Hamburger Vorlesungen über Psychoanalyse und Erziehung,* ed. Birgit Warzecha (Hamburg: Lit Verlag 1999), 137–158.

representation,[5] i.e. the mediatedness of that which it represents. This is why the cinema audience jumped off their seats when the train engine came towards them on the screen,[6] and this is where all the talk about losing touch with reality, or about the undecidability between simulation and so-called reality, stems from. Yet the appeal lies precisely in the fact that, for the length of a settling-in period, what is produced is a mere amazement, followed by the pleasure taken in the minimal difference between the previous form of experiencing reality, which was equally mediated, and the new one, as being slightly more perfect. The other effects, while producing a sense of helplessness concerning the status of representation, can be put down to the problem of lying and trust, to a problem, therefore, that is much older than the new media.

As soon as one starts to believe in the better possibilities of the media – better with each innovation, that is, new forms of awkwardness arise: All of a sudden, the old media are seen in their unsurpassed qualities which are taken to be irreplacable, dangers are recognized, side effects. But even adjusting the effusive promises will not prevent a sense of deficit from emerging.

One is tempted to assume that the media themselves owe their existence to this worried uneasiness, indeed, that they are this awkwardness, in as much as they confront us with the mediatedness of our relation to the world, to the "Nebenmenschen",[7] and to ourselves. They show us

5 The term is here understood as the presentification of something not, or no longer, present. What is at work in the process of representation is desire. It is only through the overlapping with the symbolic that the trace of that which is remembered [*Erinnerte*], the trace in the inside [*Innere*], can be represented. This representation will be marked by a loss. That which is represented has to be thought of as being inaccessible, unreachable.

6 This is what happened when the film "L'arrivée d'un train à La Ciotat" ("The arrival of the train to la Ciotat") by the brothers Lumière was shown in Paris more than one hundred years ago (in 1896).

7 Translator's note: "Nebenmensch" (plural form: "Nebenmenschen") is a term coined by Freud, and has been translated into English as "a fellow creature", "the neighbor", the "nearest human being". Translated literally, it is "a human being on the side". This is about the Other, but as next *and* foreign to the one who (also) stands beside the *Nebenmensch.*

our 'referredness', which is to say the fact that we have to refer to, and to relate to something or to someone, and that we do not have ourselves, nor each other.

May it be allowed to speculate here:
A history of two thousand years, that of Christianity, has implanted an expectation within us, namely, that each text is grounded in an authority capable of giving an answer, and even if we do not always quite understand it, we can still make an effort.

This is the basis of any missionary work: We know [all about it], we want to spare you your uncertainty, your insecurity, your state of deadlock. Paul instituted Jesus as a universal medium, as a true God and man at once, as someone whose divine existence, coinciding as it does with his bodily human existence, guarantees mediation. This is then passed on to his representatives. In the case of emergency this happens through transubstantiation, not through – by means of – a relation of referral, or of relegation, but through a hierarchized chain of embodiments.

Vote of no-confidence

Thus, each search for a new medium is per se already – and/or is turned into – a vote of no-confidence vis-à-vis the absolute medium as it is described in Christology. There are two tendencies which have led this way of thinking – a thinking that has become an attitude – to a crisis, the beginning of which dates back, at least, to the Enlightenment. For one thing, it is becoming clear that Christianity itself depends on a considerable amount of media whose human representative guarantors do not comply with the high demands; secondly, there is an increasingly distinct awareness of the violence of this discourse, its exclusions, and the projective elements it contains. Some things could not or were not allowed to be thought, and some of the people who disagreed had to be excluded or physically annihilated. Metaphysics, then, having developed in the course of this thinking, and having received parts of it from Greek beginnings, can hardly be saved, not even by enlightened thinking: Not only does the capability of connecting the medial manifestations, the texts and the words, to things vanish, but so does the hope for this to be possible in the first place.[8]

Return of the repressed

Now, what occurs in such a situation – and this can only be articulated in the mode of *Nachträglichkeit*[9] and by means of psychoanalytic devices – is the return of the repressed. That which was repressed – including, time and again, in the real and actual sense of the word[10] – was the older Jewish tradition which knew that nothing and no one guarantees the truth of the text, that there can be no final, conclusive settlement, no infallibility. While leading (back) to a different way of dealing with the text as its prevailing medium, psychoanalysis has nonetheless also absorbed "Christian" history, if in an internally fractured and compromised way. By no means do we have the sort of synthesis here that would be working out nicely; rather, what we are dealing with is a processing conflict, a conflict in process, one that has not yet found a form of institutionalization which would be able to settle and immobilize it. According to hitherto valid standards, there is no other appropriate name for this than "failure". To the extent that the attempt at institutionalization has been unsuccessful, psychoanalysis remains of high interest and productivity. Where, on the other hand, it finds its way back – back, that is, into the demands of enlightened scientificity, of known mechanisms of institutionalization and of treatment techniques – it becomes uninteresting. Wherever it has followed, for lack of fantasy, the models

8 In the field of physics the Einsteinian theory of relativity is only indicative of this tendency.

9 Translator's note: To render the Freudian concept of "Nachträglichkeit" by the usual "belatedness" risks missing the point, since the concept refers to the idea of something's being "deferred" or "carried over" *from* the past, implying, furthermore, and for the understanding of what occurred, that something could *only* retroactively be "added on" or reinterpreted.

10 [i.e. *verdrängt* also in the literal sense of someone or something being pressed back or down effectually: to push, to shove, to urge (urgent: *dringend*, insisting: *drängend*), to oust, to drive away, to crush down or out (Translator's note)].

of church and state institutions, psychoanalysis participates in their perversions. In a way somewhat different from art since modernity, psychoanalysis confronts us with mediality, with the unanchored mediatedness of any act of speaking, of any text; it confronts us with a relation of referredness that cannot be settled or concluded.

In his expertise "'Les Juifs se livrent à des interprétations insensées'"[11] ("the Jews surrender themselves to senseless interpretations"[12]) Pierre Legendre, French law historian and psychoanalyst, investigates the novella 146 (dated to the year 553) of Justinian's Code, the *Corpus Juris Civilis*, and comes to the following assessment: With this law the Jews are taken into ["*encaissés*"] the Christian history, while, simultaneously, they are signified as being deficient. Whereas the Christians had found an answer to all questions concerning mediation, namely in Christ, the Jews stuck to not knowing something, which is why they kept on having to comment, on and on, in more and more ludicrous ways, and, often disputingly, they had to interpret and thus could not do any missionary work. Here, the existence of the text becomes the occasion for its performance and vocalization, and the performance, while being spoken and pronounced, brings something from the inside to the outside; the (participating) subjects no longer have themselves, they are being separated from themselves by a third instance, which is the medium. Yet this medium remains equally unincorporable, outside, in difference to the incorporation of the Body of Christ through communion.

11 Pierre Legendre, "'Les Juifs se livrent à des interprétations insensées' – Expertise d'un texte", *La psychoanalyse, est-elle une histoire juive?* Collloque de Montpellier, ed. Adélie Rassial and Jean-Jacques Rassial (Paris: Seuil 1981), 93–113.

12 Translator's note: The present text is based on the German translation of Legendre's "expertise", the title of which, quoting the Justinian Latin phrase in German, reads "Die Juden interpretieren verrückt" (trans. Anton Schütz). Whereas the English translation of Justinian's novella uses the adjective "senseless" – "...by surrendering themselves to senseless interpretations, they [the Hebrews, U.D.] still err from the true doctrine...". *Medieval Sourcebook: Justinian: Novella 146: On Jews.* 25 April 2004: <http://www.fordham.edu/halsall/source/novel146.html>.) – the German adjective "verrückt" emphasizes the aspect of madness more strongly, so that, in view of Schütz's rendering, the Jews' way of interpreting is "crazy", "insane", or literally "removed" (from sense, and from the senses). For more details, see note 31.

Mediation, in the context of the Jewish tradition, only takes place by way of a third and common instance, by means of the text as its medium. But this medium has no other guarantor than that of having previously been used by others, who in turn have left their medial imprints. Here, the function of the medium is to turn an act into a scene.

This trait of the medium is that which is suggestive: At best, you can decide to let yourself in for, that is, to get involved in, such a medium, in which case, however, you are involved – and come out as someone else, altered. The construction of medium and subject becoming one is no more than a comforting illusion, shielding one as it does from the anxiety of losing oneself.

Legendre's interpretation of the Justinian law comes to the following point: The novella, he writes,

> shows in a remarkable way what one could call the blind spot of the Occidental discourse: [It shows] the space of the question devoid of an answer, the space where the responder to the questions of human life shines with sheer absence. This space is occupied, abundantly filled, and faultlessly mastered by the incarnated power. In other words, juridically speaking, that is from the side of that which founds the discourse of a universal normalisation, the incarnated power stands surety and answers for the impossible. A divinely insane [*divinement aliéné*] body answers for everything and everyone, and guarantees all truth for all knowledge.[13] [...]
>
> ... [T]his telescoping [*téléscopage*] of a human body with the absolute Other, with a supreme [*ultime*], and, logically, last Other, with The only One to guarantee for all, this telescoping of a body with the divine signifiers, with God himself, entails consequences for the handling of writing, and for the very concept [*idée*] of 'text'.[14]

The Jews know of no such anchoring of the text. They have no 'auctorial' teaching profession that would be embodied in a human being; they know nothing that would be comparable to the Pope.

13 Compare Commenius' programmatics for his didactic efforts, which is in principle still valid today: To teach everything to everyone, in every way. KJP

14 Legendre, "Les juifs", trans. U. D., 99.

It is precisely in this sense that

> psychoanalysis is more Jewish than one would imagine. As a consequence, under reference to the Jewish (Hi-)story, we are having to do with something radical concerning that which founds a system of thought; we are having to do with that which, through Freud, led the logic of interpretations – one that had until then been inscribed in the only authorized law – to be refuted, and a different logic – the space of the unconscious, where texts are at stake, the very space of castration – to be acknowledged.[15]

Psychoanalysis then, according to Legendre's reading of Freud, for instance, becomes a critique of the knowledge about the appropriate means for obtaining an answer, and for the subversion of satisfying certain demands. It becomes a theory of mediation, a critique of identification, and a way of emphasizing the necessary third instance, located as it is between the subject and its image, but which remains unidentifiable. Thus, psychoanalysis becomes a (discussion in the sense of a) 'setting apart' [*Auseinandersetzung*] of mediality.

15 Legendre, "Les juifs", trans. U.D., 98.
For those who are only familiar with the German version of psychoanalysis this statement can seem incorrect. But it is precisely the German version of psychoanalysis that is marked by having delegated the risk of unconcludable and unauthorized speaking to the state: This delegation operates by way of a legalization, of a recognition, that is, which consists in being admitted to participating in the public medical or health care system. The legalization entails full authorization to treatment, and, therefore, to a responsible and authorized text interpretation. What is at stake here is not the fact that one form of work of a psychoanalyst is paid by the compulsory health insurance system, but rather the effects generated by the condition of the possibility of such a payment. In this vein and with respect to both professional education and evaluation psychoanalysis, then, has to prove itself as a science that responds to any kind of set demands, which is to say it has to bow to a [state directed] curative ["salvation"] plan [*Heilsplan*].

Scepticism against suggestion

From here stems Freud's justified scepticism against the suggestion of a specific kind of access to the other: Namely the suggestion of an access that is thought of as being immediate, one that would be controllable and allow for manipulation, in short, inviting arbitrariness. One could call it instrumental suggestion. At this point Freud constructs a concept of transference which characterizes a relation that neither of the parties involved is able to handle consciously.[16] Instead, those involved in transference are being turned around by it, revolved back and forth, '-verted', as it were. To take the risk of interrupting this well-rehearsed communication [in transference] – by smuggling in some craziness, some nonsense, and by submitting oneself [*Unterwerfen*: "subjecting"] to language, belonging as it does to no one – is the only way to allow for some scope, for some room to move, for "play" [*Spielraum*]. Thus, psychoanalysis refers to mediality as a fact that has effects, i.e. that acts and works ("*wirkt*"), rather than being a mere instrument of understanding. Accordingly, it didn't take long before the amazement as to the working of words set in: That mere – or nothing but – words were supposed to be able to heal. Moreover, psychoanalysis warns of the attempt and of the illusion of mastery through suggestion, as it does of the controllability of suggestion.

In the epicrisis of his "Analysis of the phobia in a five year-old boy" (1909) Freud defends himself against the claim that his work with the five-year-old boy, which had been arranged for[17] by the boy's father, could be based on mere suggestion. There is no arbitrariness in the realm of the psyche, Freud writes, statements made by children are not marked by "unreliability", but can be traced back to the surplus of fantasy, and therefore to a wish-situation. In addition, he says, one can well follow the boy's resistence, his distinctness, and the situations during which, once freed of pressure, he would communicate his inner truth.

16 In this context Lacan more than once talks about transference being one, which is to say that the distinction between transference and counter-transference can, if at all, only be made in a far from simple way.

17 Translator's note: Ironically, "arranged for" renders what the German calls "mediated" ("*vermittelt*").

Charlatanry

The term "suggestion" is initially employed by Freud in such a way as if it concerned a conscious, arbitrary influence exerted by the suggesting person, without any active and conscious cooperation coming from the person to whom something is being suggested. It is this (mis-)understanding that he makes the psychoanalytic process stand out against. This is a clear distinction of the analytic technique, then, in contrast to hypnosis as a different technique.

Beyond this distinction, however, suggestion is nonetheless a momentum in and of the psychoanalytic technique, but one that is less subject to a conscious will than it is concurrent with any act of speaking, with any text. In this sense this also applies to pedagogic situations. Neither [the participants'] wishing nor desire can be switched off by a decision for this or that technique; rather, both wishing and desire support the formulating process of everything that is being said – indeed, they condition its expressiveness. Suggestion produces a subtext which, instead of being considered as a disturbance (which it cannot), can be conceived of as a condition of the possibility of an effectiveness.

This situation is not, therefore, about specific and content-related matters that could be articulated with more precision, but about their colouring, the forming of their materiality, and their mediality. In the moment when things happen none of these can be suspended by any intention or resolution. This is the touch, or dash, of charlatanry in psychoanalysis – as it is seen from the perspective of science.

No perception without suggestion

What is at stake is something that travels and breeds next to, through, and between what is being shown and said. These are the imaginary ingredients of, or the necessary extras to that which is said, read, seen, smelled, felt, and which, as concerns the real of the organs of the senses, get these going in the first place.

When watching a film, for instance, the imagination [*Vorstellung*] of one's own image becomes gradually filled with some of the characteristics of the main actor. This can be noticed from the atmosphere, sometimes even from one's posture.

It also seems to be the case that suggestion, being as it is induced in one and by a medium, or, in particular, by a person, produces states of attachment and/or dependencies; yet if one nonetheless longs for it, this is precisely because of the effects triggered off by this process. And there is more: This longing generates suggestion. This makes for part of that which convinces, on the borderline to that which persuades, i.e. that by which "you are talked into something". This is seduction away from, off the same old groove. Such experiences refer back to the source of suggestion, that is, to one's own imperfection. What remains unclear, though, is how suggestion 'works', i.e. how it effects one the way it does. The effect cannot be produced without the corresponding medium, without the corresponding human being. It has to be looked for again. This is where both the demand of presence and the danger of addiction lie.

This is precisely the reason that led Freud to renounce the methodical use of instrumental (hypnotic) suggestion – without, however, being able to entirely abandon it as a momentum in his analytic work.[18] It was only by thematizing the mediality of psychoanalysis itself, in both the analytic setting and the basic rule, that he could open up the chance to retroactively – *nachträglich* – deal with and work through that which is suggestive. He crossed out the analyst as someone who possesses a knowledge about the way to healing, thus trying to thwart the analysand's demand to be healed.

While the analytic setting did become a memory aid for that, it was not a guarantee. Although there is the couch (*kline*, in Greek), the analyst does not stand beside it, there is no laying on of hands, nor any other manual manipulation, at least this would be against the commitment. Apart from the short moments of welcoming and saying goodbye he or she remains invisible. This is how the suggestive fine-adjust-

18 See Sigmund Freud, "Introductory Lectures on Psychoanalysis" (1917): "Analytic Therapy", trans. J. Strachey, *The Standard Edition*, vol. 16 (1916–1917) (London: The Hogarth Press 1963), 448sq. [Orig. "Vorlesungen zur Einführung in die Psychoanalyse" (1917), *Gesammelte Werke*, vol. XI (Frankfurt am Main: Fischer 1972), 466sq.]

ment of any kind of vis-à-vis is being interrupted, opening up, in turn, the chance to experience suggestion.

Accordingly, the Freudian formulation of the difference between suggestion in hypnosis and in psychoanalysis, respectively, reads as follows:

> The transference of a person who is to be hypnotized may be negative or, as most frequently, ambivalent, or he may have protected himself against his transference by adopting special attitudes; of that we learn nothing. In psychoanalysis we act upon the transference itself, resolve what opposes it, adjust the instrument with which we wish to make our impact.[19]

The wish for immediate connection, far-reaching as it is in the situation of transference, becomes itself an issue. This is how not only suggestion, as something which is taking place, but also the instituting or establishing of the *Nebenmensch* in the well-worn wish fulfillment, and the longing for an answer to demands, get the chance to be interrupted. More often than not this interruption is nonetheless initially experienced as a threat.

Wish for connection

The interest in the media results from the wish for connection and for immediacy, but as a connection that would – or is to – be mastered and handled. This is the ambivalent wish when it comes to media-related achievements.

Thus, what cannot be ignored is the currently prevailing focus on unification leading to a "global village", on networking, on communication, and on the participation and access of all, by all possible means, to all sources of information. The wish for connection – ties and links – for breaking out of isolation is what generates the interest in ever more sophisticated media. At the same time this longing for a tie also causes the fear of appropriation, the fear of seduction.[20]

19 Sigmund Freud, "Introductory Lectures": "Analytic Therapy", SE, op. cit., vol. 16, 451 [Orig. 469].

20 See Freud, who writes to this point:
We will try our fortune, then, with the supposition that love relationships (or, to use a more neutral expression, emotional ties) also constitute the essence of

Time and again the media are suspected of something. Television is a case in point. It is supposed to be bad that people watch TV so much. It is also supposed to be bad to be sitting in front of the computer for hours, surfing through the net. Books make you lonely. Films distract you from reality, and besides, watching them leaves you no time to read books.

The suspicion lies in the fact that the media do something to people that cannot immediately – and therefore not outside the medium – be comprehended.

This suspicion is justified.

This suspicion has come to be extended to those who teach, for they also exert effects that are not immediately comprehensible. This leads to the following demand: Teachers are to keep in the background, they are to act as if the students were doing everything on their own. Maybe the tendency to favour e-learning doesn't fit too badly in this context.

Suspicion

Where does the suspicion come from? What is it grounded in? I have a suspicion: Media are sub-gestive. They are underlaid by something, they bring forth something, they are the ground of a scene, the floor of a stage.[21]

Every medium looks at you, penetrates the ears, and has other effects. It is these other effects that arouse suspicion. All media – not just the electronic, the digital, and the computer-based media – are faster than our apprehension, faster than our consciousness; so something has

the group mind. Let us remember that the authorities make no mention of any such relations [amongst those who are named are: Tarde, Le Bon, McDougall, Bernheim, KJP]. What would correspond to them is evidently concealed behind the shelter, the screen, of suggestion.
Sigmund Freud, "Group Psychology and the Analysis of the ego" (IV: '"Suggestion and Libido"') (1921), trans. J. Strachey *The Standard Edition*, vol. 18 (1920–1922) (London: The Hogarth Press (1955–64), 91–92 [Orig. "Massenpsychologie und Ich-Analyse (1921), *Gesammelte Werke*, vol. XIII (Frankfurt am Main: Fischer 1972), 100].

21 See the derivation of "suggestion" from the Latin *suggero*: "to underlay, put under, furnish, let follow" and *suggestum*: "rostrum", or *suggestus*: "tribune, stage".

always already changed, and it is only selectively that we are able to make it potentially conscious – and in the mode of *Nachträglichkeit.* We can only imagine or form an idea about that which is going on in us at the time (to which and) when we are connected – and only after the event is already over. The imaginary was faster.

Disappointment

Moreover, suspicion also seems to have something to do with a disappointment: When they first came out, many media were hoped to be able to produce something perceivable which would offer us the chance to provide a reproduction (*Abbild*) for the imaginary process, for the process of imagination that goes on inside us. For this purpose, we increased the speed of medial reproduction techniques, in order to simultaneously produce duration and omnipresence, which would be a relief for the raging effort that the being-present, the presentness, of consciousness demands from us. Maybe new and different media will eventually be invented in order to expel the unconscious. So far, this is a hopeless race, since unconscious production operates much faster, given that the unconscious is timeless and does not seem to know causality. Its "timelessness" is not to be understood as ahistorical, though, but as being timeless with respect to a sequence that would allow us to follow cause and effect.

Let's arrest the usual suspects, then

The media are the usual suspects. As were the Sophists in their time. They knew how to turn the weaker word into the stronger one. They had something suggestive about them. The Sophists were the first paid pedagogues one could rent, at a time when the division of labour in society began to be differentiated, when, in other words, what had to be learned could no longer be learned by way of immediate following. Plato reacts by suspecting writing as a medium in written dialogues.

A rivalry emerges – the pattern of which can be followed to the present day – between the living media and those which are materially and, subsequently, machine bound.

A mistrust emerges against the written text – see Justinian – and its successors and extensions in representation. Yet this only turns into a drama if and when medial recordings and productions are actually considered to be complete representations of an original. What follows then is the problem of authenticity, of credibility, and, therefore, of authorship.

But if, for instance, a text is used as a supporting or footholding device for a performance, a vocalization – the latter being necessary time and again, such as is the case, to a large extent at least, in the Jewish tradition, then what is being created is a relational net of referral which needs no representative, and no incarnation of the originator/author [*Urheber*]. As a consequence, fulfillment and conclusion are missing, leaving interminable expectation.

This does not amount to conjuring away suggestion. But suggestion is turned into an actual performance, into a staging without which the word or the text – or any medium, for that matter – would exert no effect. It confronts one with finitude and incalculability, with the repetition of expectation, with a structure, that is, that Freud metaphorically calls the death drive.

Openness in principle

The lever for suggestion to set about in the first place is the fact that humans are in principle marked by openness, which is why we are immersed in media like in protective clothing. One of these media is language. It is only by being in it that we can become aware of our openness. The effects of the media are immemorial, because without them we are neither able to think nor to act or feel.

Hence the high-speed trip [*Geschwindigkeitsrausch*]. [In contrast to the "trip"] *Rausch* pertains to hearing,[22] not to seeing. Hearing grants less certainty in the sense of the possibility and/or expectability of a

22 Translator's note: The German noun *Rausch* – i. e. the state of being "on a trip" due to the influence of any kind of drug – is directly related both to *Geräusch* ("noise"), and to the verb *rauschen*, meaning any acoustic movement from roaring to murmuring, hissing, 'whooshing', etc. Hear "rush".

repeated occurrence. But it also envelops us more, since we can also hear what comes from behind us.[23] Thus, the media will always have power over us, forming as they do part of our constitution [as human beings, as subjects], owing to which we can awake to the awareness of something in the first place. It is precisely for the purpose of waking up – elsewhere – that we have constructed them, and this is how they construct us.

The suggestive is that which makes us cry, sympathize, cheer up, or which puts us in states of tension or excitement, when watching films. It has reached us before we perceive it.[24] Its power depends on the demand we can become aware of if or when the suggestion has 'hit'.[25] Seen in this light, one can also feel ashamed of such reactions, and at times only bashfully admit to them. On the other hand, this form of suggestion can make one addicted – the form, that is, which appears due to a momentary demand, after something that corresponds to a lack has occurred. It is here that the phenomena of addiction occur. You only wanted to watch the news, and all of a sudden it is three hours later, and you wake up because the remote control fell on the floor.

This is precisely the form of demand that Freud recognized, and which, as a result, made him give up hypnosis. Continuous effects of treatment hardly occurred, and there was resistance because hypnosis was the wrong drug.

Only a longing for the other, for the unknown, is what can trigger off suggestion; and while this helps to overcome resistance, it will later have to be propelled through the grid of signifying chains. What is decisive for the occurrence of suspicions is not the medium, then, but it is the risk of wishing that triggers them off, and the fear of tension that suspects fraud.

We are not at the mercy of these effects in an unbridled way. Just how deep the effect of suggestion can be, how long it will last, and to what extent we can become aware of it, if only *nachträglich*, will depend

23 The psychoanalytic setting makes use of this.

24 The fairy tale [told by the Grimm brothers, trans.] of the hare and the hedgehog reported about it.

25 The hare paid for the hit with his life.

on our structure.[26] Defence mechanisms, previous experiences, play a role here. But this is exactly what we have no precise awareness of. What remains is being at the mercy of, being handed over to [*Ausgeliefertsein*] mediality, and a delivery of, an extradition to, and a handing over to [*Auslieferung*] mediality.

> The hypnotic subject will make small sacrifices, but, just as though he were awake, he hesitates before making great ones. If, then, we are dealing with a patient, and urge him by suggestion to give up his illness, we perceive that this means a great sacrifice to him and not a small one,[27]

Freud writes. The sacrifice that would have to be made is to renounce a known and repeatable form of momentary relaxation that was reached by way of fulfilling a demand.

Suggestion, if it is not to cause an addiction, requires renouncing a previous belonging, a possession one used to be in control of. While suggestion does dissolve [*auflösen*] and give way to something [*ablösen*], it cannot spare one the renunciation, not even that of being open to suggestion.

Hypnosis

Now, in the passage quoted above, Freud writes about a specific form of suggestion, which is that of suggestion during hypnosis. Here, the [message of the] suggestion is articulated by the hypnotist in a conscious and controlled way, and after the hypnotized person's level of awareness has been reduced with the latter's prior consent.

This is how we have to imagine not just a movie-goer who wants to get something out of the film, but also – on varying levels of openness – the student in a lecture. Otherwise (s)he wouldn't hear or see a thing.

26 On our individual media history, that is.

27 Sigmund Freud, "Psychical (or Mental) Treatment" (1905), trans. J. Strachey. *The Standard Edition*, vol. 7 (1901–1905) (London: The Hogarth Press 1953–1964), 300–301 [Orig. "Psychische Behandlung (Seelenbehandlung)" (1905). *Gesammelte Werke*. 1904–1905. 5th ed., vol. V. (Frankfurt am Main: Fischer 1972), 313].

The hypnotized person exposes him or herself as a wishing person. This is what a paranoid is not able to do. He will shield himself, and try to take hold of all possible influences, out of sheer fear of suggestion. This is the basic presupposition needed in order to fulfill the ideology of an autonomous, self-identical subject. One trait characteristic of pedagogues goes in that direction. To push autonomization in this direction does in fact make teachers dispensable.

A person willing to undergo suggestion, and to take the risks it implies, wants something to change, something that was unchangeable until then. He consents to defence-mechanisms being bypassed. Otherwise suggestion has no lever to set about. Autistic people cannot be influenced by suggestion.

Tendency to translation

Therefore, intensive wishing is the condition of suggestibility. Now, what it is that happens after the agreement cannot exactly be determined, no exact dose can be measured out. Like all medicines, media have side effects.[28]

Without these side effects no imaginations set in, linking up as they do to the smallest scraps of metaphoric qualities. There would be no tendency to translation, to bridging. Bridges use up landscape on both sides of the shore. They occupy free space.

Signs of imaginary production, of relational connections, are being communicated not only through content, but also through style, through the gestures of language and of speaking, through that which has imagined itself – not without some conceitedness – into the material of the texture, of the spoken and of the written word, of the images and of the 'musics'. This is to say the motives for the imaginary productions have

28 Science, as well as some of the arts or music, struggle to cast off the imaginary. This might account for all the efforts made by Duchamp, for instance, and, later on, by conceptional art. This is a never-ending, Sisyphean task, even in mathematics. When it comes to formulating texts that would seem to be devoid of the imaginary as a spontaneous ingredient, mathematics do not manage either. – "One must imagine Sisyphus happy", writes Camus.

deposited themselves in the [act of] speaking and in the accompanying gestures, but they tend to have done so in the form of a negative, which in turn is to be probed and filled. This is about projection. Such minimal traces, marking the gestures of language and of speaking, are instances which, in the process of transference, have a structuring effect with respect to the content. They have often already been elsewhere, they are parasites the speaking person has caught. This phenomenon does not only occur in the situation of personal addressing, but also, although in different dimensions, in machine-based medial forms.

It is also from this perspective that McLuhan's phrase *"the medium is the message"* gains a truth.[29]

Leaps over abysses

When connected to wish production, the media, in whichever form – be it as writing, as film, or in the form of a recorded computer monitor – become powerhouses producing energy in order to keep the dynamics of association going. In this process, associations are leaps over abysses, over and beyond the interface. However, if set up permanently, both become bridges, fixed connections.[30] What is essential for generating such bridges – be they fixed translations or automatized associations – are the mechanisms of the respective medial form, regardless, at this point, of any specific content. In order for new connections and associations – leaps – to be able to happen perpetuously, any fixed connection must be prevented from being generated, or, put differently, the possibility of (the risk of) a change is to be kept open. Such changes are motivated in a similar way that fashion is: Even though it corresponds to an initial wish, it is nonetheless tiring to constantly perceive that which is well known, to always perceive certainties. Seen from this perspective, fashion, as the change of that which is familiar, takes the place of the other and can lead to desire by way of seduction. The sheer functioning of the media suffices

29 Marshall McLuhan; Quentin Fiore, *The Medium is the Massage. An Inventory of Effects.* (New York: Random House 1967) [quoted in English in the original, trans.].

30 This is what is called a symptom.

to maintain connections between the shores. It is by means of this functioning that all kinds of things, the meaning of which cannot be assessed, leap, hop, and bounce, back and forth.

Hasty transfer

Art starts where media seem to throw a solid bridge. It arranges the use of the bridge in such a way that the bridge is itself affected detrimentally. The way – or version (literally: "turn") – in which the medium is thematized by art differs from the one brought forth by psychoanalysis. In contrast to what happens to the leaps (or versions) performed by art, in psychoanalysis it is only the stories told about these versions that become public. Stories, that is, the all-valid truth of which no one can embody, occurring as it does in a relation only.

In this way, parts of contemporary art and psychoanalysis work against perversion. When pronounced in French, to work against "pèreversion" means to work against a 'turning to the father', that is to say to one who is imagined to (be able to) make everything possible. The perverted scenario serves to fight castration anxiety, it serves to maintain the illusion of mastering the medium as one which would be immediate. The figure of the pope is constructed in just this way: As infallible.

In contrast, the intentions of contemporary art or, for that matter, of psychoanalysis, lead to a different relationship to the medium: Both interpret madly, *verrückt.*[31] Always shifting and shifted a little – a bit (re-)moved, their interpretations allow for some scope, which, while it releases (a structuring) anxiety, prevents apparent death, the (deceptive) appearance of plenitude.

This is precisely what the commandment "Thou shalt not make unto thee any graven image" tried to teach its listeners and readers. It owed

31 Translator's note: The argument that will follow alludes to the double meaning of the German adjective *verrückt* ("mad"), which is derived from *Ruck* ("jolt, jerk": implying, precisely, the aforementioned notion of the "leap"), and forms the past participle of the verb *verrücken* ("to (re-)move something little by little (e.g. furniture), to disarrange"). Thus, "mad" is to be heard as "removed from reason and/or sense", as in being "jolted out of one's senses". See also note 12.

its being heard to the accompanying thunder and to Moses' choleric fits. That which is suggested starts moving beneath the fixed and consciously wished image, it cuts the ground from under the feet of the image, and this leads to the destruction of the golden calf. That which is suggested awakes reason: Reason [*Vernunft*], initially to be understood as the ability to perceive [*vernehmen*][32] something, without knowing what it does [to you], and without knowing its author.

The momentum of suggestion as pertaining to the medium is that which corresponds to the real of the subject; it is that which speaks to the subject, that which accords it. The nucleus of the subject belongs to the register of the real,

> in so far as the identity of perception is its rule. At most, it is grounded on what Freud indicates as a sort of deduction, which assures us that we are in perception by means of the sense of reality that authenticates it. What does this mean, if not that, as far as the subject is concerned, this is called awakening?[33]

This is what happens when a sensual stimulus, an addressing of the real nucleus, that is, succeeds in occurring. This can happen when facing a painting, which in its gesture, by way of an incursion, blows the proofing wall made out of conscious fragments of language and fixed imaginations; or when the painting steals past this wall, or makes it vibrate in such a way that the nucleus will start to vibrate with oscillations of resonance; in other words, in such a way as to "remind" the nucleus of something that does not, or not yet, have a symbolic representation.

Translation from the German by Ulrike Oudée Dünkelsbühler

32 Translator's note: *Vernunft* – the German word for (the faculty of) "reason" – is, grammatically speaking, an abstractum of the verb *vernehmen* ("to perceive"), and, the latter being derived from *nehmen*, it implies some kind of "taking (in)".

33 Jacques Lacan, "The Split between the eye and the Gaze". J. Lacan, *The Four Fundamental Concepts of Psychoanalysis*; ed. Jacques-Alain Miller; trans. Alain Sheridan (London: Hogarth Press 1977; here: Penguin Books 1977), 68. [Orig. *Le Seminaire de Jacques Lacan, Livre XI*, "Les quatre concepts fondamentaux de la psychanalyse", ed. J.-A. Miller (Paris: Editions du Seuil 1973)].

Bibliography

Camus, Albert. *The Myth of Sisyphus and Other Essays* (Orig. 1942). Trans. Justin O'Brien. New York: Vintage Books, 1961.

Freud, Sigmund. "Analysis of a phobia in a five year old boy". *The Standard Edition of the Complete Psychological Works of Sigmund Freud.* Vol. 10 (1909). Trans. J. Strachey. London: The Hogarth Press, 1955–1964. 1–150. [Orig.: "Analyse der Phobie eines fünfjährigen Knaben" (1909). *Gesammelte Werke* (1906–1909). Vol. VII. Frankfurt am Main: Fischer, 1972. 243–377.]

Freud, Sigmund. "Group Psychology and the Analysis of the ego". *The Standard Edition of the Complete Psychological Works of Sigmund Freud.* Vol. 18 (1920–1922). Trans. J. Strachey. London: The Hogarth Press, 1955–1964. 65–144. [Orig.: "*Massenpsychologie* und Ich-Analyse" (1921). *Gesammelte Werke.* Vol. XIII. Frankfurt am Main: Fischer, 1972. 71–161.]

Freud, Sigmund. "Introductory Lectures on Psychoanalysis" (1917). *The Standard Edition.* Vol. 16 (1916–1917). Trans. J. Strachey. London: The Hogarth Press, 1963. 241–477. [Orig. "Vorlesungen zur *Einführung* in die Psychoanalyse" (1917), *Gesammelte Werke.* Vol. XI. Frankfurt am Main: Fischer, 1972.]

Freud, Sigmund. "Psychical (or Mental) Treatment" (1905), *The Standard Edition.* Vol. 7 (1901–1905). Trans. J. Strachey. London: The Hogarth Press, 1953–1964. 281–302. [Orig.: "Psychische *Behandlung* (Seelenbehandlung)" (1905). *Gesammelte Werke.* 1904–1905. 5th ed. Vol. V. Frankfurt am Main: Fischer, 1972. 287–315.]

Lacan, Jacques. *The Four Fundamental Concepts of Psychoanalysis.* Ed. Jacques-Alain Miller; Trans. Alain Sheridan. *London*: Hogarth Press, 1977.

Legendre, Pierre. "'Les Juifs se livrent à des interprétations insensées' – Expertise d'un texte". *La psychoanalyse,* est-elle *une histoire juive?* Ed. Adélie Rassial and Jean-Jacques Rassial. Collloque de Montpellier. Paris: Seuil, 1981. 93–113.

German version: "'Die Juden interpretieren verrückt' – Gutachten zu einem klassischen Text". Trans. Anton Schütz. *Psyche. Zeitschrift für Psychoanalyse und ihre Anwendungen,* No. 1, 1989. 20–39.

McLuhan, Marshall; Fiore, Quentin. *The Medium is the Massage. An Inventory of Effects.* New York: Random House, 1967.

Packard, Vance. *The Hidden Persuaders.* London: Random House, 1957. (German translation: *Die geheimen* Verführer. *Der Griff nach dem Unbewußten in Jedermann.* Düsseldorf: Econ, 1958.)

Pazzini, Karl-Josef. "Über die Produktivität von Unsinn. Ex- und Implosionen des Imaginären". *Hamburger Vorlesungen über Psychoanalyse und Erziehung.* Ed. Birgit Warzecha. Hamburg: Lit Verlag, 1999. 137–158.

International MA programme*
ePedagogy Design – Visual Knowledge Building

STEFAN SONVILLA-WEISS

Introduction

A neologism like *ePedagogy Design* commonly sounds a bit fashionable and I would assume that not everyone who sees that particular linguistic creation automatically understands its meaning. In terms of pedagogical definition ePedagogy is neither easy nor exhaustive but is perhaps a more extensive Pedagogy.

We certainly make some steps ahead in "debabelizing" the word if we consider the undergoing paradigm shift in current pedagogical action and thinking.

The use of Information Communication Technology (ICT) has increased tremendously in education and learning. The use of Web based learning environments, Open and Distance Learning (ODL) methods and materials have highlighted the audio-visual dimension of pedagogy. Regardless of the educational field pedagogical expertise requires more and more understanding and control of visual elements and their interpretations.

In various international forums such as *Prometeus* (PROMETEUS is the European Partnership for a Common Approach to the Production of e-learning Technologies and Content) and *InSEA* (International Society for Education through Art) the need for a new kind of expertise (through professional development) has been acknowledged by Art and Design professionals. The need for new expertise has also emerged from the Media-literacy and Media-competence discussions and initiatives

* http://epedagogydesign.uiah.fi
A joint university MA programme between the University of Art and Design Helsinki (Finland) as the coordinating institution together with the University of INHOLLAND Rotterdam (Netherlands) and the University of Hamburg (Germany).

(UNESCO, Toulouse Colloquy "New Directions in Media Education" 1990, E-Learning Action Plan 2001) where the lack of this expertise has also been detected by the new media industry (*Eurojournalism, Euromedia, Eurocommunications* etc.).

The accelerating "iconic turn" in our society increasingly demands the interactive representation of contextual knowledge and the transfer of information in hyper medial knowledge spaces. This does not automatically mean the general demise of "text-reading"; paradoxically it extends possibilities in the future in the areas of interdisciplinary knowledge delivery through a mixture of text fragments, concept tableaus, organigrams, pictorial elements, 3-D simulations and so on.

The redefining of knowledge construction is based on new models through research evidence in the computer games industry (*Prix Ars Electronica*). The changes in theoretical architecture could be exemplified in the boundary management that is on the boundary of disciplines and product development.

The development of future learning models will be dependent on reading images, intelligent graphical interfaces, samplings and so on. As a consequence learning and teaching organizations will readjust their delivery through core projects within a praxis-oriented curriculum.

Dilation of e-learning from in-service training to teacher training and higher education pedagogy emphasizes inter-disciplinary cooperation and expertise in visual pedagogy. There is a growing need for visually oriented pedagogical experts such as teachers, tutors, designers and developers who are capable of community knowledge building and collaboration with other experts from different fields from both private and public sectors.

The Curriculum Development for the MA programme *ePedagogy Design – Visual Knowledge Building* has been acknowledged and supported by the Erasmus program of the European Commission. The programme was officially launched in February 2004.

University Partnership – Expertise and Background

School of Art Education, University of Art and Design Helsinki, UIAH
http://www.uiah.fi

UIAH has coordinated several Socrates projects and has administrative experience in a range of European projects. At a national level UIAH is a highly reputable institution maintaining high educational standards. UIAH is well-networked and participates at national and international levels. It coordinates several international projects such as Cumulus and Cirrus in the *Nordplus* programme and has academic and student representation in most of the European and national initiatives, often at steering committee level or in working groups. UIAH has a long tradition of professionalism in implementing ICT into Art and Design processes. The key areas of expertise relevant to this project include a theoretical base (traditional, classical, post modernist contexts in Art and Design), new media and popular culture media such as comics, multimedia, hypermedia, film, television and photography. There have been several ICT oriented projects including web based ODL, in-service training courses at MA-level (*Virt@*, http://virta.uiah.fi/) and other major projects that have shaped and developed the *ePedagogy Design* project. The ePortfolio project indicates the ability of UIAH to shape and develop the portfolio content in a coherent, visually and pedagogically operative diverse format which will broaden didactical approaches by, for example, developing skills in the innovative use of ICT at a range of levels.

UIAH is participating in national curriculum developments for compulsory education and is actively participating in *Lukiodiplomi* (Finnish High School Diploma work in Arts – portfolio form) developments in Art and Media (the *ePortfolio* project will develop high school diploma works into digital format). UIAH has also managed Doctoral studies in Doctor of Arts programmes since 1978. All partners have significant operating knowledge of each other and experience in European cooperation. They represent creative providers in the European educational marketplace, each working with different aspects of Art and Design education.

Institute of Aesthetic Education, University of Hamburg

http://mms.uni-hamburg.de/home/index.php

The MULTIMEDIA-STUDIO is part of the Institute of Aesthetic Education within the Faculty of Education at the University of Hamburg. In close association with the visual arts, the studio focuses on questions of presentation and representation. Within a framework of knowledge that is (no longer) easily systematized, these questions that call representation itself into question are being worked on, in theory and practice. Art and art education provide an exemplary field for the generation, maintenance and handling of complex knowledge. From this vantage point the multitude of projects undertaken by the MULTIMEDIA-STUDIO have centred on the visualization of complex interconnections on a highly specialized level. These projects have included cooperation with Universities and other educational institutions on a national and international scale, as well as cooperation with 'free-market' corporations.

The close association with University teachers, students and external experts is vital for the work of the MULTIMEDIA-STUDIO. The results of this foundational research present themselves in the concrete production of software, while also effecting reflection on and the practice of art education and mediation. Transmissions occur here that are relevant to questions of the accessibility, the search and the collection and transformation of existing forms of order and the transference of information into knowledge and action. Today's aspects of knowledge management are moreover strongly influenced by economic interests and social, political, educational, and aesthetic dimensions.

INHOLLAND University

http://www.inholland.nl

On 1 January 2002, Alkmaar University of Professional Education, Haarlem University of Professional Education, Hogeschool Holland University of Professional Education and Ichthus/Delft University of

Professional Education merged to form INHOLLAND University. The INHOLLAND organization is one with many students (40 000), staff (3000) and teaching sites, but above all an educational institution that is close to the students. The University offers students a choice from almost all conceivable programmes at ten sites in the provinces of Noord- and Zuid-Holland.

In the period up to 2006 INHOLLAND is focusing on three areas that reflect its ambitions: *the development and implementation of an educational model which focuses on individual students and the market, knowledge creation and borderless education.*

INHOLLAND focuses on the development and implementation of a competence-based educational model for the simple reason that students and the market demand a clear and varied range of programmes tailored to the individual. Innovation and the developments of the competences of students and teachers are key concepts in this development.

INHOLLAND invests in blended learning, the use of an electronic learning environment in which students, independent of time and place, acquire knowledge and experience with a familiar group of students.

INHOLLAND and its legal predecessors are (and have been) active in many cooperation projects (nationally via the NL Digital University and SURF, regionally and internationally) in the domain of eLearning, innovation, professionalism of staff, quality assurance and technology. INHOLLAND also participates quite actively in ERASMUS and for instance in Leonardo programmes.

MA in *ePedagogy Design* – Credits and Areas of Expertise

Major and minor courses (56 ECTS)

Major: 36 ETCS (mandatory)
Minor: 20 ECTS
Advanced Credits (64 ECTS):
Field practice, study project: 16 ECTS
Research methods: 4 ECTS

Thesis seminar: 4 ECTS
Master thesis: 40 ECTS

Areas of expertise Helsinki:
Visual knowledge building
Copyright issues
Learning Objects
Hamburg:
Pedagogical media theory
Knowledge formation
Hypermedia
Rotterdam:
Project management
Issue management
Didactical analysis and design of VLEs

Minimum Student Requirements

The specification of the applicant's minimum requirements has been decided in the following way:

- BA or equivalent level
- Questioning visualization and media theory
- A range of ICT skills through work or study
- Interest and/or experience in education theory and practice

Entrance Examination

Entrance requirements

- BA or equivalent level
- Practical and theoretical skills in media and visual literacy
- A range of ICT skills through work or study
- Interest and/or experience in education practice and theory
- Social communicative competence

- Contextual abilities in visual knowledge building
- Curiosity, openness and basic knowledge in electronic media and educational processes
- Openness to socio-cultural diversity
- Disposition to challenge the ongoing paradigm shift in the knowledge society
- Flexibility and attendance to work and practice in collaborative environments

Purpose of the degree programme

The purpose of the MA in ePedagogy Design – Visual Knowledge Building (120 ECTS[1]) is to improve the quality of higher education and strengthen its European dimension. It will accomplish this by encouraging trans-national cooperation between universities, fostering the European mobility of students and teachers, and contributing to improved transparency and academic recognition of qualifications and studies throughout the European Union.

This includes mobility grants to students and teachers and a strong mandate to create a Virtual Campus of Visual Knowledge Building in European Higher Education that will support those students who cannot directly participate in exchanges.

Descriptions of the programme

The MA programme aims at a broad spectrum of professional qualifications offered by the three universities involved. Thus the focus lies in multidisciplinarity with special emphasis on communication theory and practice, issue management, visual knowledge building theory and practice in contextual media culture, hypermedia and knowledge organization.

In addition the MA in ePedagogy Design fosters international research and community building, student and teacher exchange, field practice and qualifications for an international job market.

1 ECTS = European Credit Transfer System

Structure of studies/methods of teaching and instruction

The studies leading to the MA degree consist of major courses (obligatory), minor courses, field practice, research methods and the MA thesis. ePedagogy Design study advocates individual study plans supported by Blended Learning, Open Distance Learning, Tutoring and Portfolio Management.

A major part of the programme deals with international research projects that should strengthen the multidisciplinary research strands and junior research among the joint university partners.

The study programme language is English.

Entrance examination criteria

1. Online registration, http://epedagogydesign.uiah.fi/register.html
2. Survey, http://epedagogydesign.uiah.fi/survey.html
3. CV no longer than 1 page (A4, pdf file)
4. Portfolio of your expertise and interests, e.g. theoretical articles (max. 1000 words), examples of visualization and design strategies (max. five jpeg or gif files), hypermedia projects (max. three works), weblink references (max. three web links)

The entrance examination committee highly appreciates portfolio submissions.

Eligibility criteria

Currently only students from INHOLLAND University and University Hamburg are entitled to apply for the MA programme. In Finland persons or students at the University of Art and Design or any other university with BA-level or equivalent are entitled to register for the entrance examination. In future the study programme intends to take in students from around the world.

Evaluation criteria

Students will be selected based on the entrance requirements, examination criteria and eligibility criteria.

The student selection consists of two parts: pre-selection for the final entrance examination is based on the reply to the survey, CV and portfolio of an applicant.

Interdisciplinary Approach

The interdisciplinary approach of *ePedagogy Design – Visual Knowledge Building* embraces media and communication theory, visual pedagogy, hypermedia and educational science. With regard to scientific coherence and consistency the biggest challenge has been the process of finding a well-balanced mixture among the academic traditions and expertise available.

Evidently the changing paradigm shift that has emerged through media convergence across all scientific disciplines has simplified knowledge and information exchange. Creating novel forms of cross-disciplinary studies potentially bears some risk in losing control over consistent development, research, distinction and validation among the disciplines within the framework of a highly competitive knowledge economy that continuously proliferates regulation over educational policy. Inevitably a dichotomy occurs in the economic validation within scientific disciplines in higher education, whether they would fulfil the new challenges of a global knowledge economy or lose terrain.

Although the disciplines that constitute *ePedagogy Design* are closely related, academic traditions, learning cultures, and so on in different countries vary significantly. In that respect the interdisciplinary approach envisages to encompass training and development of soft skills as well.

Curricular Topography – Visual Knowledge Building

The historical mapping of visual knowledge building in Fig. 1 encompasses the visual – didactical, mediatheoretical and epistemological aspects of scientific visualizations up to collaborative knowledge building processes with an underlying concept of the semantic web approach.

Different semantic and ontological visually-oriented web paradigms enhance human accessibility to current Semantic Web technology by enabling the visualization of knowledge. Arguing against the claim that humans and machines need to look at different knowledge representation formats, new methodologies are shown to enable modelling of systems in a single graphic and textual model. The human centred approach of better understanding and communicating knowledge encompasses equivalent graphic-text knowledge representation, visual navigability, semantic sentence interpretation, specification of system dynamics, and complexity management. The ability to use such bimodal knowledge representation that is both human – understandable and machine-processable is a major step forward in the evolution of the Semantic Web.

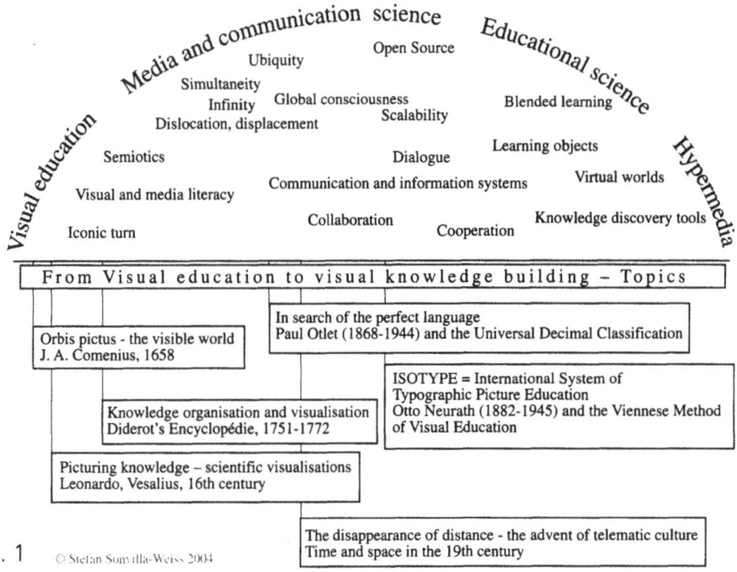

Fig. 1 © Stefan Sonvilla-Weiss 2004

The following text and image-based reflections envisage drawing a bow from the early steps of Enlightenment up to the advent of telematic culture and the digital revolution. It suggests a chronological order encompassing the various historical traces of visual representation, knowledge organization and communication that led to the paradigmatic changes of media convergence based on computer generated information.

1. Orbis sensualum pictus - the visible world

Seeing is forgetting the name of the things one sees
Paul Valery

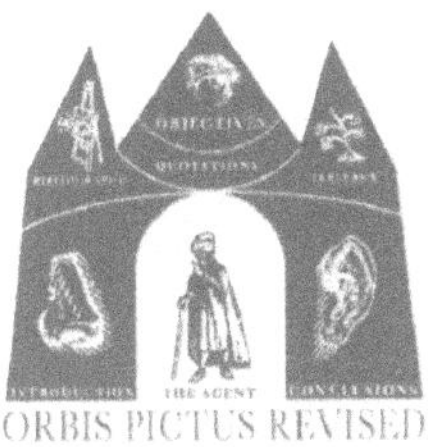

Fig.1

Jan Amos Comenius 1592-1670

1996 Orbis Pictus Revised

The Orbis Pictus Revised wants to demonstrate the development, through time, of the process of making the world understood, by means of duplicated imagery - how objects and ideas, through sound and words become language.
Milos Vojtechovsky and Tjebbe van Tijen

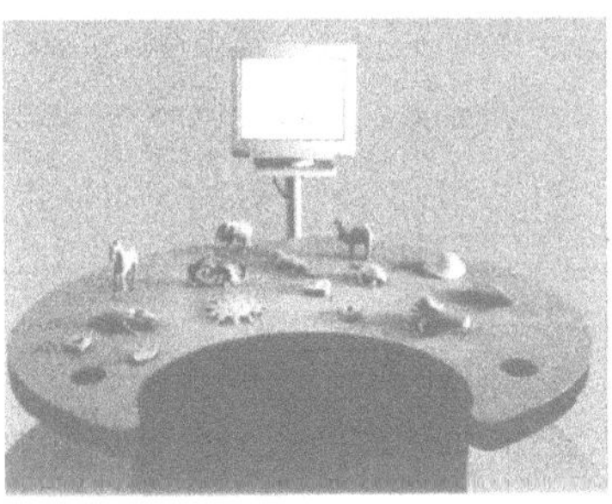

Fig. 2

- Objects can be put on sensor spots
- Opening image/tableau/detail
- Language sensor spots lit from above

A learning process involving different senses, looking, touching and speaking, connecting object and image with language and vice versa.

1658 Orbis sensualum pictus

III RICHES OF THE EARTH [9 tableaus]

009:TERRAE-FOETS/The Fruits of the Earth
010: METALLA/Metals
011: LAPIDES/Stones
012: ARBOR/Tree
013: FRUCTS ARBORUM/Fruits of Trees
014: FLORES/Flowers
015: OLERA/Pot-Herbs
016: FRUGES/Corn
017: FRUTICES/Shrubs

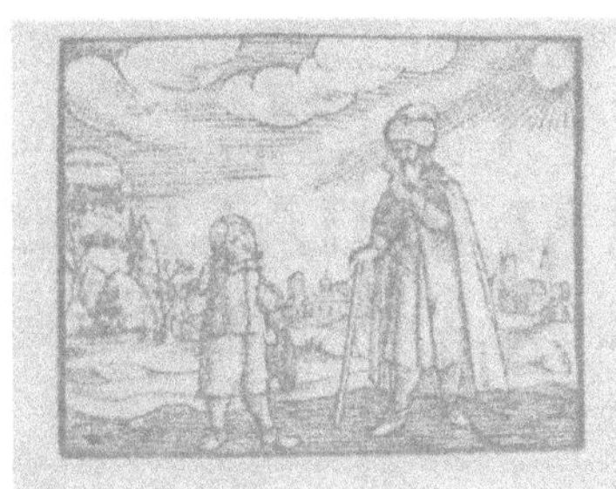

Fig. 3

Master to the pupil: "Postea ibimus Mundum , et spectabimus omnia "
"We will go into the world and we will view all things"

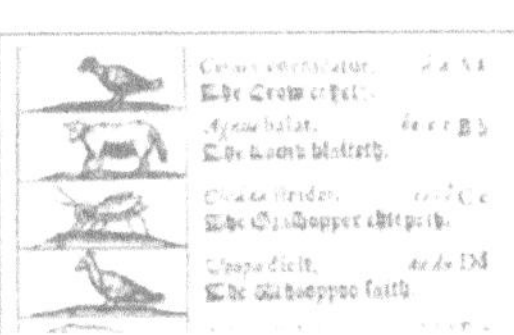

Fig. 4

2. Knowledge Organization and Visualization

Diderot's Encyclopédie (Diderot & d'Alembert, 1751-1772)

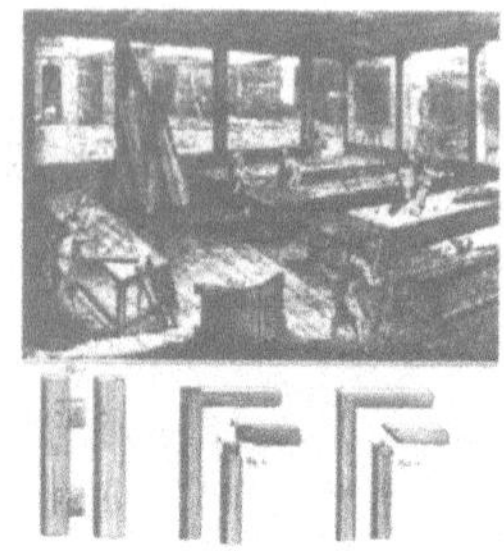

The method of describing each mechanical art grew out of Diderot's concept of a science, which he viewed as "a system of rules or facts relative to a certain object".

In the letterpress volumes, each craft was described in a major article such as glassmaking, ironworking, or tanning. In addition, important technical terms had separate entries, which were published in alphabetical order. In principle, each major article in the text was complemented by a series of illustrations (copperplate etchings) and a commentary in the volumes of plates. Ideally, the article was to refer to the objects depicted in the plates by a system of code numbers and letters, thus integrating texts and images; however, there was considerable variation among contributors in their use of this method (cp. Gendzier, 1967).

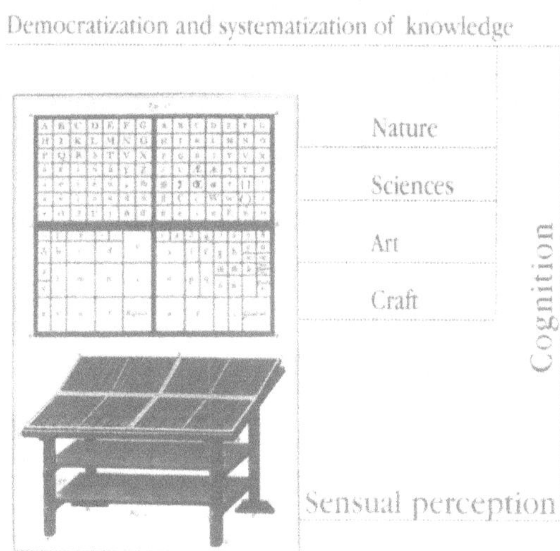

Leibnitz: No one can any longer read all books

Gutenberg-Galaxis (McLuhan): The printing press caused a reordering of our thinking, by elevating the written text as organisation form above other forms of information transmission.

3. The liberation from human imagination

René Descartes (1596-1650), Discours de la méthode pour bien conduire sa raison, et chercher la verité dans les science

pars pro toto

There are four rules:

1. Never accept anything as true for any reason, unless you have **seen** that it is doubtlessly so;
2. Every problem should be divided into parts. This makes it possible to find the best solution;
3. Direct your thoughts. Start with the simplest and easiest to understand, and move to more and more complex questions little by little, as by stairs. Accept order even among that which in the natural course of things do not come one before the other;
4. Make the most complete lists and the most general reviews as possible, so that you are sure nothing has been left out.

Methodological reductionism

Regulae ad directionem ingenii
REGULA XV
Juvat etiam
It is also useful in many occasions to describe these figures and to show them to our external senses, so that in this way our thought might maintain more easily its attention

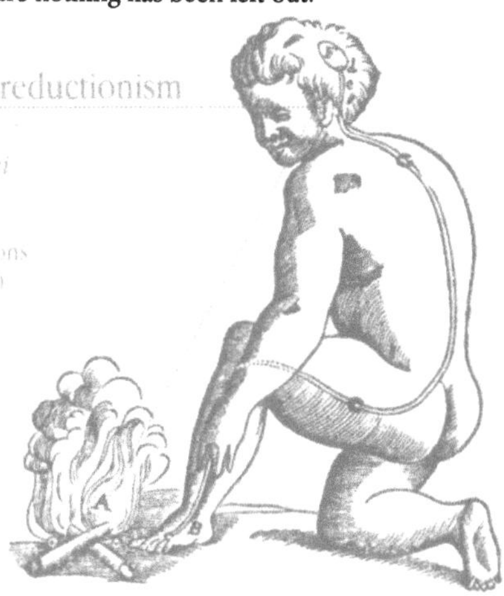

Visualization of virtualities

Encyclopaedia is never interested in words but in what words mean and refer – the world behind the words.

That is why the encyclopaedia always reflects the cultural and scientific situation in which it is created. To update an encyclopaedia is not just to add new entries but to diminish the importance of some and to foster others.

Leibnitz conception of encyclopaedism
late 17th, early 18th century

.is a..." trésor publique qui seroi d' un usage incomparable dans tous les besoins de la vie"

4. In search of the perfect language

G.W. Leibnitz: Characteristica universalis

The terms Character and Symbol will be used synonymously.
This implies, for example, that the picture of a man can be used as a symbol in a script, and it can represent a character of a Character System (CS).
Thus a CS can also be called a Symbol System.

Abbreviations:

AC:	Ars Characteristica
AL:	Adamic Language
CS:	Character System or Characteristica
CU:	Characteristica Universalis
FCS:	Formal Character System or Symbolic Machine
UL:	Universal Language
UT:	Universal Thinker or Universal Thinking
ST:	Specialist or Scientific or Expert Thinker or Thinking

In 1679 Leibnitz introduces binary arithmetic
2=10, 4= 100, 8=1000 ...

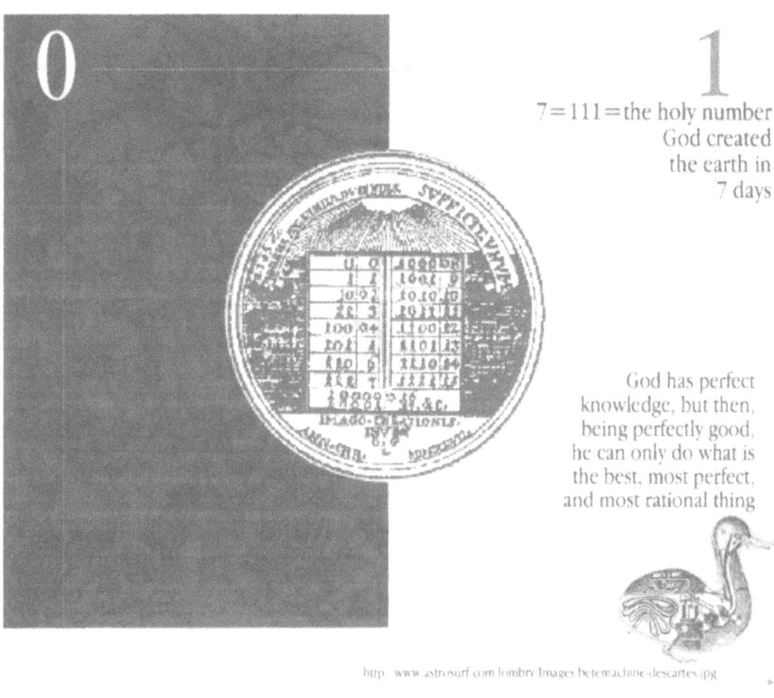

http: www.astrosurf.com lombry Images betemachine-descartes.jpg

5. The organizational context of knowledge

Paul Otlet (1868-1944) and the Universal Decimal Classification (UDC)

UDC = A document may be classified under a combination of different categories through the use of additional symbols.
For example:
\+ (plus)
Addition, e.g. 59+636 = Zoology and animal breeding
/ (stroke)
Extension, e.g. 592/599 = Systematic zoology (everything from 592 to 599 inclusive)
: (colon)
Relation, e.g. 17:7 Relation of ethics to art

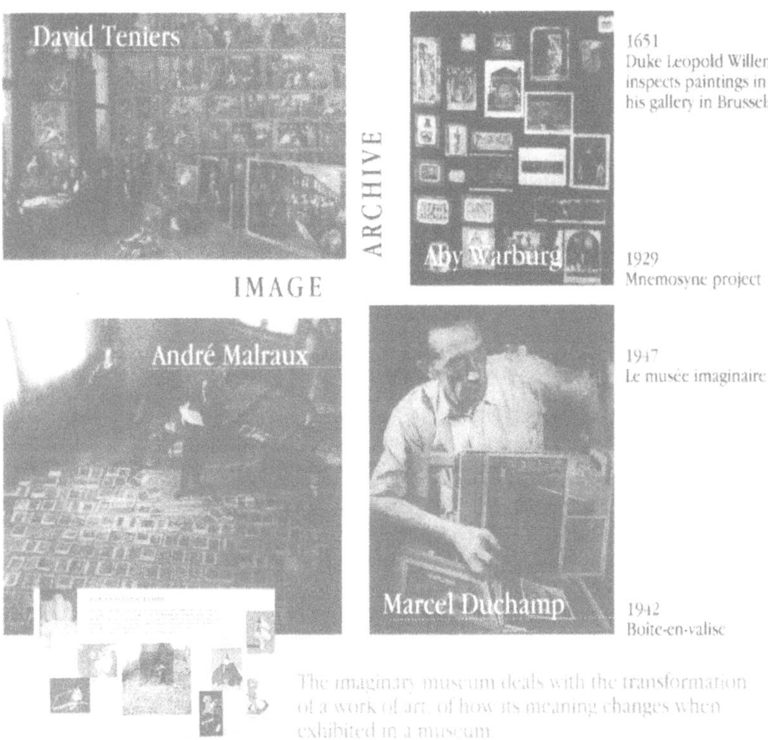

The imaginary museum deals with the transformation of a work of art, of how its meaning changes when exhibited in a museum

In a museum, a crucifix becomes a sculpture, an image of the Virgin is a picture, a sacred effigy a statue

Malraux deeply questions the ultimate meaning of this great transformation.

6. Picturing knowledge - scientific visualizations

Scientific visualizations and artists

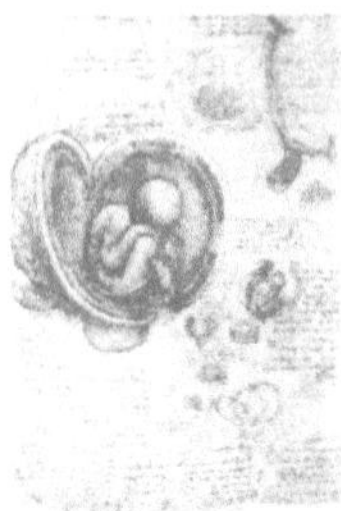

LEONARDO

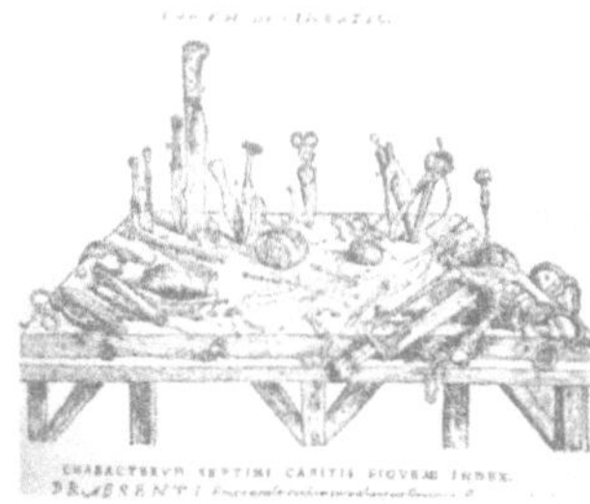

VERSALIUS

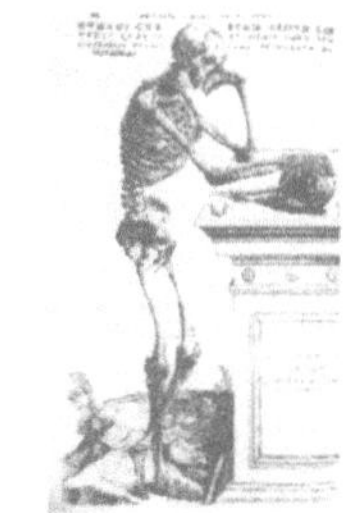

Study of the foetus and the womb, with optical and mechanical diagrams. Leonardo da Vinci 1510-1512

Tools for dissection. Andreas Vesalius 1543

Skeleton from the side. Andreas Vesalius 1543

The conception of the virtuoso, the rational artist aiming at reasoned and examined control alike of his own thoughts and intentions and actions and of his surroundings, seems to me to be the essence of European morality, meaning both habits and ethics, out of which the European scientific movement was generated and engineered. In this context the rational artist and the rational experimental scientist appear as exemplary products of the same intellectual culture (Crombie 1985, pp.15-16).

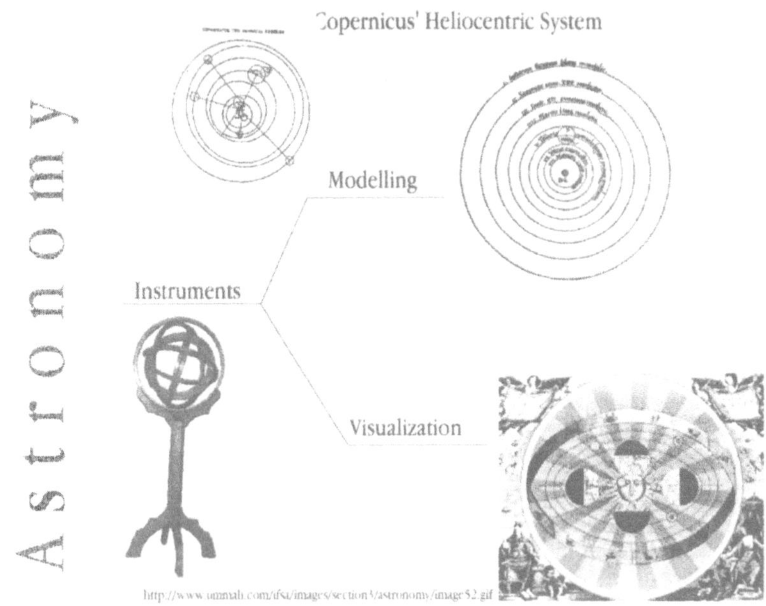

7. The disappearance of distance - the advent of telematic culture

Time and space in the 19th century

Unleashing production machinery and the mechanical acceleration of communication and transportation caused a deep change in human experience of time and space during the 19th century's industrial revolution. Though the objective distance remained the same, travel time decreased tremendously through faster transportation. The subjective experience of the spatio-temporal relationship could be exemplified at that time: the faster one traversed a specific distance the more it seemed to him that the distance would disappear. Thus space turned into a perceivable temporal dimension.

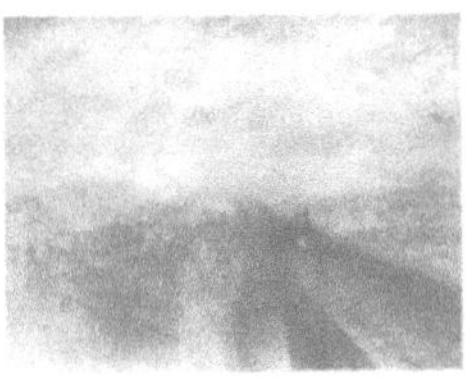

In *Rain, Steam and Speed*, (before 1844) William Turner contrasts the drama of nature with the awesome power of human invention.The blurred details not only suggest the downpour, but also the experience of the passengers, in the open-topped carriages, travelling at 30mph - break-neck speed in the 1840s.

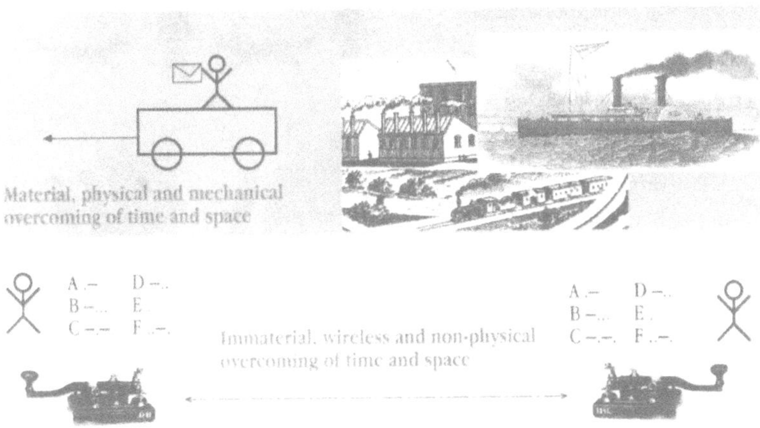

TELEGRAPHY
TELEVISION

Samuel Morse (1791-1872) was a famous American inventor and painter. He received the patent for the first successful electric telegraph in the United States and also invented the Morse Code, used for many years to send telegraphic messages.

The '**Nipkow Disk**' invented by Paul Gottlieb Nipkow, 1884, was a first attempt to transmit pictures by wire – Nipkow's development led to the first public demonstration of television in 1926.

8. ISOTYPE = International System of Typographic Picture Education

Otto Neurath (1882-1945) and the Viennese Method of Visual Education

Otto Neurath was a pioneer in many respects - his contributions are in socialist politics, political economy, the theory of science, sociology and social philosophy.
His revolutionary access to communication theory based
on investigating the role of communication in the making of modern man was remarkable. Within the wider context of a Wissenschaftliche Weltauffassung (= scientific world conception), he developed early steps in media literacy, conceived as a continuation of enlightenment, the struggle against metaphysics following a practical turn to the iconic form of communication, in the terms of ISOTYPE, a new pictographic design system. The starting point for this project was the 'Viennese Museum for Society and Economy' founded in 1924; Neurath's endeavour was mainly to visualize social and
economic relations also for the uneducated receiver, and therefore to design the museums of the future.

The best foundation for a comprehensive visual education would be to let all children learn their own language and also foreign languages by this method.

If a German, for example, wants to learn English it will help him to perceive that the English language, far more than German, is based on opposites, or antonyms. It is more instructive to *show* the fact of opposition than to try to explain it in words.

Any child can understand a picture showing a coming and a going dog. By such symbols we can help children learn to use words readily.

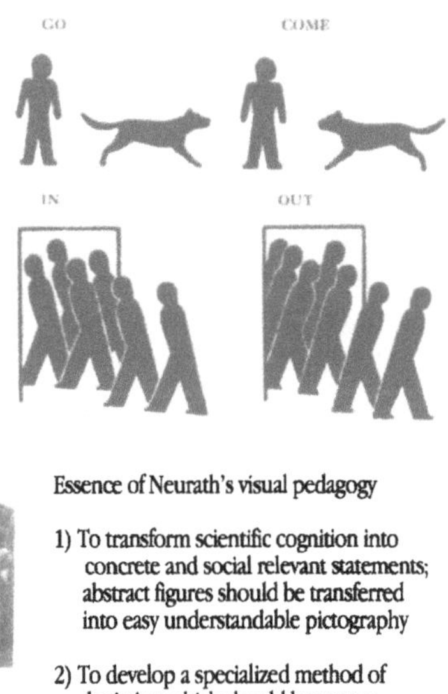

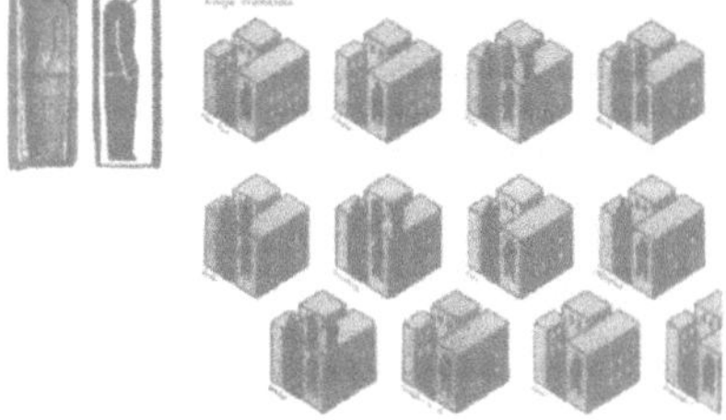

Essence of Neurath's visual pedagogy

1) To transform scientific cognition into concrete and social relevant statements; abstract figures should be transferred into easy understandable pictography

2) To develop a specialized method of depiction which should become a systematized visual language

3) To apply logistic usage of iconic form of communication in the concept for the "museum of the future"

9. Messenger and message - about telephone pictures and global thinking
Transmission models of communication

The telephone, the automobile, the airplane and, of course, radio, were for the avant-garde artists of the first decades of this century a symbol of modern life, in which technology could extend human perception and capabilities. The dadaists, however, diverged from the general enthusiasm for scientific rationalism and criticized technology's destructive power. In 1920, in the"Dada-Almanac", edited in Berlin by Richard Huelsenbeck, they published the irreverent proposal that a painter could now order pictures by telephone and have them made by a cabinet-maker...

"In 1922 I ordered by telephone from a sign factory five paintings in porcelain enamel. I had the factory's color chart before me and I sketched my paintings on graph paper. At the other end of the telephone the factory supervisor had the same kind of paper, divided into squares. He took down the dictated shapes in the correct position. (It was like playing chess by correspondence.) One of the pictures was delivered in three different sizes, so that I could study the subtle differences in the color relations caused by the enlargement and reduction" (Laszlo Moholy-Nagy, The New Vision and Abstract of an Artist, New York: Wittenborn, 1947, p. 79).

Shannon-Weaver Model of communication, 1948

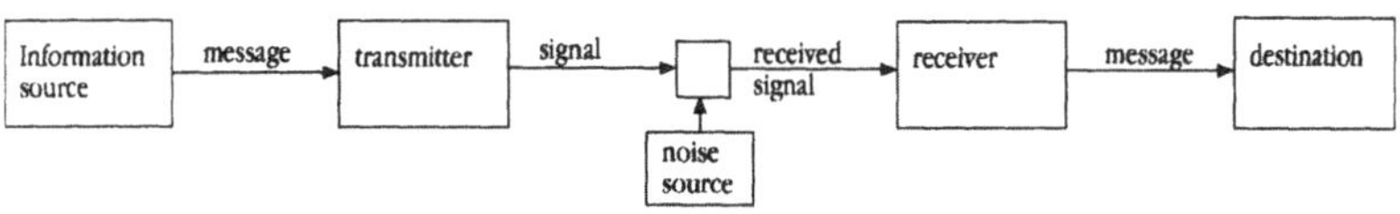

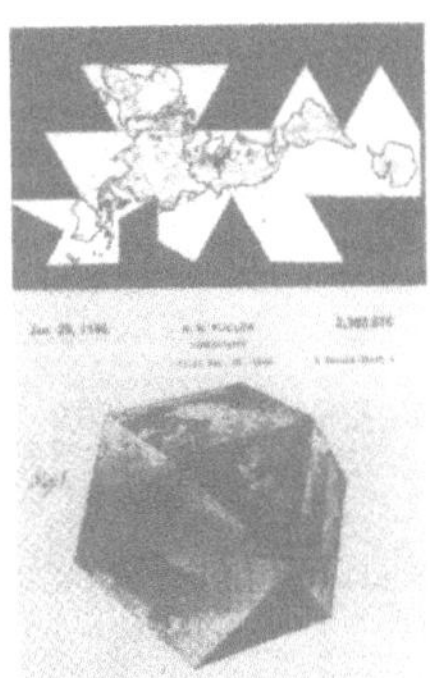

Dymaxion world map

Every world map projection must make certain compromises as information is transferred from a spherical globe to a flat surface. In 1927 Buckminster Fuller, an educator, engineer, architect, author, cartographer and futurist, set out to develop the world's most accurate two-dimensional world map. He wanted to provide a view of the whole Earth at once which would have the ability to reveal major trends in world affairs and show the shortest air routes between land masses. Fuller predicted even then that global travel would shift from the sea to the sky.

Buckminster Fuller proposed to cover the surface of the globe with 4 D twins, delivered by Zeppelin to remote locations. The plan is a proposal for an "omnidirectional transportation device", to allow people to reach their homes by means of jets.

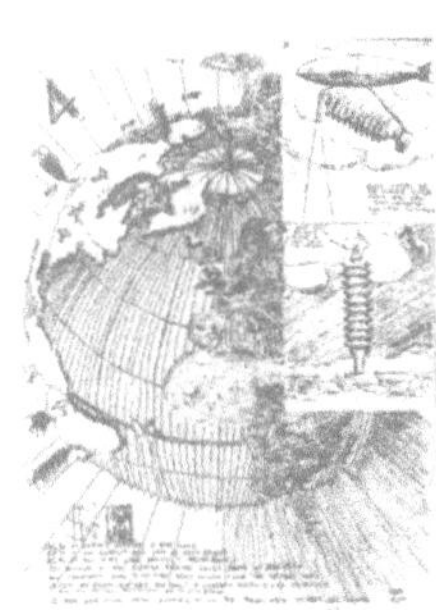

10. The medium is the message

The new age of education is programmed for discovery rather than instruction. Art as radar environment, radar feedback, early warning system: the antennae of the race. Marshall McLuhan

In a culture like ours, long accustomed to splitting and dividing all things as a means of control, it is sometimes a bit of a shock to be reminded that, in operational and practical fact, **the medium is the message.**
(Marshall McLuhan, Understanding Media: The Extensions of Man, 1964)

The medium is the message; the message is the medium.

Document/ Purposes Visual Matrix	Tables	Line Graphs	Bar Graphs	Pie Charts	Schematic Diagrams	Flow Charts	Maps	Photo	Tree Diagrams	Illustrations	Blueprint
Costs	X	X	X								
Causes/ Effects	X					X		X			
Trends	X	X	X	X			X				
Organizational Relationships	X					X			X		
Policies/ Procedures	X								X		
Decisions/ Alternatives	X		X	X			X		X		
Work Flow						X			X		
Chronology	X	X	X			X					
Design Parts/ Apparatus					X			X		X	X
Comparison/ Contrast	X	X	X	X				X			
Advantages/ Disadvantages	X		X	X				X			

The type of visual you use in visual communication depends upon the message, the situation, and the technical level of your audience.

Keep illustrations simple. If necessary, remove surrounding detail. When appropriate, provide a perspective to facilitate reader understanding. – When illustrating a process, structure the process from top to bottom and left to right.

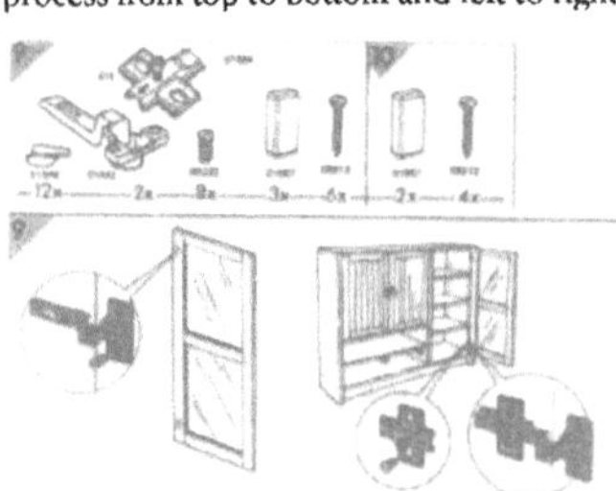

Don Norman's (***Human Centered Design***) motto:
"The human-centered approach puts people's needs first, technology second. It focuses upon human activities."

11. Concepts and strategies of telematic art in the 70's and 80's

It was a technologically utopian structure of feeling, positivistic, and "scientistic." David Mellor

The term 'telematic' has been appropriated by the electronic arts community to describe artwork which employs modern communications medium as part of its structure, or process.

Roy Ascott, one of the pioneers in telematic art, drew on cybernetics to theorize a model of how art could transform culture. He was particularly insistent that cybernetics was no simple prescription for a local remedy to the crisis of modern art, but represented the potential for reordering social values and reformulating what constituted knowledge and being.
In 1968 he wrote:
As feedback between persons increases and communications become more rapid and precise, so the creative process no longer culminates in the ***art work***, but extends beyond it deep into the life of each individual. Art is then determined not by the creativity of the artist alone, but by the creative behaviour that his work induces in the spectator, and in society at large. . . . The art of our time tends towards the development of a ***cybernetic vision***, in which feedback, dialogue and involvement in some creative interplay at deep levels of experience are paramount. . . . The cybernetic spirit, more than the method or the applied science, creates a continuum of experience and knowledge which radically reshapes our philosophy, influences our behaviour and extends our thought.

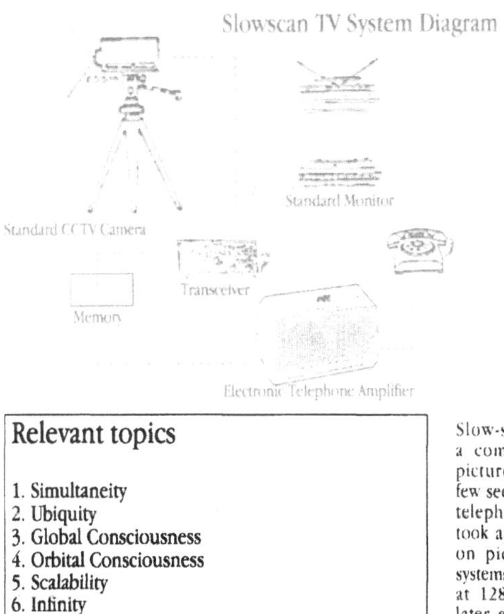

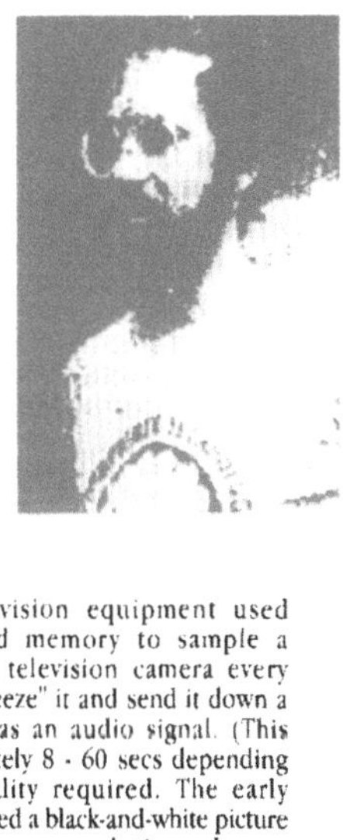

Relevant topics

1. Simultaneity
2. Ubiquity
3. Global Consciousness
4. Orbital Consciousness
5. Scalability
6. Infinity
7. Non-materiality
8. Semiotics
9. Acceleration of time
10. Time-based media
11. Dislocation, displacement
12. Communication and information systems
13. Disconnection between message (sign) and messenger (body)
14. Virtual worlds

Slow-scan television equipment used a computerised memory to sample a picture from a television camera every few seconds, "freeze" it and send it down a telephone line as an audio signal. (This took approximately 8 - 60 secs depending on picture quality required. The early systems transmitted a black-and-white picture at 128 lines/screen resolution whereas later equipment operated at 256 or 512 line resolution in colour.) The machines could only be used between two points at a time. At the receiving end, the signal was decoded and slowly scanned out a still frame on a television monitor.
http://www.hss.uts.edu.au/oth/telematic_art/tech.html

12. Multimedia CD-Rom - enclosed cosmos of interactive information access

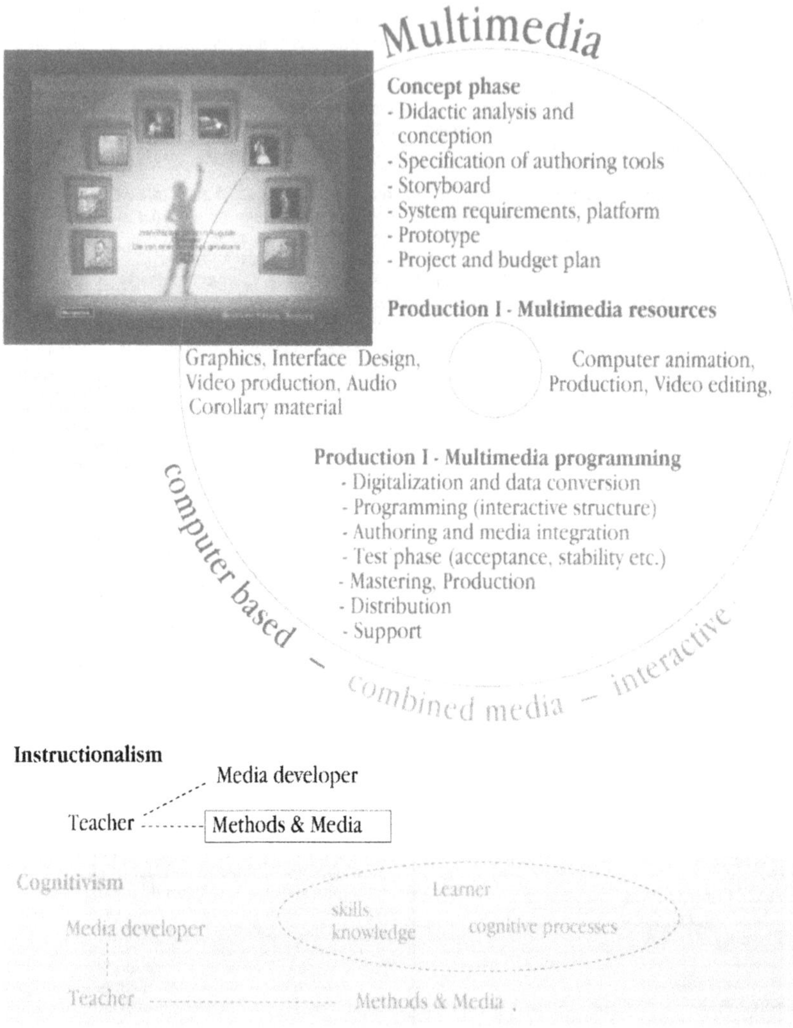

13. Internet aesthetic – Programming, Interface, Interaction

Programming = Technology

Meta-Rules

1. Rules must be either funny, whimsical or true.
2. You are not expected to understand these rules.
3. The rules as a whole may be self-contradictory.
4. Rules may have exceptions.

Don't whine unless you are going to implement it yourself.

If you don't work on your project, chances are that no one will.

A project is never finished.

The user is always right unless proven otherwise by the developer.

Release early, release often. Clean compilation is optional.

When a developer says he will work on something, he or she means "maybe".

Open-Source is not a panacea.

Backward compatibility is your users' best friend.

You are your best tester.

Duplicate effort is inevitable. Live with it.

Open code = Good code

Models of collective creativity

Interface = Aesthetic

[illegible]

Interactivity = Social action

Cooperation
various settings of temporary, project-oriented compositions of webdesigner, programmer, content-provider etc.

Dialogue
open for all users, no editorial conrol, MUDs, e.g. www.banja.com

Communities
provision of infrastructure such as webspace, chat, content management system etc.
e.g. www.thing.de

Participation
Monitoring aspect included, mostly temporary projects, e.g. www.keo.org

Collaboration
Concept frame based on collective teamwork, individual authorship replaced by co-authors, process oriented and dependent on constant input, e.g. http://telezone.aec.at

14. From implicit skills to explicit knowledge
visual strategies for shared construction of knowledge

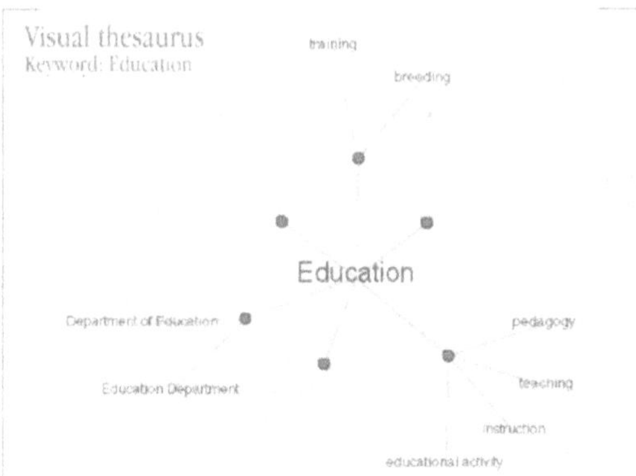

Relationships
- antonym
- see also
- is similar to
- attribute
- is derived from
- entails
- is a participle
- pertains to
- verb group
- is a type of
- is a part of
- is a member of
- is made of

Nouns

Adjectives

Verbs

Adverbs

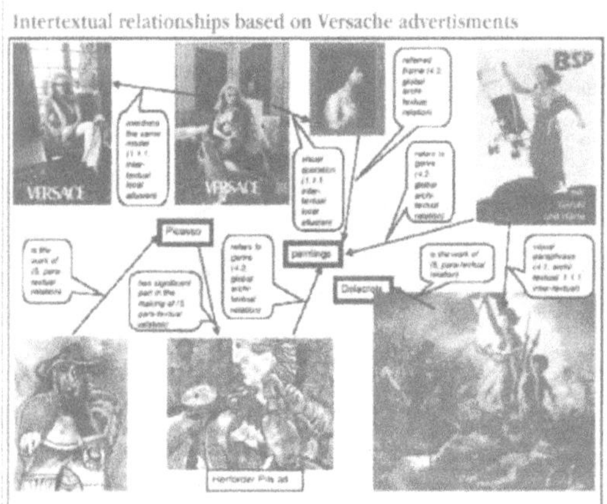

Sketch illustrating intertextual relationships on a certain topic.

- interrelationships
- intrarelationships
- intertextual relationships

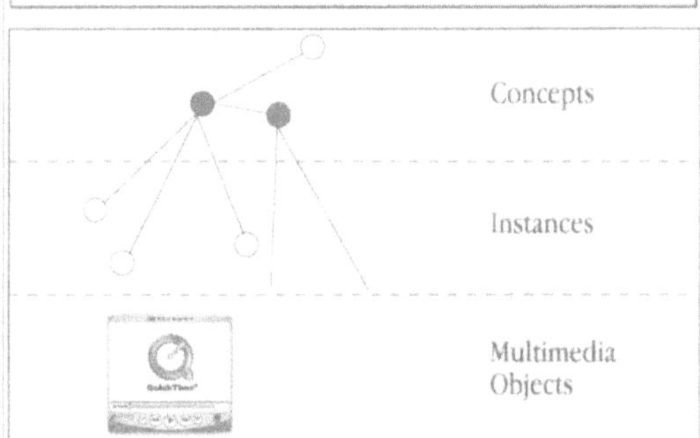

Ontology builder

Concept

Threads

Semantic relationships

media rich content

reflexive visualization

ubiquitious access

Reference system
Collaborative knowledge construction

Communication and Collaboration

The students' backgrounds vary from educational to media- and art-related previous studies. Most of their expectations and motivation to take *ePedagogy Design* lay in the international dimension, improvement of English language skills and mutual knowledge sharing. Within a setting of three different cultural backgrounds and languages – none of the students are native English speakers – the whole approach began to be a challenge in itself. Thus the main focus has been on the process of collaborative communication: how the students create a shared meaning and understanding from which to pursue common interests. Synchronous communication processes among students and teachers started rather ambitiously from the first discussion based on the online seminar "Iconic Turn – Iconic Clash".

Progressively personal time management and synchronization of binding dates became restrictive to workflow and continuity. One of the main reasons synchronous communication among the students became gradually less frequent are the different schedule lines of academic years of each of the universities involved in the MA programme.

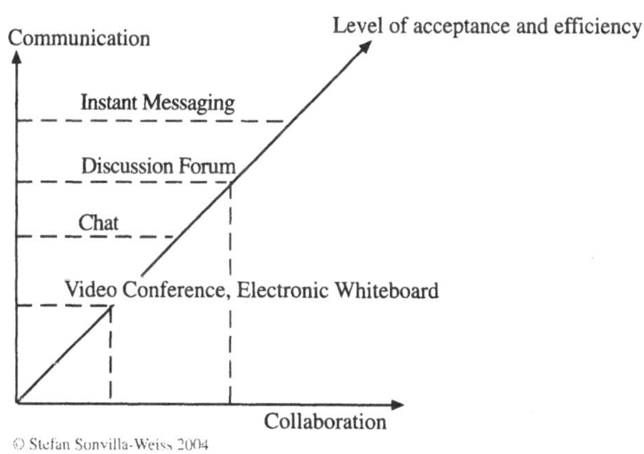

Fig. 3

Figure 3 gives an overview of acceptance and efficiency of communicative and collaborative tools during the online seminar within a two-month period of time.

Main pedagogical and didactical approaches and concepts

Knowledge building pedagogy in *ePedagogy Design* supports VLE-activities with the following characteristics:

- Problem focus versus topic focus – students need to understand and to identify the knowledge they want to research;
- Production of knowledge objects versus media objects – ontology model;
- Contributions versus display – media rich database entries are valued for their contribution to a joint knowledge-building effort;
- Sustained versus single-pass knowledge creation – preservable and traceable good ideas generated by student discussions;
- Public versus person-to-person communication – promotion of moderated discussion forums and person-to-person communication;
- Opportunity for reflection – asynchronous discussion forms let students "take their time in formulating a contribution." *ePedagogy Design* emphasizes situated, authentic learning in a collaborative context and the encouragement of research, experimentation and the generation of the students' own-problem solving activities, rather than those defined by the lecturer or tutor.

The didactical design contains cross-reference to problem based learning settings with threaded discussion boards, online resources, tele-lectures and synchronous communication facilities.

A collaborative Learning Object is the result of a collaborative knowledge building process that includes key information written by the discussion attendees. This kind of information could be used to ease decision making, to familiarize new students with the past working methods or as a learning object (Fig. 4).

Research focus

A knowledge organization strives towards virtually integrated Knowledge Organization Systems (KOSs) and subject metadata. Of paramount interest are intersubjectively validated knowledge structures, i.e. social or cultural constructs: the view (conceptualization) a discourse com-

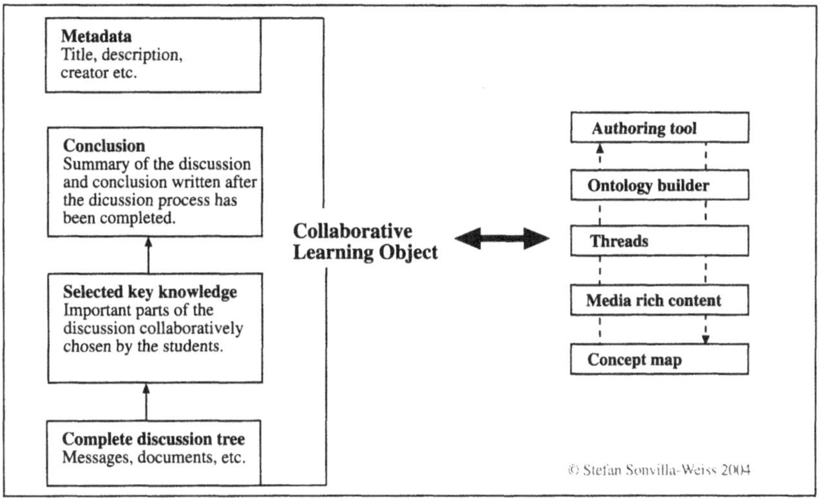

Fig. 4 Fig. 5

munity shares on relevant objects of discourse, and how such a community thinks that those objects are interrelated (Fig. 5).

Topic Maps or Concept Maps allow expressing knowledge structures as structured link networks, and to share and merge them. They can be employed to both express contradictory discourse community views, and subject metadata for knowledge repositories. KO is therefore about how to arrive at and represent appropriate conceptual access structures to aid working with knowledge (knowledge networks or knowledge spaces). Topic or concept maps are a special paradigm and technology to handle such networks, particularly models of representation and knowledge structures, and are thus able to create sophisticated finding aids that allow one to semantically search and visually browse those complex knowledge structures.

Our research and project developments stress the need to merge existing VLE-developments with Open Standard based multimedia knowledge management tools.

Thus the main activities concentrate on

- Customization of an integrated authoring environment that supports portable meta-data objects;

- Specification of relevant media didactical properties of these portable meta-data objects;
- Delivery and deployment of these objects in different learning scenarios;
- Specifications and implementation of support tools for dual mode workflows;
- Definition of an ontology for the domain of interdisciplinary studies, which will be proposed as a enriched model of visual knowledge building to support teaching and learning.

Another research strand in *ePedagogy Design* focuses on didactical ontologies in blended learning, development of innovative dual mode/blended learning activities and deployment of co-operative objects such as:

Online tutoring	Clarifying the role of the online tutor and establishing effective strategies for supporting students' learning online
Learning discussions	Clarifying the proportion of on and offline teaching methods and establishing effective strategies for students' dual mode learning
Learning conferences	International seminars and exploration of effective methods for transferring seminar materials, video documentation, reports and student presentations into online resources
Role-playing	Creative modes of moderation, tutoring, mentoring among students, teachers and experts in on and offline settings
Working groups	Clarifying the structure and methods of collaborative project approaches among students, experts and teachers and establishing effective methods of facilitating such cooperation

Future Steps in *ePedagogy Design* – *Visual Knowledge Building*

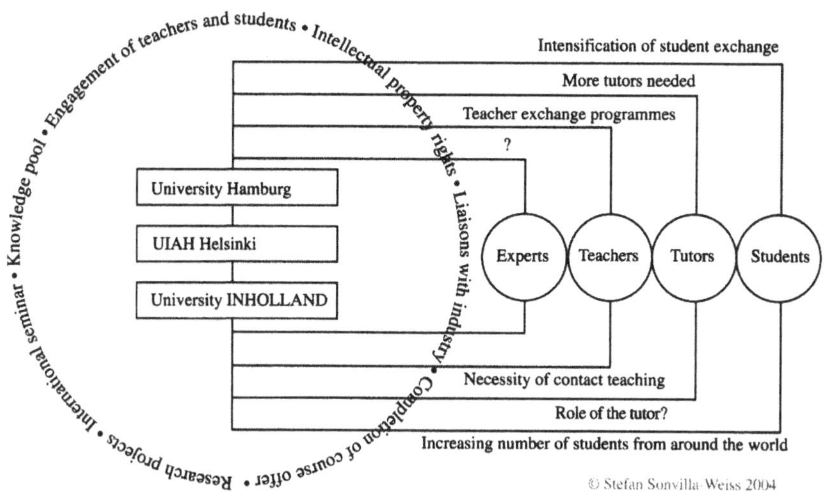

Fig. 6

The ongoing curriculum development process depicted in Figure 6 covers major aspects of improvements in collaborating more concisely and efficiently between the institutions. The next steps include amplification of various kinds of cooperation among the universities and liaisons with private/public enterprises.

Furthermore the entire approach of bringing together students, teachers and experts to create an interlinked knowledge sharing culture demands a broader view on the changing paradigm shift in formal and informal education. Virtual communities support the acceleration of knowledge externalized in documents or repositories, but evidently will not be able to substitute social interaction and skills among individuals.

References

AI Topics – a dynamic library of introductory information about Artificial Intelligence, Education, http://www.aaai.org/AITopics/html/education.html.

ANDERSON Terry and Denise Whitelock (2004): The Educational Semantic Web: Visioning and Practicing the Future of Education, http://www-jime.open.ac.uk/2004/1/editorial-2004-1.pdf.

BAUMGARTNER Peter, H. Häfele, K. Maier-Häfele (2002): Evaluierung von Lernmanagement-Systemen (LMS). In: Handbuch E-Learning. Fachverlag Deutscher Wirtschaftsdienst: Köln 2002.

BRITAIN, Sandy; Oleg Liber (1999): A Framework for Pedagogical Evaluation of Virtual Learning Environments, http://www.leeds.ac.uk/educol/documents/00001237.htm.

CULTOS – Cultural Units of Learning – Tools and Services Multimedia knowledge management tools for culture and arts, http://www.cultos.org.

DICOLE – VLE, http://www.dicole.fi.

REINMANN-ROTHMEIER Gabi (2003): Didaktische Innovation durch Blended Learning. Leitlinien anhand eines Beispiels aus der Hochschule. Unter Mitarbeit von Frank Vohle, Frederic Adler und Heidi Faust, Bern 2003.

SEMANTIC WEB, http://www.w3.org/2001/sw/.

WILEY David (2000): Learning Object Design and Sequencing Theory, Dissertation, http://wiley.ed.usu.edu/docs/dissertation.pdf.

Communication in Creative Processes

Notes towards the facilitation of creative-artistic autonomy

PETER TRUNIGER

A. Communication in Creative Processes

1. Language in Design and Art Education

> "I can't model a figure properly." "I have no ideas." "I just can't draw!" "I wish I could walk away from this." "I can't decide which alternative to choose."

Anyone who teaches design and art, whether at the primary or high school level or in courses for adults or seniors, is familiar with these complaints. Most teachers instinctively respond to such outbursts of frustration by rushing to help. They give well-intentioned advice and cheerful encouragement with qualifying comments like "this is not nearly as bad as you think…" Another way of responding would be for teachers to ask themselves questions such as: "Does he/she always see things this way? Does he/she sometimes react differently in similar situations? Is there something that might change this assessment? What could be done to facilitate his/her decision-making process?"

For the purpose of our discussion about the facilitation of learning and communication in creative processes, we need to distinguish between two basic scenarios. In the first situation, techniques are explained, procedures ARE taught and technical knowledge is conveyed. These activities typically take the form of lectures, instruction, and tutorials. Communication serves a different function when the object is to facilitate learning in creative processes. In the first case the teacher usually delivers a straightforward description of a technique or explains how one must proceed to achieve a desired result. The second case calls for a more restrained approach and a respectful exploration of the student's creative intentions. Learning to distinguish and implement these two types of communication skills is part of the training that students undergo in order to become teachers themselves.

Those who decide to attend a school of art and design usually have a creative talent and specific abilities in the field of two and three-dimensional expression. In the course of their studies, students hope to refine this talent and develop a creative-artistic language or authentic expression of their own. Ultimately this process is about the development of what Selle (1988) calls the aesthetically intelligent subject (see below).

At the start of the semester the students sit in their studios and workshops with the best creative intentions, hoping to translate the plans or fantasies in their head into a tangible and appropriate materiality. They are ready to embark on a journey of creativity and transformation that will profoundly affect their thinking, feelings and motivation. They would like to create and develop something that will redefine and expand the limits of their potential.

From a psychological-educational perspective we are interested in the ways that teachers have to facilitate the creative-artistic development of their students: that is, to facilitate it in such a way that the students feel encouraged and emboldened in moments of creativity and reassured in moments of doubt or potential failure. Whatever form it takes, this support should always respect the original idea of the student. Hopefully the students will carry these experiences into their future educational activity in the arts and there apply the same care in guiding and instructing their students.

In the pages that follow we will deal mostly with situations focusing on interactions that encourage and promote the autonomous expression of the creative individual. Let me illustrate this with a brief case study.

1.1 Particulars of the creative process

A case study

It is the start of the summer semester. Tom and Paul have to pick their segment of a larger project called "Weight-less". They are asked to choose between three different takes on the theme of weightlessness: purely artistic, experimental and physics-based, and functional and design-oriented. This last one is part of a project that will be realized in the city park: designing a play structure for children that conveys a "feeling of weightless floating". Criteria like child safety, play quality, materiality, stress resistance and visual appearance are important aspects. The allotted time frame is nine three-day working weeks. The specific requirements for this project-segment are:

A Floating freely like an astronaut – moving through space in giant steps – exploring an alien world.

B The structure can easily be adjusted for different weights. It withstands the usual wear and tear of play structures and meets current safety requirements. It provides a visually attractive addition to the playground.

C In the allotted time, produce either a 3D-animation or a 1:15-scale model.

Tom and Paul settle on this project segment. Having immersed themselves in mechanical and physical phenomena for some time, they have no trouble relating to the overall theme. From the start they know theirs will be a large structure with levers and springs. They take spontaneous delight in searching for ideas and quickly assemble an assortment of promising concepts. They investigate the resilience of various materials, test their weather-resistance and do further research on *weightlessness* and *physical levers.*

In various meetings with their teacher, the students discuss technical solutions and materials. She offers valuable tips on the mechanical implementation of their ideas and advises them on the selection and application of materials. They also enlist the support of a professor for 3D-design software who helps them with the animation.

Tom and Peter initially disagree on the formal design of the structure. Given the limited time allocated for the realization of the project, Paul and Tom need to make a quick decision. This decision-making situation causes a crisis for the two students. While two project ideas quickly emerge as clear favorites, Paul and Tom are unable to settle on a final choice, since the general requirements for both proposals are similar and the technical and material complexity of both structures is daunting. Also, following conversations with fellow students, they have come to doubt the artistic merits of their proposals. For more than a week, they are unable to continue. An extended talk with their advisor eventually helps them break the deadlock.

Listening patiently, the teacher explores the various aspects of the two project ideas and with specific questions supports and facilitates the students' search for a solution. They finally select the project *Luna-Tandem,* a structure that would allow two children at once to float through a crater-like landscape. Their confidence and motivation restored, Paul and Tom proceed with the visual and technical implementation of their idea. They almost get bogged down in design difficulties two more times but both situations are resolved after a brief conference with their advisor. The final result of their research and development process eventually elicits a positive response from both fellow students and teachers (see illustration "sketches and models").

Back and Forth

As this case illustrates, creative-artistic processes typically involve very specific procedures and work modes. Frequently the object of such processes is to create prototypes or unique copies. Most artistic production does not progress in a straight line – from initial idea through planning to production and the finished object, image, installation, etc. – but tends to resemble a dense tangle of advances and retreats. Creative processes involve numerous searches, decisions, choices, surprising insights and moments of elation, but also obstacles and detours. For the designer or artist this is frequently a source of considerable emotional stress. Also important are questions of motivation and processes of reflection, testing, reviewing, and revising. The facilitation of such processes by a teacher engaged in a dialog with the student requires a meaningful methodology focused on solutions and expectations. It is this dialog that we will focus on now.

1.2 'Meisterlehre' (Master Apprenticeship) and Independent Learning

There is a rich tradition in art and design education and related occupations of ways to transmit skills, techniques and procedures from master artists to their apprentices. The copying of existing works is a widely used method (see Peez, 2002, p.110). As a rule this is called Meisterlehre (master apprenticeship) (see Stebler, Reusser & Pauli, 1994, p.232). This type of skills transmission is based on the premise that all relevant technical information is in the possession of the master. The master gradually transmits his knowledge to the eager apprentice, who absorbs important elements into his/ her own thinking and creative processes. After a certain time the apprentice will possess a wide-range of technical knowledge and progressively emancipate him/herself from the master. Thus, important artistic concepts, practices, and procedures are transmitted over generations.

Facilitation and Self-Reliance

The exploration of new creative-artistic paths follows a different pattern. As participants in larger projects or in their studio-based work (see Peez, 2002, p. 113), students often focus on a particular theme for an extended period of time. Here the acquisition of process-related skills is merely a means to an end. The main focus is on the realization of a creative intention. Artistic or aesthetic activity assumes value if one's own ideas become reality. Teaching and learning processes that allow this to happen stimulate the development of the aesthetically intelligent self (see Selle, 1998).

According to Selle, aesthetic learning takes place primarily within the self-educating self. Educational interventions provide impulses and support that facilitate an indvidual's exploration and subjective interpretation of aesthetic phenomena and events (1990, 35). The teacher's task is 'to instigate or abet aesthetic action and (self) awareness, and – if successful – to cooperate in aesthetic processes' (p. 26).

The development of the individual into a fully formed aesthetic self is completed once the individual is:

> im besonderen Masse wahrnehmungsfähig und selbstwahrnehmungsfähig, kontemplativ und geistesgegenwärtig-handlungsfähig, bewusstseinsproduzierend-reflexiv und sinngenerativ [...] und wenn es in besonderem Masse zum aufmerksamen Zuschauer jenes im biografischen Material der Erinnerung und im Augenblick der Wahrnehmung verankerten Bewusstseinsprozesses werden kann, dem es seine Erzeugung verdankt – wenn es also ästhetisch intelligent genannt werden kann (Selle, 1998, p. 112).[1]

In light of current theories about teaching/learning this means that the attitude of instruction in *one* direction – from teacher to student – gives way to the notion that teaching and learning constitute a reciprocal exchange of knowledge, perceptions, and procedures that guides students to independent and responsible action (see Guldimann, 1996). In this view, educational intervention consistently attempts to promote the development of the student.

In many teaching/learning situations the methods of the Meisterlehre work well. On the other hand, there are situations or personal relationships in which they do not achieve the optimal results: the flow of information is too one-sided and the knowledge of the expert looms too large. In the pages that follow we will present forms of interaction that promote dialog and encourage novices to develop and refine their own ideas even as they venture into a new area of expertise. Here the know-how of the specialist represents a valuable resource.

1 The individual has become highly perceptive and self-perceptive, contemplative and alert/ready to act, capable of producing consciousness through reflection and generating meaning, and once it can become, to an extraordinary degree, the attentive observer of that process of consciousness, which is rooted in the biographical data of memory and the instant of perception, and to which it owes its existence – in other words, once it can be called aesthetically intelligent (Selle, 1998, p. 112).

1.3 Teachers and Students in Creative-Artistic Processes

In the following chapters I will propose a number of attitudes, procedures, and methods of communication that may be used to guide/advise learners at certain stages of the creative process. We will begin with a look at some basic parameters and, in particular, some important concepts like autonomy, emotions, roles, judgment and evaluation.

Autonomy and Originality in Creative-Artistic Expression

Knowledge is acquired in different ways. We learn many things from experts who instruct us or through the more or less precise imitation of a model (see Peez, 2002, p. 110). Knowledge is also gained from practical experience (with an object) and/or through operations of logic. This is as true for art as it is for other areas of knowledge and experience. What sets creative-artistic practices apart from all others is that they claim to create something unique. As a rule, creative people claim originality and individual expression. Facilitating creative processes therefore requires styles of communication and interaction that strengthen the students' sense of independence, self-reliance and self-confidence in thinking and action.

The following reflections are based on the assumption that non-directive[2] design instruction significantly supports the creative-artistic expressiveness of each student. In this context, the teacher sees him/herself as coach, mediator, and facilitator who is above all interested in the ideas, intentions, and plans of the student.

Person and Emotion

Art and design classes, more than other parts of the curriculum, devote considerable attention to the individual's way of being in the world, of coping with emotions and creative expression. Creative activity – if motivated by a serious concern – also involves feelings and moods. For example, students in art and design classes often work through *bio-*

2 Directive instruction: prescriptive, teacher-dominated instruction, featuring the voice of experience and demonstrating the teacher's superior knowledge.

graphical or *pressing personal matters.* They are touched or affected by the theme of their work and often confront aspects of their own personality. Then there are the theme's cognitive components, its technical aspects and procedures, for instance.

It is easy to see how being focused on issues relating to the self can lead to tensions and conflicts between personal concerns and artistic questions and requirements. In situations like these, reviewing student work requires great skill on the part of teacher. Among other things it is important to distinguish clearly between feedback on general procedures or technical aspects *and* comments on matters of content.

Role change

Traditionally, teachers put great store in having a thorough grasp of the subject matter they teach. This ambition is valuable and important. Drawing on a wide-ranging expertise, it is the source of a considerable potential for motivation that manifests itself in the teacher's enthusiasm for the subject matter discussed in the classroom: intimate knowledge of a particular subject allows me to relate anecdotes, offer specific insights and show connections. The teacher's fascination becomes palpable (see Spitzer, 2002, p. 194). Among the drawbacks however of having this knowledge is the temptation to propose premature solutions, offer unsolicited advice and short-circuit processes of understanding by revealing partial solutions. Students are discouraged from thinking for themselves and taking responsibility for the acquisition of information, and independent thinking is not given sufficient space.

In order to promote student responsibility, the teacher needs to step back and leave his/her charges a good deal of freedom. His/her own suggestions and inputs should be seen as options, i.e. possible other ways in which a problem *may* be solved (see *facilitator*, Rogers, 1988).

Under these circumstances the teacher's self-image is transformed: the all-knowing expert becomes a mediator between subject matter and learning, a kind of coach (see Stebler et al., 1994). One-way communication gives way to an interaction that questions and probes. Joint investigation and discovery, judiciousness and the suggestion of possibilities are the mainstay of the encounter between teacher and student.

What we call learning process facilitation includes all the actions performed by a teacher aimed at enabling students to solve problems independently. People who facilitate the learning process of others put their experience of difficult working and learning situations at the service of the students by analyzing such situations with them and assisting them in developing suitable solution-generating strategies. From among these established and reliable procedures, strategies, and methods, the students select those, which they find useful, helpful, and promising under the circumstances and assimilate them into their own mental and technical repertoire (see DenkBAR, 1996, p. 2). Judgmental, prescriptive, or authoritative pronouncements and directions are of secondary importance here.

Communication Training

Being an effective facilitator requires special communication skills. Art and design teachers are motivated to test various specific forms of communication and interaction, which, if effective, will be applied and improved continually.

Below, we will discuss some aspects of the facilitators' attitudes, perception of and interaction with students, and then propose a number of approaches and methods of communication/interaction with students in creative processes. Most of these suggestions are adapted from the field of therapy.

2. Communication in Creative Process Facilitation

The following proposals for communication/interaction with individuals engaged in creative processes are based on established procedures, methods, and reflections about the proper attitudes for dealing with people engaged in learning, decision-making and transformation processes. Most of these approaches were developed by psychologists and therapists.

First we will introduce the "attitudes which facilitate learning", originally developed for a therapeutic context and later adapted for the field of learning by Carl Rogers. They are, in my opinion, fundamental for every kind of dedicated, interested interaction between two or more people. Afterwards we will examine the active listening technique, one of the basic counseling tools and a standard in professional communication since the eighties. Two other approaches – systemic counseling and solution-focused counseling – are still virtually ignored in education and represent a true innovation, notably in the creative field.

2.1 Attitudes in Interpersonal Interaction

Carl Rogers, an important representative of humanistic psychology and the founder of client-centered therapy and counseling,[3] spent many years exploring the question of what quality or element actually initiates and sustains change in the therapeutic encounter. The most important supportive element in the development of the client, he concluded, is the *atmosphere of the encounter* and thus the nature of the relationship between therapist and client. And nothing has a greater influence on this climate than the attitude of the therapist. In later years Rogers adapted the lessons from his extensive therapeutic work to the field of learning (see Rogers, 1988). In terms of *humanistic psychology*, the attitude of the facilitator in his/her interaction with the student requires three fundamental qualities: genuineness of one's own manner (alternative terms congruence/realness), the unreserved acceptance of one's counterpart and a willingness to show empathy for the other person (ibid. 117–124). Especially for teachers in creative disciplines, where the emotional aspects of the student's personality requires special attention, these three fundamental attitudes are indispensable for successful teaching.

Genuineness

Being oneself and being able to communicate one's feelings, e.g. about the work and the comments of the other, is the basis for a cooperation based on trust. There is reason to assume that such genuineness promotes artistic development: the teacher communicates, with all due sensitivity, what he/she feels, thinks, how he/she assesses certain facts, with-

3 Today: person-centered counseling/therapy.

out putting on a façade or resorting to empty phrases, embellishments or sweeping judgments (see Rogers, 1983).

Acceptance and Appreciation

Feeling accepted and appreciated by one's teachers is a highly motivating experience and demonstrably increases the student's performance (see studies on classroom atmosphere). Acceptance and appreciation is expressed through attention, care, praise, criticism, humor etc.

Empathy

An empathic attitude, i.e. the ability of putting oneself in the shoes of the other and understanding the student's reactions and intentions from the inside, increases the likelihood of meaningful learning. The point is to see an event or object with the eyes of the student who is creating something. Sentences like: "I can imagine that this irritates you," or "I'm trying to understand how you feel about this" give verbal expression to the fact that one is assuming the perspective of the student, i.e. showing empathy (see ibid., 23).

Empathy requires an intimate understanding of how the other experiences things. This understanding is achieved through careful listening (see active listening).

The I as Expert

Humanistic psychology also assumes that individuals have the innate capacity to develop answers and solutions to most questions and problems concerning their person, experience and behavior. These solutions are usually quite effective: the chances of them being realized are generally better than those of proposals coming from someone else. For the teacher this means that he/she should assist the student in finding and realizing his/her own solutions and refrain from giving advice or suggesting solutions. Such restraint requires self-discipline and self-confidence (see ibid. 41, 138).

Teachers may propose other approaches or ideas as long as it is clearly understood that they are merely alternatives to the solutions envisioned by the student, or are additional options aimed at expanding the realm of the possible.[4]

2.2 Basic Rules of Communication

An essential ingredient of any respectful and professional culture of communication is the technique of *active listening.* It includes the use of *I-messages* in all utterances addressed directly to the other person or persons and a high level of attentiveness in receiving their messages (see Fittkau, Müller-Wolf & Schulz von Thun, 1994). These two behaviors and manners of response are essential for the creation of an atmosphere in which facilitation of learning becomes possible.

I-message

I-messages signal to the student that he is hearing a personal statement and not merely a truism (using "one", "we"). They convey something of the emotional state of the speaker/teacher, such as his/her response to a specific event or statement. I-messages are *not* accusatory, condemning, or judgmental ("you always do this and that...!" "You are like this or that...").

Active Listening

Active listening, the careful, attentive way of listening described by Gordon (1981), implies the use of I-messages. An attitude of undivided attention is a valuable instrument in any creative learning situation, but it is a particularly effective form of listening, questioning and responding in circumstances that require a mentor to explore the progress of an

4 The realm of the possible means the total range of options available to the person who is trying to solve a specific problem.

ongoing project, facilitate decisions and identify incongruities and inconsistencies.

For the facilitator, active listening includes:

- eye contact and regular gestures signaling attentiveness (nodding, confirming..)
- patience, leaving sufficient time for reflection, waiting for answers
- asking questions without rushing the respondent ("Can you be more specific?")
- verbalising emotional aspects of the process ("I see you're happy about that?!")
- paraphrasing or mirroring statements to eliminate misunderstandings
- abstaining from judgments (interest is focused on the perspective of the student)
- Using incomplete sentences...that can be completed by the other person

For the speaker, active listening signals that he/she is being accepted, understood and given space to grow. Students often respond to exploratory exchanges of this nature with comments such as: "I feel secure, understood, taken seriously, accepted. My reaction to your question made me aware of how I work. I learn things because I am expected to express myself with precision. I don't have to defend or justify myself."

One important active listening skill is the ability to paraphrase or mirror student statements by *repeating the essence of their message* back to them in *one's own words.* This serves to:

- avoid misunderstandings (Did I hear you right?)
- convey acceptance and interest (What you're saying interests me!);
- ascertain how the other person sees him/herself or his/her ideas/concerns (How do you rate yourself/your work?);
- build a trusting relationship (see Culley, 1966, p. 77).

2.3 Systemic View

Systemic counseling is an important psychological counseling approach influenced by systems theory and closed-circuit processes, as well as by assumptions about the networks that exist among individuals and their organization into larger and smaller systems (s. von Schlippe & Schweitzer, 1997).

This approach is based on the premise that people do not exist in isolation from each other but are constantly moving through a social field or system. In reality, people move in several parallel systems simultaneously – in their family, peer group, class, workplace or business. These systems have a circular organization, i.e. they affect the affiliated individuals and are, as a whole, affected by them. Systemic counseling focuses on the patterns, rules, roles and structures that emerge in such systems.

In psychological counseling the system is included in the mapping and problem-solving process. One of the ways in which this happens is through a *change of perspective*, by inviting the client to consider a particular phenomenon from a different angle. Another way would be to put oneself in somebody else's shoes, e.g. by reflecting on what person B thinks, if A behaves in a certain way. A special questioning technique serves to initiate the change of perspective: circular questioning (see chapter 4.1).

Another important feature of systems is their self-referential and autopoietical[5] organization. As a result, systems provide important *resources* in the form of strategies, assistance, knowledge and materials. This support – some of it from individuals with specific know-how, some from technical literature or from access to collections etc. – needs to be mobilized and used in problem-solving (see von Schlippe & Schweitzer, 1997 and chapter 2.4 below).

Perturbation is another starting point. The term was introduced by Varela and Maturana (1984) to highlight the potential for change inherent in the perturbation of a system: if a situation cannot be con-

5 Autopoiesis: self-organization, i.e. the system has the ability to shape, organize, and produce itself (see Barthelmess, 2001).

trolled by the usual behaviors and algorithms, i.e. if a disturbance or irritation arises, then the system and the individuals acting within it are forced to develop new strategies for coping. This is often a starting point for change.

These three aspects are important for the facilitation of learning in the creative-artistic context. In a slightly modified form, change of perspective, resource orientation and perturbation can be helpful in resolving many of the difficulties that arise in learning processes.

2.4 Solution-Focused Perspective

Solution-focused counseling assumes that looking for a viable solution to a problem is more efficient than attempting a detailed exploration of its origins (see Walter & Peller, 1994; de Jong & Kim Berg, 1998). A possible *outcome is anticipated* at the beginning of the problem-solving process. Situated within the frame of reference of the person seeking counsel, this outcome is pursued as the intended goal throughout the counseling process. Therefore, every solution-focused interaction begins, explicitly or not, with the question: what would be a desirable outcome of today's session?

The focus of the interaction is on the search for a viable path, for possible first steps in the direction of the anticipated solution.

A teacher engaged in learning facilitation is less interested in what may go wrong or why something did go wrong along the way than he is in uncovering the resources, i.e. the ideas, strengths and viable strategies that allow a project to move forward. Thus, a student struggling with a problem may try to recall similar situations in the past and how he/she went about finding a solution. To prompt a student to go in this direction, the teacher may inquire about possible *exceptions* ("Can you recall similar situations in which you reacted differently, proceeded differently?").

Abandoning the *problem-focused* perspective ("Why *didn't* it work? When did things also go *wrong*? How can you avoid these *mistakes*?)" for a *solution-focused* view ("When did you succeed in doing something similar? Can you make more of these?") is the essence of this approach. Implicit in this approach is the search for personal *resources* and *strengths* that might serve as a basis for progress and can be modified or expanded. On a practical level this means asking questions about personal strengths and abilities, knowledge and skills, persons, archives, collections of materials, etc. known to the student and available as sources of motivation and inspiration.

During the interview it is important to persist in the search for resources and to make repeated inquiries about other possible means of support: "Can you think of anything else? Is there something else? … and then?" … Often, truly important things only surface after repeated questioning.

The solution-focused approach progresses in small steps. The facilitator makes sure that the chosen objectives are feasible. The outcome of different behaviors can be anticipated in advance. This is a safe way for the student to probe different variants of a problem-solving procedure. The resulting objectives and ideas for their implementation need to be discussed and possibly revised, limited, or reformulated. To avoid frustration, it is important to keep a balance between what is desirable and what is possible. The solution-focused approach is really quite easy on the student, and yet allows him/her to steadily advance in the direction of development and change.

To increase the odds of realization it makes sense to insist on specifics. Questions like: "How should I picture that in actuality? … How can you tell that you're realizing this idea? … What is the first thing you do? … What is the next step?" challenge the student to be concrete in his stated intentions and mindful of his connection to reality.

Since positive feedback is seen as empowering and motivating, *compliments* are a typical ingredient of the solution-focused approach. (I like how you do this! I am amazed at your imaginative treatment of these materials"). Confidence in one's effectiveness has a positive effect on performance (for self-effectiveness-expectation according to Bandura, s. Previn, 2000/4, p. 388; Weidenmann & Krapp, 2001/4, 391; Stettler, 2002, p. 22).

2.5 Using Therapeutic Methods in the Counseling of Creative Individuals

One may wonder at this point how much sense it makes to invest the facilitation of creative processes with so much psychology. Actually, certain phases of creative processes are very similar to the therapeutic situations described above. My interactions with students confirm the assumption that careful communication is particularly helpful in discussing theme- or content-related questions because the creative person is often deeply involved and emotionally invested in the process. In order to complete a work the student may have to choose between several options. It is often not clear in the beginning just where the journey should end. In some situations it is important to take stock of one's resources and use whatever know-how and support is available in one's surroundings. Used in combination with the conventional directive instruction of technical aspects, procedures adapted from the field of therapy frequently offer enriching alternatives in the facilitation of these process steps.

To be sure, the use of therapeutic methods in creative processes must not be generalized. To demonstrate procedures or impart technical knowledge, a clear and directive instruction by the expert is clearly the best choice. But whenever teachers are advising students on the thematic or aesthetic aspects of their work, an extended repertoire of communication skills is advisable.

3. The Role of Educators in Creative Processes

Creative processes are many-layered, multi-dimensional and multi-level developments that may be extremely challenging for the student on a personal level and require an intense cognitive, emotional, and motivational involvement. Metaphorically speaking, many creative processes are not unlike high wire acts or tightrope walks and often they are borderline experiences.

In teaching/learning situations the creative individual is not alone but is supported by an educator who instructs and facilitates. The teacher who is familiar with the complexity of creative processes assumes a number of very different functions in deploying the skills that allow him to facilitate this process.

Multi-Dimensionality

In the creative process the teacher assumes a number of different *roles*. The different phases[6] of the creative process and other situations within the creative activity require him to adjust his role. So, occasionally, does the nature of a particular classroom session. Whether I teach my students about material properties by lecturing them or by letting let them discover and explore these in an experimental setting affects my role as a teacher or facilitator:

- *Introducing a technique*, a software, a procedure, a medium (e.g. water colors) – the teacher switches between instruction, colloquy, experiment or lab work, etc. and serves as a model.
- *Framing a problem or task*, e.g. what are the basic elements of a homepage? – the teacher suggests the exploration of the subject, assists in research and resource analysis, supports the search for alternative approaches, stimulates interest and lectures the basics, etc.
- *Using a technique*, a procedure, a construction, e.g. processing images in Photoshop – the teacher facilitates, offers criticism, organizes individual, tandem, group work, etc.
- *Social facilitation*, empathy, e.g. in a creative slump – the teacher demonstrates understanding, comments on mistakes with a positive spin, praises, encourages, and supports cooperation, etc.
- *Analysis of a process (whole or in parts)*, e.g. a photo reportage – the teacher advises, coaches and critiques, assists metareflection and suggests phenomenological reflection, etc.
- *Evaluating* a creative-artistic project, e.g. a semester thesis – the teacher critiques, evaluates and suggests a meta-analysis, etc.

6 The phases of the creative process – access, planning, incubation, production and reflection (see Sinner & Lunin, 2002) are analogous to the creative problem solving process (Csikszentmihaly, 1997; Haseloff, quoted in Edelman, 1996, 324).

3.1 Role Elements and Role Aspects

The role of the teacher varies slightly depending on the state of the work, the progress of the student or his own intentions. When *presenting* a task or *giving instructions* for a procedure, a method, a piece of equipment or a machine, the teacher usually assumes the position of an expert who lectures what is *understood to be his view* of things clearly and succinctly. He may do this in the form of statements, rules or norms, instructions, etc.

When *framing a problem* at least two roles are imaginable: he is again the *expert*, presenting a clearly structured set of requirements, or else he is the *facilitator* of an exploratory process in which he merely dispenses advice. In the one case, the activity is narrowly defined and leaves little room for student input (example: introducing egg tempera), while in the other the stated task or problem is little more than a label for a search process (example: find ways to bind, process and preserve pigments).

In the case of an *analysis* of parts or the whole creative process the teacher chooses between playing the *expert* with a narrow or wide perspective or participating as a critical-constructive *facilitator* (example: find criteria for the stability of soldering joints/for the use of novel materials in felt production).

In an ongoing *development process* the teacher turns into a *facilitator*, *moderator* and *coach* of the student. He/she supports him/her in searches, experiments, material explorations, preliminary evaluations, etc. by asking questions, pointing out particulars, contradictions and incongruities, and being supportive in the reflection or metacognitive analysis of the process[7] (example: find natural pigments; test the suitability of various source materials).

In *evaluating* a creative-artistic project or a partial process, the teacher assumes primarily the role of the expert in the field of art and design. The best way to do this is as an openly subjective observer: "From my perspective …/ For my taste …/ The way I see it …" Remarks alluding

7 Metacognitive reflection denotes the activity of thinking about one's thinking (see Weinert 1994).

to an imagined public should be prefaced as hypotheses: "I can imagine, that .../ I would suppose viewers will be surprised ..."

If he/she wants to find out how a student evaluates his/her own work, the teacher becomes an expert who listens with interest. By listening attentively, asking critical questions, and questioning unreasonable self-assessments the teacher supports the student in learning to assess him/herself accurately.

3.2 Unusual Types of Questions

In the following section we will discuss methods of questioning and forms of questions that were transplanted to the creative field from a therapeutic context. Some readers may frown or shake their heads at some of the things proposed here. This "shock" is intended and I hope it will cause readers to consider how learners in creative processes could be treated with consideration. Some of the proposals clearly address teaching/learning situations involving people without any background in the arts. Such is the case with this question proposed in the first paragraph:

> "How do you think an 'artist' or more specifically 'artist xy' would comment on your work?"

In discussions with future art and design teachers this proposal is regularly ridiculed or simply dismissed as useless. However, we may assume that in working with lay people we can actually communicate on this level. There is reason to believe that people without an arts background hold a quasi-*archetypal*[8] image of the "artist" and are willing to answer this question. Asked to imagine the "imaginary artist's" opinion, the lay artist will make statements about his/her own work or parts thereof that may reveal important information about his/her creative intention –

8 Archetypes are original images shared by social groups (collective unconscious, see analytical psychology, C. G. Jung). It is assumed that many people describe archetypal images or figures such as "the magician" or "the wise woman" with similar abilities, characteristics, and attributes.

information he/she might never volunteer if asked directly: "What are you trying to represent? What were your thoughts with regard to color?" etc.

B. Adapting Questioning Techniques from Systemic and Solution-Focused Therapy

4. Question-Driven Learning Facilitation

In the following chapters I will present methods of communication and questioning that might be useful in the teaching and counseling of people engaged in creative artistic activities. The proposals are influenced by two widely used psychological therapies – systemic therapy and solution-oriented therapy. While our focus is on the *forms of questions* used in these therapies, some aspects of the attitudes that go with them will also be considered. My intention in proposing these sample questions is to *expand the communication culture* as it is *already practiced* in creative processes. Expansion means: *not* relying on a single form of questions (e.g. circular or resource-oriented) throughout an entire interaction. In fact, during a longer interaction one or several of the following questions *can* be used at suitable moments. The main goal is a *change of perspective* brought about by encouraging the student to see and reflect on his work from different angles.

Another objective is to explore the student's *creative intention* and to bring out and *strengthen* his/her abilities, skills, possibilities; in other words, his resources. Some of the questions also call for a self-assessment and support the evaluation of alternatives in connection with decisions that may be forthcoming.

4.1 Change of Perspective and Circular Questioning

Circular questioning is a technique developed by systemic therapists to account for the influence that people exert on each other in social systems (family, school, workplace etc.). It is used to initiate a change of perspective by encouraging the student to consider a work, an object, etc. from a different perspective than the one they are accustomed to. In the creative discourse, circular questioning works for one-on-one interactions and plenary discussions, for group analyses with people who want to undertake a project together and for the self-reflection of the creative person (see Schlippe & Schweitzer, 1997).

Consider how effective it is to merely suggest that one should look at one's work, temporarily, with the eyes of another and thus hypothetically change one's position. This changes one's position as well as the perception of one's work and how one thinks about it. This opens up a space for new ideas and views.

Examples:

> What do you think an artist/teacher at an art school would say about your work?
> Variants: a relevant person from your circle of friends; a particular artist, who may already have done similar work.
>
> What, do you think, is the first thing a viewer will notice as he looks at your work? What might he possibly overlook?
>
> If your work could speak for itself... what aspect of itself would it review favorably? What would bother it?
>
> What kind of feelings/associations/thoughts do you think your work provokes in the viewer?
>
> What part of your work would prompt an expert to offer you professional advice about color or form?
>
> Imagine that someone is interested in buying your work. What kinds of questions would he/she ask you?

Questions like these are likely to irritate and disturb the student (see perturbation, Maturana & Varela, 1984). But they will make him/her think and therefore become a starting point for new insights. The important thing in this case, as in many other situations, is to give the respondent sufficient time to reflect. It takes a few seconds until a question is properly processed and a suitable answer is found, especially with questions like these. It is a search process and patience is required.

Here are a few suggestions about how the interaction could be continued:

> The student is encouraged to give his reaction to third-party assessments of his work (self-criticism/self-assessment); the teacher may comment further on these statements.
>
> How do you deal with this? What does it provoke in you? Will it be of any use to you? Will anything you just said be helpful to you?
>
> Do you agree with what you just heard? To what extent do these comments reflect your own views? What else could the person have said?

The next paragraph lists a number of questions designed to provoke a reaction from the student, encouraging him/her to classify all or part of his/her work, evaluate the presented works and comment on the work of fellow students.

4.2 Classification, Percentage and Scaling Questions

Classification, percentage, and scaling questions for creative processes may sound irritating and inappropriate at first. Yet, tailored to a specific situation and carefully worded they provide a good alternative line of questioning for the evaluation and (self-)assessment of finished works or aspects of works. They provide the teacher with information about the student's ability to accept criticism and his/her self-perception. This is helpful in situations where students are involved in the grading process.

Shifting to a different level of symbols allows the student to step back from the core theme and take a more impartial look at his/her own work. In this situation, a student may be more willing and able to address aspects of his/her work that he/she would otherwise overlook.

Classification and Scaling

Of the sample questions presented below, the percentage question provides clues about the direction an assessment is taking and serves as a starting point for further questions about possible solutions, causes, and explanations.

Scales provide clues about the current self-assessment of the student: "where I stand at the moment..." and at the same time suggest taking a small development step towards improving the situation. After positioning himself/herself, say, at seven on a scale (of ten) the student is asked: "What if you were at eight, i.e. one step further along?" In other words, we are talking about small, feasible steps and not about a maximum.

> Which work of yours might be considered successful by experts, and which one a failure? Alternative: most successful/least successful;
>
> What part of the work would you most like to touch / take with you / wear?
>
> What do you think *I think is / like best*?
>
> If you were to start over...what would you change?
>
> In the course of your work, where would you place green dots (positive assessment) and where red ones (negative assessment)? How did you arrive at this conclusion?
>
> Looking back from the final result... would you make the same assessment?
>
> To what *percentage* are you happy with your use of color? What do you need to influence the remaining 20 %?

On scaling:

> Imagine a scale of ten. Ten means your work is perfect; zero means it is a total failure. Where would you place your work?
>
> Ten means you will procure all the information and help that you need to continue; zero means you are clueless about how to go on. How do you rate yourself on that scale?

Continuation:

> How did you arrive at this assessment? What is needed to get you from four to five? (see de Shazer, 1989).

4.3 Including the environment

If creative tasks are designed jointly by two or more people, smaller and larger systems emerge. Events within these systems are perceived differently. Exchanges among the different VARYING perspectives increase possibilities and clear misunderstandings.

Sometimes it is helpful to imagine an audience, e.g. visitors to an exhibition. Questions about the expectations of imaginary recipients are designed to provoke and irritate the author of the work and press him/her to share his/her intentions.

Subsystem Questions

Group projects do not necessarily guarantee the continuous exchange of different perceptions and perspectives in the form of collective reflection, mutual criticism, etc. Here it may be helpful if an outsider stimulates such exchanges by asking partners or parts of the system to explain their perspective or, inversely, by making conjectures about the intentions, opinions and feelings of other participants regarding the project. This kind of intervention might be called for if it becomes evident that some people (a) hardly participate in the development process or (b) obviously have taken matters in hand and dominate the proceedings.

The social aspect takes precedence over the creative proceedings!

> Can you imagine what your partners might do differently if you were not part of the group?
> Can you say something about what might happen, if from now on your partner could determine the course of action all by himself?
> As an outsider, how can I tell who did what part of the work?
> What would you say is your role in the realization of this project?

Asking for the Expectations of Recipients

To initiate a change of perspective it may help to address the changed point of view directly. Asking a student about the possible expectations of viewers is a mildly provocative way of challenging him/her to offer some insight into his/her thinking, fears, and limitations, but also his/her intentions and desires.

What kinds of explanations do viewers expect as they look at your work?

What changes would you have to make in your work to meet the expectations of teachers and fellow students?

As a viewer looking at your work, what additional information would you expect to be given? What would you want to ask the author? What's going through your head right now?
What additional information does a viewer need to fully appreciate your work?

4.4 Questions about Available Resources

The point of these questions is to determine the potential of the student and his/her possibilities and limitations, including previously acquired knowledge, experiences with materials, helpful contacts, etc. In a second step the most promising links are selected and the student is encouraged to mobilize and utilize these resources.

Here the premise is that familiar means and contacts are particularly supportive and helpful. Most people have a considerable number of useful contacts, means and strategies to help them deal with different situations. However many of these are often not uppermost in our mind and may in fact require an intense resource analysis in order to be remembered.

Among the ways to search for resources and anticipate possible solutions the miracle question represents a singular case. With the help of miracles, everything is possible. In the bright glow of a miracle all actual obstacles, fears and difficulties dissolve.

The Search for Resources

Which of your creative skills and abilities do you value the most/would you like to develop further? Are there others? And what else is there?

What have you done so far to inspire/motivate yourself and find the information you need?

What are your most trusted resources when you work? What else? And then...?

What means or strategies do you turn to if you face an impasse?

Which of your abilities are fully developed and reliable enough? What are your strengths? Are there others? Still others?

Which of your contacts are particularly promising as sources of information for your work?

Is there someone you wish you could discuss your work with at this time? Who else?

Take another work – one you successfully completed... What allowed you to succeed then? What was the crucial ingredient that allowed you to reach your goal?

The teacher should not be satisfied with just any answer. Asking over and again is an effective and supportive strategy.

The Miracle Question

The miracle question, just like the classic rate-yourself-on-a-scale question, was developed by Steve de Shazer, one of the founders of the solution-focused approach. It is a very effective tool. It encourages the client/student to imagine the "impossible" – that which requires a miracle to come about. By anticipating a desirable ideal state the student expands the range of the possible. Often, the imagined miracle is less far-fetched than one might think and may well be posted as a goal to be pursued. With the aid of the miracle question I focus attention on things (abilities, techniques, perspectives, etc.) that I know or assume to be important but that the student lacks the confidence or vision to consider just yet. Also, it offers an opportunity to *think the impossible*, the utopian thing, and then to compare this with the reality. An imaginary space for play-acting[9] is opened up (see also 4.5).

9 Mental play acting: a mental game to test solutions and examine their feasibility. In the imagination even apparently impossible solutions may work out.

Imagine: Today, after our session, your work is done, maybe you're still up for something, later you go to bed... During the night, while you're asleep, a miracle happens. It fast-forwards your creative project to completion, eliminating all your recent difficulties with the work. You didn't actually witness the miracle because you were sleeping. What would be the first thing you notice in the morning that would let you know the miracle had happened? How would others recognize that a miracle had taken place?

further questions:

How would you go on if this were to actually happen?
What part of this miraculous transformation could you conceivably realize without the aid of a miracle?

4.5 Acting as If – The Case for Mental Play-Acting

Asking a student to pretend that something is real which exists only as a vague vision or intention, is to encourage him/her to expand the limits of their mind and undertake something in the mind that in the 'real' world *still* appears doomed to failure. More specifically, the student is encouraged to focus on a problem and pretend that it has been solved -- that he has already mastered that very difficult technique which he is actually just starting to learn. As a variant, "a game with prescribed variables" is imaginable, a game based on a set of fictitious givens proposed by the teacher.

We call this *mental play-acting:* The student places himself on an imaginary stage and acts as though this were his real life. He can probe and imagine things that he would never attempt in real life. If an idea "succeeds" in his imagination, a transfer to reality moves into the realm of the possible. Even just putting something in words is a first step towards making it real.

The following questions provide a good starting point for a personal self-reflection:

Pretend you've already mastered this technique. What would you do next? How would you develop your themes?

Let's assume you're starting over... what would you change/repeat unchanged? (*variant*: same question for individual aspects)

Imagine a studio. What should it look like, how should it be equipped so you can do your best work?

Assume your work is due tomorrow (or some other deadline) ... how would you proceed/where are your priorities?

What would be a meaningful next step?

The next step is to identify the elements in these proposals and visions that are already in place, or could easily be implemented. After that, search for and agree on concrete procedures.

4.6 Solution-Focused not Problem-Focused

In therapy the term "problem trance" is used if the treatment of a problem does not progress beyond the analysis of its causes. There are several ways to break out of a problem trance. A solutions approach is helpful because it focuses on the goal and not on (the analysis of) the problem. There are methods that distract from the problem aspects of a work and encourage a change in thinking. Below I will briefly introduce the idea of reframing and the possibility of paradoxical intervention.

Focusing on the Solution

It makes sense to select an aspect of the problem that functions reasonably well to start an intervention or consultation. This ensures that the student has a certain confidence in his/her ability to perform because a particular behavior was used successfully in an earlier situation. As for the actual problem, the task is now to define small, feasible steps. Agreeing on a realistic time frame and defining an intended solution is important. A session with a student will normally require 15 to 45 minutes. It is best to agree on the allotted amount of time at the start of a session as this heightens the efficiency of the interaction. The intention to achieve a solution is typically announced in the classical opening question: "What would be a good result for our session today?" (see de Jong, Kim Berg, 1998).

Opening question: What would be a good result for our session today?
How will you continue? What's your next step? Where would you like to continue?
Do you know what it might look like when it's finished/achieved? Do you *picture* it?
As an outside observer, how will I know that the development / the creative process was successful?

Alternative:

Try to reconstruct the development of the work...where is your chief interest? Where were decisions made? What parts were the most interesting for you?

At the end of the session, it is important to return to the opening question about the desired outcome. This encourages the student to review the session in his mind and draw the balance for himself.

Reframing

Reframing is a therapeutic strategy designed to anchor a behavior pattern or a work with a negative or obstructive component in a new context. As the problem is reframed by the teacher, the student's perspective on the subject changes.

Presented with an opportunity to motivate his intentions of changing in a new context, the student will find it easier to implement these. Genuine reframing must establish a perspective that is significantly different from the earlier view of reality (see von Schlippe, Schweizer, p. 177). Continued counseling is important. Here is an example involving a decision-making crisis:

Problem:	"When I have to decide what font to use I often go in circles for hours, trying to weigh the pros and cons of the different choices."
Possible intervention:	"I gather from what you're telling me that you proceed very carefully in your decision-making! Isn't the choice of typography a particular quality of this product?"

Paradoxical Intervention

In some cases, where the teacher comes to believe that failure is caused by a *persisting* in recurrent patterns (paradoxical, obstructive pattern), he may decide to employ a counter-paradox to make the student aware of his/her behavior and allow him/her to resolve it. He makes an *unconventional*, seemingly nonsensical *proposal* for the continuation of the work (see Schlippe, Schweitzer, 1997, p. 26; see also Watzlawick, Beavin & Jackson, 1969).

Problem: "There is too much red in my paintings lately and that bothers me. Every one of my paintings eventually ends up like this, no matter how hard I try to use other colors in the beginning. What should I do?"

Possible intervention: "I suggest you only use shades of red in your painting for a while. That way you eliminate the problem of having them turn red in the end."

5. *Irritation as Opportunity – A Step by Step Approach to New Forms of Communication*

At first it may sound strange or irritating to hear someone advocating the use of methods commonly associated with therapy and counseling in an art and design education context. However, the reader will soon realize that I am not about to turn the teaching/learning process into a therapy session but am merely proposing the transfer of some widely applicable and very effective (independent of context) procedures. Take *change of perspective*, for instance.

The switch to the proposed form of learning process facilitation begins with the adoption of the attitudes identified by Rogers (1988) – communication based on acceptance, empathy and genuineness – and the understanding that people have the innate capacity to develop their own answers and solutions to problems confronting them. Through specific forms of listening and questioning the facilitator supports the search for and realization of an appropriate solution. At its most fundamental level, this involves a (partial) turning away from the model of the Meisterlehre and the practice of moving the learning process along with well-intentioned advice and tricks of the trade.

The appropriation of the various forms of counseling and questioning is a gradual process and is perfected through regular use and practice. Students report that for them a certain degree of preparation for the teacher-student interview has been helpful. They apparently read the practice-oriented sections of this paper to get into the right frame of mind and make notes on specific questions. Some of these questions actually come up during the interview while others remain unasked. After a number of sessions the new forms settle into an automatic pattern and new procedures may be added.

If successful, the general ideas and specific methods of this approach gradually expand the repertoire of interactive strategies and the range of teacher-student communication in general. This is no less true for teachers at academies and colleges than it is for educators in lower grades and continuing education courses.

If the initial premise of this article – non-directive and question-driven forms of interaction have a dynamic effect on the performance of both teachers and students – is correct, then teachers willing to embrace this method are in for a surprise. Prompted and allowed to assume full responsibility over all aspects of their work, from planning and decision-making to execution and reflection, the students develop varied and lasting skills and a deeper understanding of the creative process and their powers of expression. In a shift of emphasis that seems well worth a try, the teacher's restraint is rewarded by the visible excitement of the students about their newfound self-confidence, independence and success.

6. Bibliography

Barthelmess, Manuel (2001/2). Systemische Beratung: Eine Einführung für psychosoziale Berufe. Weinheim: Beltz Sozial.

Csikszentmihalyi, Mihaly (1997). Kreativität: Wie Sie das Unmögliche schaffen und Ihre Grenzen überwinden. Stuttgart: Klett-Cotta.

Culley, Sue (1996). Beratung als Prozess: Lehrbuch kommunikativer Fertigkeiten. Weinheim: Beltz Edition Sozial.

De Jong, Peter; Kim Berg, Insoo (1998). Lösungen (er-)finden: Das Werkstattbuch der lösungsorientierten Kurztherapie. Dortmund: Verlag modernes Lernen.
denkBAR! (ca. 1996, undatiert). Lernprozesse begleiten. Zürich: denkBAR!
De Shazer, Steve (1989). Wege der erfolgreichen Kurztherapie. Stuttgart: Klett-Cotta.
Edelmann, Walter (1996/5). Lernpsychologie. Weinheim: Psychologie Verlags Union.
Fittkau, Bernd; Müller-Wolf, H. M.; Schulz v. Thun, Friedemann (1994/7). Kommunizieren lernen (und umlernen). Aachen-Hahn: Hahner.
Gordon, Thomas (1981). Lehrer-Schüler-Konferenz. Wie man Konflikte in der Schule löst. Reinbek: rowohlt.
Guldimann, Titus (1996). Eigenständiger Lerner. Bern: Haupt.
Maturana, Humberto R.; Varela, Francisco (1984). Der Baum der Erkenntnis. München: Goldmann.
Miller, Patricia (1993). Theorien der Entwicklungspsychologie. Heidelberg: Spektrum Akad. Verlag.
Peez, Georg (2002). Einführung in die Kunstpädagogik. Stuttgart: Kohlhammer.
Pervin, Lawrence A. (2000/4). Persönlichkeitstheorien: Freud, Adler, Jung, Rogers, Kelly, Cattell, Eysenck, Skinner, Bandura u. a. München: Ernst Reinhardt.
Reusser, Kurt; Reusser-Weyeneth, Marianne (Hrsg.) (1994). Verstehen: Psycholog. Prozess und didakt. Aufgabe. Bern: Huber.
Rogers, Carl R. (1988). Lernen in Freiheit: Zur inneren Reform von Schule und Universität. Frankfurt a. M.: Fischer TB.
Rogers, Carl R. (1983). Therapeut und Klient. Frankfurt a. M.: Fischer TB.
Schlippe, Arist von; Schweitzer, Jochen (1997). Lehrbuch der systemischen Therapie und Beratung. Göttingen: Vandenhoeck & Ruprecht.
Selle, Gert (1998). Kunstpädagogik und ihr Subjekt. Oldenburg: Isensee.
Selle, Gert (Hrsg.) (1990). Experiment Ästhetische Bildung: Aktuelle Beispiele für Handeln und Verstehen. Reinbek/Hamburg: Rowohlt.
Sinner, Marianne; Lunin, Serge (2002). Werkfelder: Grundlagen zu Gestaltung und Techniken. Zürich: Kantonaler Lehrmittelverlag.
Spitzer, Manfred (2002). Lernen: Gehirnforschung und die Schule des Lebens. Heidelberg: Spektrum Akademischer Verlag.
Stebler, Rita; Reusser, Kurt; Pauli, Christine (1994). Interaktive Lehr-Lern-Umgebungen: Didaktische Arrangements im Dienste des gründlichen Verstehens. In: Kurt Reusser; Marianne Reusser-Weyeneth (Hrsg.). Verstehen: Psycholog. Prozess und didakt. Aufgabe. Bern: Huber.
Stettler, Andreas (2002). Selbstwirksamkeitsüberzeugung im technischen Gestalten. Uni Bern, Diplomarbeit NDS, unveröffentlicht.

Walter, John L.; Peller, Jane E. (1994). Lösungs-orientierte Kurztherapie. Dortmund: Verlag modernes Lernen.

Watzlawick, Paul; Beavin, Janet H.; Jackson, Don D. (1969). Menschliche Kommunikation: Formen, Störungen, Paradoxien. Bern: Huber.

Weidenmann, Bernd; Krapp, Andreas (Hrsg.) (2001). Pädagogische Psychologie. Weinheim: Beltz PVU.

Weinert, Franz E. (1994). Lernen lernen und das eigene Lernen verstehen. In: Kurt Reusser; Marianne Reusser-Weyeneth (Hrsg.). Verstehen: Psycholog. Prozess und didakt. Aufgabe. Bern: Huber.

About the Authors

Gerhard Hickisch (A)
born 1955; MA; studied art and design education at the University of Art and Design Linz (1974–1979); from 1976 on he has been teaching at higher secondary and university level as art teacher, lecturer for teaching practice and docent for "Bildnerische Gestaltung" (visual design education). Since 1999 he is professor of visual design education at the University of Art and Design Linz, Austria.

Pierangelo Maset (D)
born 1954; PhD; studied art, visual communication, philosophy, English and sociology in Kassel, Göttingen and Berlin. Since the late 70's he has worked as artist and performer and during the 80's he produced several records. His publications are mainly in the field of art, aesthetic education and aesthetics and his university teaching positions ranged from Weimar to Kassel, Hamburg, Canterbury and Linz. Since 2001 he is professor of art and didactics at the University Lüneburg, Germany.

Torsten Meyer (D)
born 1965; PhD; studied philosophy, sociology, educational science and art. He is the head of the MultiMedia-Studio in the faculty of education at the University of Hamburg. Since 2004 he is Junior Professor of "educational science with special consideration of research and teaching in the field of multimedia with an emphasis in art education" at the University of Hamburg, Germany.

Martina Paatela-Nieminen (FI)
born 1957; Doctor of Arts; she has worked at the University of Art and Design Helsinki (UIAH) since 1985 and she is currently a Finnish Academy postdoctoral researcher at the School of Art Education at UIAH, Finland.

IWAN PASUCHIN (A)
PhD; studied composition and music theory in Salzburg and media pedagogy in Salzburg. His works include compositions for festivals, music theatre, film and television, as well as didactic multimedia projects and scientific publications. He is the head of the MA-programme "New Media in Music Pedagogy" and the research project "Intermedia Art Education" at the university "Mozarteum" in Salzburg, Austria.

KARL JOSEF PAZZINI (D)
born 1950; PhD; studied philosophy, theology, educational science, mathematics and art education. He is a psychoanalyst with his own practice and cofounder of the "Assoziation für die Freudsche Psychoanalyse" and of the "Psychoanalytisches Kolleg." His main fields of work are: psychoanalysis, pedagogy, museum and education, teaching and learning in reference to art and aggressiveness of teaching; he is currently working on the research project "delusion, knowledge, institution." Since 1993 he is professor of educational science and didactics of fine art at the University of Hamburg, Germany.

STEFAN SONVILLA-WEISS (A/FI)
born 1961, PhD; studied philosophy, graphics, art and design education and communication theory in Salzburg and Vienna. During the 80's and 90's he worked as cross-over artist, multimedia producer, university teacher and project manager in national and international contexts. Since 2003 he is professor and head of the international MA-programme ePedagogy Design – Visual Knowledge Building at the University of Art and Design Helsinki, Finland.

PETER TRUNIGER (CH)
MPhil; psychologist (FSP), supervisor (BSO) and docent for pedagogy and psychology. He is the head of the study topic "Gestaltung und Kunst in der Erwachsenenbildung im Freizeitbereich" (Art and design in adult education on leisure activities) at the University of Art and Design Zurich, Switzerland.

David Barr

ICT – Integrating Computers in Teaching

Creating a Computer-Based Language-Learning Environment

Oxford, Bern, Berlin, Bruxelles, Frankfurt am Main, New York, Wien, 2004. 240 pp.
ISBN 3-03910-191-9 / US-ISBN 0-8204-7176-3 pb.
sFr. 69.– / € 47.40 / €** 44.30 / £ 31.– / US-$ 52.95*

* includes VAT – only valid for Germany and Austria ** does not include VAT

This book examines the role of computers in language learning and teaching in higher education. In particular, it considers the pedagogical and practical value of designing a language-learning environment around computer technology. Whereas considerable research has already been undertaken in analysing the value of individual computer tools and packages (such as e-mail), the study gives a broad appraisal of their individual and collective value, without being too exhaustive.

Using quantitative and qualitative data, based on research visits to three universities, Ulster, Cambridge and Toronto, this study provides examples of effective practice in the area of the exploitation of Information and Communication Technology for language learning and teaching. It draws on the experience of these three institutions, as well as the findings of current literature in this area, in order to establish a set of essential criteria that institutions need to meet when creating a computer-based environment. Although these criteria are based on experience with language-learning environments, they are essentially generic in nature and may be applied to other computer-based learning environments.

Contents: What is a learning environment? – Towards a computer-based language-learning environment – Case Study 1 - the University of Ulster – Case Study 2 - the University of Cambridge – Case Study 3 - the University of Toronto – Meeting the needs of learners and teachers: the success or failure of computer-based language learning environments – Conclusion: A framework for an effective environment.

The Author: David Barr received his BA (Double 1st Class Hons) in Applied Languages (French and Spanish) in 1999 and his DPhil in Computer-Based Language-Learning Environments in 2003 from the University of Ulster. He has a PG Cert in Higher Education Teaching and is currently teaching French at the University of Ulster, Northern Ireland. He is a member of EUROCALL and has published in the area of CALL.

PETER LANG
Bern · Berlin · Bruxelles · Frankfurt am Main · New York · Oxford · Wien

Stefan Sonvilla-Weiss

Virtual school – kunstnetzwerk.at

Partizipative Medienkultur in der virtuellen Bildungslandschaft Österreichs

Bern, Berlin, Bruxelles, Frankfurt am Main, New York, Oxford, Wien, 2003.
243 S., 8 Abb., zahlr. Tab. und Graf.
ISBN 3-03910-231-1 br.
sFr. 72.– / € 49.60 / €** 46.40 / £ 33.– / US-$ 55.95*

* inkl. MWSt. – nur gültig für Deutschland und Österreich ** exkl. MWSt.

Welche Kommunikationsstrukturen und -konzepte im Internet sind notwendig, um ein partizipatives Medienverständnis zu entwickeln? Welche Potentiale liegen in einer aktiven, kommunikativen und kollaborativen Wissenskonstruktion, die dem beschleunigten Prozess der Informationsverarbeitung und -bereitstellung Rechnung trägt?

Die Gestaltung von *kunstnetzwerk.at* und die Einbindung dieser Online-Plattform für Kunst/Design, neue Medien und Bildung im europäischen Bildungskontext der *Virtual School Europe* markieren den Ausgangspunkt für eine umfassendere Darstellung methodisch-didaktischer Konzepte im Interaktionsraum computerisierter Lehr- und Lernumgebungen.

Dieser Band beleuchtet – ausgehend von einer kritischen Analyse der Hard- und Softwareindustrie bis zu den offenen Strukturen der Open-Source-Bewegung – die bildungspolitischen Zielsetzungen und Veränderungen in Bildungs- und Ausbildungsprozessen und die dahinterliegenden Konzepte und Modelle formeller und informeller Lernumgebungen.

Eine Vielzahl von Projektanalysen und Beispielen im kunst- und medienpädagogischen Kontext in Zusammenhang mit der permanenten Weiterentwicklung von *kunstnetzwerk.at* runden diese Publikation ab.

Der Autor: Stefan Sonvilla-Weiss, geboren 1961 in Wels, ist seit 2003 Professor für ePedagogy Design an der University of Art and Design Helsinki.

PETER LANG
Bern · Berlin · Bruxelles · Frankfurt am Main · New York · Oxford · Wien

FSC
www.fsc.org
MIX
Papier | Fördert gute Waldnutzung
FSC® C083411

Kolibri 360 GmbH
Ferdinand-Jühlke-Straße 7
99095 Erfurt, Deutschland
produktsicherheit@kolibri360.de

Druck:
CPI Druckdienstleistungen GmbH
im Auftrag der
Kolibri 360 GmbH
Ferdinand-Jühlke-Str. 7
99095 Erfurt